ARROGANT DIPLOMACY

ARROGANT DIPLOMACY

U.S. Policy toward Colombia, 1903–1922

by

Richard L. Lael

The paper used in this publication meets the minimum requirements of the American National Standard for permanence of paper for printed library materials, Z39.48, 1984.

First published 1987
Printed and bound in the United States of America

Scholarly Resources Inc.
104 Greenhill Avenue
Wilmington, Delaware 19805-1897

Library of Congress Cataloging-in-Publication Data

Lael, Richard L., 1946–
Arrogant diplomacy.

Bibliography: p.
Includes index.
1. United States—Foreign relations—Colombia.
2. Colombia—Foreign relations—United States.
3. United States—Foreign relations—20th century.
4. Colombia—Politics and government—1903–1930.
I. Title.
E183.8.C7L34 1987 327.730861 87-12987
ISBN 0-8420-2287-2

Dedicated to
Ann

Contents

List of Tables

Introduction

Most Americans in November 1903, if they thought at all about the Panamanian revolution against Colombia, probably viewed it as just another in a long series of Latin American uprisings. Few, including the self-confident American president, Theodore Roosevelt, could have expected that Washington's response to this incident would create a diplomatic dilemma that would occupy U.S. and Colombian policymakers for almost twenty years. But that is exactly what happened.

Colombian and U.S. historians, including Eduardo Lemaitre Román, Dwight Miner, Joseph Arbena, David McCullough, and Walter LaFeber, have studied the impact of the United States on the success of, or the immediate repercussions of, the Panamanian revolution; however, few have questioned the long-term implications of that insurrection on U.S. policy toward Colombia.[1] By ordering units of the U.S. Navy to prevent Bogotá's efforts to suppress an insurrection in its department of Panama, the Roosevelt administration precipitated a prolonged diplomatic dispute with its Caribbean neighbor. The following consideration of that dispute and the fragile diplomatic process that eventually led in 1922 to a mutually acceptable settlement sheds light on how and why Washington policymakers acted as they did toward Colombia in the early decades of the twentieth century.

Who exactly determined U.S. policy toward Colombia? What motivated those policymakers to act as they did? Were they swayed by strategic interests, economic benefits, moral beliefs, or a combination of these or other influences? In dealing with Bogotá, how similar or dissimilar were the policies of the Theodore Roosevelt, William Howard Taft, and Woodrow Wilson administrations? How influential were business interests, governmental bureaucracies, the press, and public opinion in the policymaking process? In what way and for what reasons, if any, did U.S. domestic politics influence U.S.-Colombian efforts to resolve the 1903 diplomatic dilemma? What does an examination of

U.S. foreign policy toward Colombia reveal about subsequent historical perceptions of the Roosevelt, Taft, and Wilson administrations? These and other questions are discussed in the following study.

Writing in 1984, William H. Becker concluded that economic interests "were not generally the primary consideration in the conduct of foreign policy" at the highest decision-making levels in the United States during the first two decades of the twentieth century.[2] A study of U.S. diplomacy toward Colombia between 1903, the year Colombia lost its northernmost department, and 1922, when both governments finally resolved their isthmian dispute, clearly sustains Becker's conclusion. In dealing with Bogotá during those years, strategic, not economic, concerns were of first importance to U.S. policymakers. Not that the United States had to fear the Colombian military, for alone it would have faced annihilation in a traditional military confrontation with Washington. Rather, the United States feared, as Secretary of State Elihu Root astutely observed in 1907, that "Colombia as our enemy is a source of vital danger *if we have any other enemy*."[3] Echoing the same thought in 1917, Secretary of State Robert Lansing argued that it was of pressing importance to ensure Colombian friendship, especially since Washington had just severed diplomatic relations with Germany.[4]

While strategic interests, frequently focusing on isthmian canal security, dominated U.S. thinking about Colombia, it is not always possible to separate strategic from economic concerns, a fact P. E. Haley and Robert Freeman Smith have demonstrated in their studies of U.S. policymaking toward Mexico in the early twentieth century.[5] However, that separation is easier in the Roosevelt and Taft administrations than in Wilson's. But, even when economic pressure on, or penetration of, Colombia seemed desirable, Washington policymakers considered it more as a means to ensure achievement of America's strategic goals than as a means of answering fears of U.S. internal economic or social problems. Perhaps surprisingly, despite the popular and historic association of Big Stick and Dollar Diplomacy with the Roosevelt and Taft administrations, those governments did not generally seek to gain or use economic leverage over Colombia. On the other hand, despite Wilson's apparent repudiation of his predecessors' distasteful methods of economic diplomacy, his administration did consider using economic leverage as necessary.

One trait all three presidents shared in relation to Bogotá was their reliance on moralistic, humanitarian rhetoric to defend their respective policies. In 1903, for example, Roosevelt defended his naval assistance to Panama, his guarantee of its independence, and his opposition to Colombia's recapture of its errant department by citing a "mandate from civilization" to have the United States build an isthmian canal. When, in his view, the "jack rabbits" in Bogotá refused to ratify an isthmian agreement acceptable to the United States, his administration was honor bound to aid a "newly independent" Panama to fulfill the mandate. By levying blame on Bogotá and by justifying his actions based on the positive benefits that eventually would accrue to mankind, Roosevelt downplayed U.S. self-interest, discounted the threats and pressure his administration had placed on Colombian charǵe Tomás Herrán to sign an isthmian agreement, and ignored the fact that the Colombian legislature had as much legal right to reject the canal treaty as did the U.S. Senate. Roosevelt's moralistic justifications seemed to sanction interventionism so long as its intent was "unselfish." No matter what the justification, however, it was still interventionism.

Roosevelt, Taft and Wilson believed, as did many of their top advisers, that a U.S. presence abroad, whether in Colombia, Panama, or elsewhere, offered development and modernization, not dependence and exploitation.[6] Therefore, when Secretary Root argued in 1906 that the people and government of the United States "deem the independence and equal rights of the smallest and weakest member of the family of nations entitled to as much respect as those of the greatest empire," neither he nor Roosevelt saw a contradiction between past U.S. action and current rhetoric.[7] Nor was Secretary of State William Jennings Bryan intentionally trying to be deceptive when in 1913, the year U.S. forces seized Veracruz, Mexico, he contended that the United States "must protect the people of [Latin America] in their right to attend to their own business, free from external coercion, no matter what form that external coercion may take."[8] Nor was Wilson insincere, despite the many interventions during his presidency, when he publicly rejected selfish, narrow nationalism and materialism as a basis for U.S. foreign policy.

All three presidents not only shared a common vision of America's greatness but also a desire to use that greatness to aid civilization, restore order in chronically unstable Caribbean nations, and lessen the potentially malign European influence in the hemisphere. In achieving those goals, they sincerely believed that the United States acted, not out of selfishness, but out of a genuine desire to assist its Caribbean neighbors. They too naively assumed, however, that their vision and intent would be either automatically shared or, at least, understood by their neighbors, and that Caribbean states would respond to U.S. policies accordingly. Alas, as Mark Gilderhus's study of Mexico has shown, when Wilson's moral rhetoric and beliefs clashed with his actual policy toward Mexico and when that country failed to respond to his policies as anticipated, the president appeared surprised and confused about a future course of action.[9] Similarly, in relation to Colombia, he, Roosevelt, and Taft were puzzled when Bogotá did not accept Washington's views. None of them seemed to realize, or seriously consider, the possibility that U.S. actions, as seen from Colombia, could legitimately be perceived as interventionist, dangerous, and imperialistic.

William Appleman Williams, in his thought-provoking *Tragedy of American Diplomacy*, has criticized policymaking based on such naive assumptions.[10] Washington policymakers would do well, he advised, to evaluate carefully how closely their actual use of power conforms to their rhetoric. Based on their Colombian policies, Roosevelt, Taft, and Wilson were motivated less by humanitarian concerns, unselfishness, world "mandates," and a belief in equal sovereignty than by strategic or economic interests considered vital to the United States. All three were committed to peaceful diplomatic negotiations with affirmations of equal sovereignty so long as those negotiations conformed to basic U.S. desires. However, when Colombia proved obstinate, both Roosevelt and Wilson were willing to consider coercion, or threats of coercion, to achieve their goals. They, along with Taft, never seriously questioned the basic underlying assumption of their policymaking: that Washington's decisions served the best interests of not only the United States but also of Colombia or Latin America as a whole. Neither did the presidents nor the vast majority of their diplomatic subordinates really consider on a sustained basis how Colombia perceived U.S. actions and policies, or how well such actions and policies were working to achieve the preeminent goal of a more secure hemisphere friendly to the United States.

When Wilson's foremost biographer, Arthur S. Link, asserts that Wilson sought no monopolistic concessions or preferential treatment in foreign trade and investment during his years as president, that he "utterly detested the exploitative imperialistic system," and that he was "the first antiimperialist statesman in the twentieth century," he is therefore missing an important point.[11] While Wilson may have been guided by a different vision than his predecessors and while he may not have sought monopolistic concessions, he was an imperialist. In opposing a Colombian petroleum agreement with a British firm in 1913, in opposing proposed platinum legislation in 1918, and in opposing Colombian petroleum legislation in 1919, the Wilson administration clearly intervened in legitimate Colombian domestic affairs, just as Roosevelt had done in 1903. As Smith has so persuasively argued in his study of U.S.-Mexican relations, Wilson and his advisers never seriously considered that the same international law on which they relied reflected the "legal norms and economic practices" that benefited industrial-creditor nations, such as the United States, rather than newly developing nations like Mexico or Colombia.[12] They assumed once again that a Caribbean state would understand the rationale behind U.S. actions and would not overreact to Washington policymaking. Wilson's Colombian policies confirm not only Smith's observation of his administration but also that of Joseph Tulchin, who has argued that all too frequently after 1917 the U.S. government "formulated and executed foreign policy without reference to the demands or responses of the Latin American nations."[13] However, in this regard then Wilson, Taft, and Roosevelt were no more or less astute than the bulk of the American people, whether in 1903 or 1919, or for that matter in 1986.

Consideration of the Roosevelt and Wilson administrations' management of the Colombia question leads this author to question the sympathetic treatment accorded these two presidents by such historians as Arthur Link, John Milton Cooper, Jr., Robert A. Friedlander, Frederick Marks, and Richard Collin.[14] Marks's work in particular distorts Roosevelt's handling of the Panama-Colombia-U.S. crisis of 1903 and unjustly levies responsibility for it on the Marroquín government in Bogotá, virtually exonerating Roosevelt of any culpability. Furthermore, Collin, writing in 1985, not only perpetuates that erroneous interpretation but also concludes that imperialism is "unrecognizable as an American phenomenon during Theodore Roosevelt's presidency."[15] Link, especially in his more recent studies, obviously shares the view with Cooper that Wilson "deserves better from posterity." Perhaps to redress that, both fail to view Wilson's weaknesses with the same enthusiasm as they view his strengths. Despite their comments to the contrary, U.S. policymaking toward Colombia reveals imperialistic Roosevelt and Wilson administrations.

Nor can responsibility for imperialistic decision making easily be shifted to other groups. In formulating Colombian policies, the three presidents and their top policy advisers after November 1903 operated virtually free of outside pressure from either the press or the public. Similarly, American business interests rarely tried to influence U.S.-Colombian policy. American business generally neither sought nor received substantial U.S. aid in securing Colombian concessions between 1903 and 1922. This observation, as historians of the early twentieth century realize, comes closer to the views of business-government relations as discussed by Carl Parrini, Joan Hoff-Wilson, and Robert D. Cuff than those espoused by Burton Kaufman.[16] Petroleum exploration and negotiation of Colombian petroleum contracts, at least during this period, for example, were still functions performed by private enterprise with minimal U.S. government involvement. The United States had not yet embarked on either a policy of petroleum exclusivity or cooperation with potential foreign rivals.[17] Despite opposition to their policies in the U.S. Senate, the absence of other vigorous external pressures perhaps should have granted the presidents greater leeway in formulating policies more fully reflective of their rhetoric supporting the concept of equal sovereignty and genuine respect for the rights even of the weakest of nations. It apparently did not.

While this study of U.S. policymaking toward Colombia reveals not only the importance of strategic, economic, or moral factors, it also demonstrates the significance of domestic politics and personalities in understanding the U.S. treaty-making process. No study of U.S. policymaking toward Colombia would be complete without considering the role of Senator Henry Cabot Lodge, who emerges here not as intransigent nor as anti-Democratic as he sometimes has been portrayed. One of his biographers, John Garraty, argues, for example, that by 1914 and 1915 Lodge had come to hate Wilson and was his "implacable enemy."[18] In fairness, Garraty then offers a counterexplanation, posited by Henry Cabot Lodge, Jr., which argues that his father's attitude toward Wilson was not characterized by a personal hatred but merely reflected legitimate political differences of opinion. Even if Garraty is correct, the senator's feelings toward Wilson did not prevent him from working closely with the Wilson administration to secure an acceptable Colombian settlement in 1919 while he was simultaneously battling the same administration over the Treaty of Versailles. In this study, Lodge is shown as a more sensitive, patient, and compromising politician, one closer to the portrayal by William C. Widenor than of earlier historians.[19]

The rivalry of Lodge and Wilson over the Versailles Treaty is legendary; less well known is their six-year rivalry over the Thomson-Urrutia Treaty, signed between the United States and Colombia in 1914. Wilson's response to Lodge's initial and successful resistance to that treaty sheds light on the president's ability to learn from history. Ernest May's conclusion that American policymakers "ordinarily use history badly" clearly applies to Wilson in relation to the process of treaty ratification.[20] He apparently learned no useful lesson from his struggle to secure U.S. Senate ratification of the Thomson-Urrutia Treaty between 1914 and 1919. A more astute president might have considered how he had been outmaneuvered by Lodge in almost every phase of the ratification battle and how his defeats in the Senate Foreign Relations Committee had come at the hands of the minority membership, not the majority. And he probably would have reconsidered his belief that the Senate might feel committed to a treaty, even if it disapproved, once an agreement had been negotiated and signed by the president and the prestige of the U.S. government had been pledged to ratification. Had Wilson carefully reflected on his Thomson-Urrutia struggle, he might well have gained valuable insights he then could have applied to his decisions relating to the negotiation and ratification of the potentially much more important Treaty of Versailles. But inexplicably Wilson ignored the earlier Colombian episode. Therefore, in late 1919, just as in the preceding years, he discovered once again that the U.S. Senate was not automatically committed to a treaty negotiated by the executive branch.

Just as President Wilson failed to ensure that his actions fostered the correct counterreactions in 1919, so too were the Roosevelt, Taft, and Wilson administrations unable to develop a systematic policy to ensure that U.S. actions fostered the correct counterreactions in Colombia or in the U.S. Senate. Their failure to adopt a long-term, coherent, and consistent Colombian policy, coupled with their inability to grapple successfully with the distinction between U.S. rhetoric and action, helped prolong the Panama dilemma for almost twenty years.

Without the generous assistance of many fellow historians, librarians, archivists, and friends, this study would not have been possible. I am particularly grateful for the thoughtful and constructive criticisms of the following historians: Samuel F. Wells, Jr., Joseph Arbena, William Beezley, Joseph Tulchin, R. Don Higginbotham, and George Mowry. Ernest Hillard also provided invaluable assistance during the final stages of this work. To these and to all the others whom I have not specifically named, I express my deep appreciation.

Notes

[1]Lemaitre Román, *Panamá y su Separación de Colombia* (Bogotá: Banco Popular, 1972); Miner, *The Fight for the Panama Route* (New York: Octagon Books, 1966 [1940]); Arbena, "The Panama Problem in Colombian History" (Ph.D. diss., University of Virginia, 1970); McCullough, *The Path between the Seas* (New York: Simon & Schuster, 1977); LaFeber, *The Panama Canal* (New York: Oxford University Press, 1978).

[2]"America Adjusts to World Power: 1899–1920," in William H. Becker and Samuel F. Wells, Jr., eds., *Economics and World Power: An Assessment of American Diplomacy since 1789* (New York: Colombia University Press, 1984), 174.

[3]Comment attached to a 20 June 1907 cable from Bogotá, Numerical and Minor Files, 1906–10, Department of State, Record Group 59, vol. 582, 7804, National Archives, Washington, DC (author's emphasis).

[4]Robert Lansing to Woodrow Wilson, 6 February 1917, RG 59, 711.21/ 535 (hereafter cited as SD, followed by decimal file number).

[5]Haley, *Revolution and Intervention: The Diplomacy of Taft and Wilson with Mexico, 1910–1917* (Cambridge: MIT Press, 1970); Smith, *The United States and Revolutionary Nationalism, 1916–1932* (Chicago: University of Chicago Press, 1972).

[6]Emily Rosenberg demonstrates in *Spreading the American Dream: American Economic and Cultural Expansion, 1890–1945* (New York: Hill & Wang, 1982) that many American businessmen shared the same belief.

[7]Quoted in Robert Bacon and James Scott, eds., *Latin America and the United States: Addresses by Elihu Root* (Cambridge: Harvard University Press, 1917), 10.

[8]Bryan to Wilson, 28 October 1913, Woodrow Wilson Papers, series 2, reel 51, Library of Congress.

[9]Gilderhus, *Diplomacy and Revolution: U.S.-Mexican Relations under Wilson and Carranza* (Tucson: University of Arizona Press, 1977).

[10]Williams, *The Tragedy of American Diplomacy* (New York: Dell Publishing Company, 1962 [1959]).

[11]Link, *Woodrow Wilson: Revolution, War, and Peace* (Arlington Heights, IL: AHM Publishing Company, 1979), 8–9.

[12]*The United States and Revolutionary Nationalism*, 25–28.

[13]Tulchin, *The Aftermath of War: World War I and U.S. Policy toward Latin America* (New York: New York University Press, 1971), vi.

[14]Link, *Wilson: Revolution, War, and Peace*; Cooper, *The Warrior and the Priest: Woodrow Wilson and Theodore Roosevelt* (Cambridge: Harvard University Press, 1983); Friedlander, "A Reassessment of Roosevelt's Role in the Panamanian Revolution of 1903," *Western Political Quarterly* 14 (1961): 535–43; Marks, *Velvet on Iron: The Diplomacy of Theodore Roosevelt* (Lincoln: University of Nebraska Press, 1979); Collin, *Theodore Roosevelt, Culture, Diplomacy, and Expansion: A New View of American Imperialism* (Baton Rouge: Louisiana State University Press, 1985).

[15]Collin, *Theodore Roosevelt*, 103.

[16]Parrini, *Heir to Empire: United States Economic Diplomacy, 1916–1923* (Pittsburgh: University of Pittsburgh Press, 1969); Hoff-Wilson, *American Business and Foreign Policy, 1920–1933* (Boston: Beacon Press, 1973 [1971]; Cuff, *The War Industries Board: Business-Government Relations during World War I* (Baltimore: Johns Hopkins University Press, 1973); Kaufman, *Efficiency and Expansion: Foreign Trade Organization in the Wilson Administration, 1913–1921* (Westport, CT: Greenwood Press, 1974).

[17]For insight into U.S. petroleum policy during this period see Michael J. Hogan, *Informal Entente: The Private Structure of Cooperation in Anglo-American Economic Diplomacy, 1918–1928* (Colombia: University of Missouri Press, 1977).

[18]Garraty, *Henry Cabot Lodge: A Biography* (New York: Alfred A. Knopf, 1953), 311–12.

[19]Widenor, *Henry Cabot Lodge and the Search for an American Foreign Policy* (Berkeley: University of California Press, 1980).

[20]May, *"Lessons" of the Past: The Use and Misuse of History in American Foreign Policy* (New York: Oxford University Press, 1973), xi.

Chapter I

Panama: Bone of Contention

The dream of an interoceanic canal linking the Atlantic and the Pacific had tantalized American leaders since the days of Thomas Jefferson. Obviously the route for such a canal should lie somewhere along the narrow isthmus connecting the continents of North and South America. One potential site of particular interest to the United States in the nineteenth century was Panama, a department within the Republic of New Granada. Anticipating the future importance of that area as a conduit for trade and travel between the two oceans, the United States in December 1846 signed a treaty of peace, friendship, commerce, and navigation with New Granada. In addition to defining trade relations, establishing the nature of future customs duties, and outlining the mutual rights of their citizens, the treaty, under Article 35, assured the United States full access to all means of communication and transportation then in existence across the isthmus, "or that may be hereafter constructed."[1] Furthermore, the treaty guaranteed the United States that, in the assessment of any levy for isthmian passage, American and Granadan citizens would be treated equally. In consideration for these provisions relating to trade, transit, and preferential treatment, the United States guaranteed "the perfect neutrality" of the isthmus, "with the view that the free transit from the one to the other sea may not be interrupted or embarrassed in any future time." Such a guarantee did not mean that either New Granada or Panama were in any sense American colonies. Washington specifically had promised in the treaty to guarantee New Granada's "rights of sovereignty and property" over the isthmus.[2] While the United States militarily intervened on the isthmus at least seven times during the remaining years of the nineteenth century to protect isthmian neutrality or to maintain uninterrupted railroad service between the Atlantic and Pacific, it continued to acknowledge New Granadan sovereignty over the increasingly important department of Panama.[3]

Although Washington officials during the nineteenth century understood the benefits that would accrue to the nation upon completion of an interoceanic canal, they were unable to secure an acceptable isthmian construction agreement with either Colombia or Nicaragua, the two nations with the considered canal sites.[4] Although Colombia and the United States signed two canal treaties, one in 1869 and the other in 1870, the Colombian legislature formally rejected the first, while the U.S. Senate refused to approve the second.[5]

Before those two aborted treaties were even negotiated, the United States and Great Britain, each suspicious of the other, agreed in April 1850 to the Clayton-Bulwer Treaty, which guaranteed that neither nation would assume exclusive control over an interoceanic canal in the Caribbean. Perhaps at that time Washington assumed that only the British had the financial resources and military power to construct a canal without the assistance or cooperation of the United States. Whatever the rationale, the United States signed no such agreement with other major powers. Therefore, in 1878, when Colombia granted the Türr syndicate a canal concession across the Isthmus of Panama, Washington officials expressed concern that a non-American group planned to undertake the canal project.[6] Only the French organization's engineering and financial crises between 1882 and 1890 calmed those concerns. By 1890 the syndicate's financial problems virtually assured that there would be no French canal.[7] Relieved officials in Washington utilized this reprieve to reinstitute an examination of possible routes for an American-built canal. Once again congressional and administrative leaders debated which route to support: the one through Nicaragua, or the one through Panama.[8]

The Spanish-American War in 1898 dramatically reminded the United States of the potential importance of an isthmian canal. At the end of only ten weeks of fighting, the United States had extended its control further into the Caribbean and the Pacific. With this expansion into noncontiguous territory, the American navy needed to play a more active role in maintaining U.S. sovereignty and influence abroad. Yet naval maneuverability and effectiveness would be seriously curtailed if during a crisis either individual vessels or the entire fleet had to be shifted from one ocean to the other. Without a canal, naval units had to travel the 14,500-mile route around Cape Horn or through the Strait of Magellan. The problems of such a course around South America were graphically demonstrated during the war with Spain, as the battleship USS *Oregon* tried to shift quickly from the Pacific to the Atlantic in order to strengthen naval forces in the Caribbean. The *Oregon*, steaming at full speed, reached Florida only after a grueling sixty-six-day voyage in which, to save time, it took the more dangerous but shorter route through the strait.[9]

In Washington the dramatic voyage of the *Oregon* incited the vigorous pursuit of a policy that would ensure sole U.S. control over a canal route. Shifting attitudes and world power had occurred during the fifty years following the signing of the 1850 Clayton-Bulwer Treaty with Britain. By the end of the century a confident and increasingly powerful United States desired to eliminate the restrictions imposed on canal construction by that treaty. Secretary of State John Hay, therefore, began talks in 1898 with British representatives to modify the earlier agreement. His preliminary concessions to the British, including an understanding not to fortify an American-built canal, so angered certain U.S. legislators in 1900 that they threatened construction of an American canal despite the existence of the Clayton-Bulwer document. British and American negotiators avoided such a radical alternative and the resulting diplomatic furor it would have sparked by signing a new agreement in November 1901, which allowed the American government to construct, control, and fortify an interoceanic canal without British participation. The U.S. Senate overwhelmingly ratified that treaty by a vote of 76 to 6.[10]

The settlement cleared the way for the United States to negotiate with either Nicaragua or Colombia for an isthmian route. In June 1899, President William McKinley had established the Walker Commission, composed of respected engineers, to determine the preferable route. In their final report of November 1901, the commissioners unanimously supported the Nicaraguan route, citing its lower projected cost as a decisive factor. Acting upon the Walker report, the House of Representatives in mid-January 1902 voted 308 to 2 in favor of the Nicaraguan canal. A shaken New Panama Canal Company, which had replaced the Türr syndicate, quickly decided to lower the price it had sought originally for the transfer of its Panamanian canal concession to the United States.[11]

The lowering of the New Panama Canal Company's price to $40,000,000 decisively influenced President Theodore Roosevelt, who had heretofore withheld support from the Panama site.[12] He already had convinced himself of the importance of, and need for, an interoceanic canal. In his message to Congress shortly after assuming the presidency in 1901, he noted that "no single great material work which remains to be undertaken on this continent is of such consequence to the American people as the building of a canal across the Isthmus connecting North and South America."[13] Once he had decided the Panamanian site was preferable, he convinced Walker to reconvene the commission in order to examine its previous decision in light of this newest development. Walker took little convincing. Personally committed neither to Panama nor Nicaragua, he had believed all along that the United States should choose the most advantageous route. Since in Walker's view both were equally feasible, cost was a crucial determinant.

Within four days of reconvening, the Walker Commission reversed its earlier selection and urged construction at Panama. While Roosevelt's desire for a reconsideration of routes had led to the reassembly of the commission, the president had not dictated its choice. Writing months later to Senator John T. Morgan, an archfoe of the Panama route, Commissioner Lewis Haupt revealed that Roosevelt neither had communicated with individual members, except Walker, nor had coerced the commission as a group.[14] The pro-Nicaraguan forces in Congress, led by Morgan, had suffered a mortal blow, although they would continue to argue their case through June.

On 28 June 1902, Congress delegated to Roosevelt, under the Spooner Act, the authority to supervise negotiations for a Panamanian route with both Colombia and the New Panama Canal Company. Should either of these two interrelated negotiations fail, the act authorized the president to meet with Nicaraguan and Costa Rican officials to gain access to the Nicaraguan route.[15]

Responsibility in 1901 and 1902 for negotiating an acceptable isthmian agreement with the United States rested on Colombian Ministers Carlos Martínez Silva and José Vicente Concha.[16] While Bogotá desired a Panamanian rather than a Nicaraguan canal, it was reluctant to grant the United States all the concessions Washington policymakers deemed essential for such a large-scale enterprise. Hoping to delay any agreement until it ended an internal civil war, the José Marroquín administration refused to send detailed proposals to either Colombian minister on what an isthmian agreement should or should not contain. To no avail, Silva specifically requested instructions in June and December of 1901 and in January of 1902. Lacking guidance, he then decided to develop his own proposals, granting the United States use of a canal at Panama in perpetuity, the right to employ its own police force in the canal zone, and the right to establish a separate civil and criminal judicial system. Upon replacing Silva as the chief negotiator, Minister Concha believed such grants were an erosion of Colombian sovereignty and wanted his government to renounce them. When the Marroquín administration failed to act on his suggestions and when, invoking the 1846 treaty, it invited U.S. military intervention on the isthmus in 1902 to protect the isthmian railroad, Concha resigned in protest.

Following passage of the Spooner Act in June, Roosevelt found Colombian delay increasingly unacceptable; he was anxious to conclude an agreement and to proceed with actual construction. Secretary of State Hay, therefore, orally informed the Colombian chargé, Tomás Herrán, who assumed control of the legation upon Concha's resignation, that Roosevelt sought a categorical decision over the terms currently under discussion by January 1903. Herrán was also aware that Senator Shelby Cullom was urging the Roosevelt administration to ignore Colombia and to seize Panama, citing "universal public usefulness" as its justification if Colombia did not soon conclude an acceptable canal agreement. While neither the State Department nor Roosevelt had made such direct threats, Herrán believed that the president's impetuousness might lead him to accept the Cullom approach if a treaty was not signed.[17]

Considering Herrán's reports from Washington, Colombian Minister for Foreign Affairs Felipe Paúl informed his chargé to continue working for "pecuniary advantages." However, he cautioned, if this is not possible and "you see that you might lose all by delay, sign the treaty."[18] Facing the growing restlessness and pressure of the Roosevelt administration, Herrán signed the document on 22 January.[19] Writing ten days later, he observed to a friend that he was likely to receive abuse "for not having quite satisfied the exaggerated expectations that [were] entertained" in his homeland.[20] Ironically, unaware of Herrán's actions, Vice President Marroquín ordered him on 24 January to await further instructions from Bogotá before signing a treaty with the United States.

Colombia was in a poor position to resist further the isthmian aspirations of the United States. Political factionalism, as well as departmental resistance to strong control from Bogotá, limited the freedom of action and maneuverability of top governmental leaders during the entire negotiating process. After three years of bloody civil war, Colombia had managed to reestablish peace only in November 1902, the month Concha resigned. The conflict that had begun in October 1899 was the culmination of years of struggle between Colombian Liberals and Conservatives. After gaining power the Conservatives had abrogated the Liberal constitution in 1885 and had written a new document effectively curbing the great autonomy of Colombian states and centralizing governmental power in Bogotá. Under the leadership of President Rafael Núñez (1884–86), they also began instituting wide-ranging measures extending federal power, curtailing civil liberties, levying new taxes, and restraining Liberal participation in the elective process. (A minor Liberal revolt in 1895 against Conservative rule had been quickly suppressed with no major reprisals.) During the next four years the Liberal factions had been unable to effect changes in the government and, as a result, again had revolted in 1899. Seven months after this uprising, Conservative forces had decisively defeated the Liberals at Palonegro. However, instead of conceding defeat, the mortally weakened Liberal forces had initiated guerrilla warfare, thereby extending the conflict for another two years. Not until late November 1902 did the last of the three major Liberal armies finally surrender.[21]

The fighting had ended, but at immense cost. Between 75,000 and 100,000 Colombians had died in the three-year conflict. The national treasury was empty. The government was unable either to pay its employees or even the interest on the national debt. In fact, as early as mid-1898 it owed 7 million pesos which it could not repay. Add to this financial instability a long, costly civil war and the result was devastating. The struggle disrupted commerce, destroyed farms, tied up manpower, siphoned needed funds, and created rampant inflation, as well as spreading terror, bloodshed, and fear.[22]

By delaying negotiations under Martínez Silva and Concha, Marroquín had hoped to postpone talks until Colombia resolved its civil war and thereby strengthened its negotiating position. However, in view of growing U.S. pressure for an agreement after June 1902, the Colombian executive faced a dilemma.

> As far as the question of the canal is concerned [he lamented to General V. M. Salazar in July], I find myself in a horrible perplexity; in order for the North Americans to go ahead with the work it will be necessary to make to them concessions of territory, sovereignty, and jurisdiction which the executive power has no power to give, and if these concessions are not granted and the North Americans determine to open the canal, and to open it without being bothered by triffles, then we will lose more sovereignty than that which we would lose if we make the concessions that they ask. Of me history will say that I ruined the isthmus and all of Colombia, not permitting the Panama Canal to be opened or that I permitted it to be done, scandalously injuring the rights and reputation of my nation.[23]

Plagued by party and personal rivalries, by governmental division and instability, Marroquín was unsure that, if he accepted the Herrán treaty on behalf of the Colombian people, he could survive politically. While legally only the vice president, he had exercised the full powers of the executive since seizing power in a coup in July 1900. Well aware that, even in more peaceful times, a canal treaty with the United States would be a politically explosive issue, Marroquín did not want to bear full responsibility for the Herrán document. The most controversial sections of the agreement included the transfer of the concession held by the New Panama Canal Company without requiring the company to compensate Colombia; the size of U.S. compensation to Colombia ($10 million plus a $250,000 annuity); and the right of the United States to make and enforce "police regulations" and to establish U.S. courts in the canal zone. Marroquín had reason to worry. British Minister Claude Mallet estimated that only 20 percent of the educated inhabitants of Bogotá favored the treaty.[24] Since the Colombian constitution granted both houses of Congress the right "to approve or reject treaties entered into by the Government with foreign powers," Marroquín avoided a decision by convening Congress for the first time since 1898.[25]

His message to the new Congress on 20 June 1903 was reminiscent of his earlier lament. If Congress ratified the Hay-Herrán Treaty, it would relinquish sovereignty without sufficient indemnification, Marroquín informed the legislature. While "the just wishes of the inhabitants of Panama and other Colombians would be satisfied," he continued, "the Government would be exposed to the charge afterwards that it did not defend its sovereignty and that it did not defend the interests of the nation." If, on the other hand, Colombia rejected the treaty, the government would be attacked for not obtaining a canal at Panama and for losing the benefits and revenue such a canal agreement would bring. As vice president, what did Marroquín suggest? He announced that he believed the canal should be opened at Panama, and that Colombia should not put obstacles in its path, "even at the cost of sacrifices." But, he quickly added, whatever the decision, Congress must make it, not the executive. "Once I have let fall upon you all the responsibility that the decision over this subject brings with it, I will not try to make my opinion influential."[26] In his message, Marroquín neither urged Congress to ratify nor reject. In an attempt to disassociate himself further from the treaty, he even refused to place his signature on the proposed convention as was the custom.[27]

Officials in Washington should not have been surprised by signs of Colombian discontent with the details of the agreement. The American minister, Arthur N. Beaupré, already had warned that the treaty would face stiff opposition in the Colombian Congress.[28] He also noted that the press, as well as the public, sharply criticized the proposed terms. In addition, Beaupré seemed to doubt the Marroquín administration's commitment to the agreement. "It seems altogether probable," he wrote on 30 March, "that unless the Government is thoroughly in earnest in its desire to have the convention ratified, it will not be done; and there is a possibility that it may not go through in any event."[29] By mid-April, Beaupré thought that the treaty could in fact be ratified if, and only if, it received full support of the Marroquín government.[30]

Beaupré's analysis corresponded to that of the British legation's. As early as March 1902, Mallet had warned London that, while Colombian officials favored a canal, they were sensitive to the issue of sovereignty. Four days before Beaupré informed Washington of his uncertainty concerning Marroquín's commitment to the treaty, the British minister reported that the three lawyers Marroquín had asked to evaluate the proposed treaty had opposed it. Furthermore, based on his own evaluation of the attitude of "influential natives," Mallet concluded that the "opinion is unanimous that the projected treaty is unacceptable as regards the provisions both for compensation and sovereignty." Nevertheless, he was convinced that many believed if Colombia rejected the treaty they might lose both sovereignty in Panama and the $10 million offered by the United States. In phrasing remarkably similar to Beaupré's of 30 March, Mallet added: "I am persuaded in my mind that unless the Colombian Government is in earnest and determined to have the treaty accepted, its ratification by Congress is extremely improbable."[31]

After considering the disappointing communiqués from Beaupré, Secretary Hay instructed the American legation, in a telegram of 9 June, to express concern over the prospects for ratification:

> The Colombian Government apparently does not appreciate the gravity of the situation. The canal negotiations were initiated by Colombia, and were energetically pressed upon this Government for several years. The propositions presented by Colombia, with slight modifications, were finally accepted by us. In virtue of this agreement our Congress reversed its previous judgment and decided upon the Panama route. If Colombia should now reject the treaty or unduly delay its ratification, the friendly understanding between the two countries would be so seriously compromised that action might be taken by Congress next winter which every friend of Colombia might regret.[32]

Not only was Beaupré to transmit this message orally to Minister for Foreign Affairs Luis Carlos Rico, but, if requested, he also was to present it formally to Colombia as a written memorandum.

Facing a hostile Congress, which had opened its special session on 20 June, Rico, hoping to divert the criticism of the Hay-Herrán agreement to the United States, transmitted the Hay-Beaupré memorandum to the Senate. If Secretary Hay's purpose was to intimidate the Colombian government into rapidly approving the Hay-Herrán Treaty, he failed. For almost two weeks the Senate debated whether or not even to consider the treaty since Vice President Marroquín had withheld his signature. Finally, on 15 July, the Senate appointed a committee of nine to study the proposed agreement and decide whether it was acceptable or needed to be amended.

The committee reported its conclusions on 4 August, with seven of its nine members agreeing to the proposed document on the condition that the United States accept nine modifications aimed at limiting American control of the canal area. The senators found unconstitutional that section of Article 13 of the Hay-Herrán Treaty which permitted the United States to establish judicial tribunals in the zone to resolve all controversies relating to the construction, maintenance, and operation of the canal. In addition to the elimination of that particular section, the committee suggested no clear grant be given the New Panama Canal Company to sell and transfer its rights to the United States. Instead, it recommended that the company reach an acceptable agreement with Bogotá, including possible monetary considerations, after which it could legally transfer its rights to the United States. The senators also agreed to modify Articles 2 and 3 granting the United States the exclusive right to the zone for 100 years, "renewable at the sole and absolute option of the United States, for periods of similar duration so long as the United States may desire." The committee further suggested that

> Colombia [concede] to the United States only the right to use the zone of the canal and such part of the adjacent territory as may be necessary for the work; it must be clearly set forth that the rights conceded to the United States are in the nature of tenancy, excluding any idea of transfer of dominion by establishing clearly and peremptorily the perpetuity of the concession.[33]

If the United States adopted these three amendments, as well as six less serious modifications, the committee would then recommend passage by the full Senate.

In a letter to the minister for foreign affairs, Beaupré, acting without instructions, denounced the committee's modifications.[34] In a second letter of the same date, he warned that "any modification whatever of the terms of the treaty" could be legitimately considered by the United States "as practically a breach of faith on the part of the Government of Colombia, such as may invoke the very greatest complications in the friendly relations which have hitherto existed between the two countries."[35] The American minister hoped such language would deter the full Senate from accepting the committee's alterations, but Beaupré's calculations proved seriously in error. The twenty senators who had indicated their intention to accept the treaty with modifications withdrew their support altogether when informed of the legation's response. As a result, on 12 August the Senate voted 24 to 0 to reject the unamended Hay-Herrán Treaty.[36]

Within twenty-four hours, Rico cabled Herrán, citing the issue of sovereignty over the isthmus and Beaupré's impolitic remarks as reasons for the defeat. In closing, however, he added that "it is considered probable that Congress will give bases for renewal of negotiations." Three days later Rico explained in more detail Colombia's position: "The Senate, considering that the people of Colombia wish to maintain the most cordial relations with the U.S., and that the completion of the canal is of the greatest importance to general American commerce, has appointed a commission of three members to study the manner of satisfying the vehement desire for the excavation of the Panama canal in harmony with national interests and legality."[37] He then ordered Herrán to inform the United States that the debate over canal construction at Panama was not dead. Discussions in the Colombian Senate over possible modifications to the Hay-Herrán document continued into September and October, although the senators reached no agreement. Finally, on 31 October, the Senate adjourned, postponing indefinitely further consideration of the treaty.[38]

The Colombian legislature's refusal to ratify the Hay-Herrán document, considered vital by Panamanians for their future well-being, provided the catalyst for revolution. Fearful that the Roosevelt administration, following the terms of the Spooner Act, might abandon Panama and construct a canal in Nicaragua, and angered by Bogotá's apparent indifference to the needs of the Panamanian people, the revolutionaries acted. Bogotá's rejection of the treaty simply had reinforced a conviction already prevalent among Panamanian elites, a conviction that they, not the government, should control their own destiny.

Such a conclusion was not unique to the revolutionary generation of 1903. Seeds of Panama's rebellion had been planted as early as the 1830s when Panamanians first opposed Bogotá's political and economic control. Nor did newly won independence from Spain ensure that Panama and other New Granada political departments would welcome a strong central government. Quite the contrary was true. Throughout the nineteenth century, New Granada officials faced civil insurrections and secessionist attempts. Personal political rivalry, the absence of an integrated national transportation network, provincial isolation imposed by the physical geography of the nation, and fear of an arbitrary central government unsympathetic to the economic and political needs of diverse regions led to a deep suspicion of centralized control. By the early 1860s those Colombians favoring strong departmental governments, rather than a powerful central one, had emerged victorious. Panama, for example, chose its own governor and exercised considerable autonomous power. Even then, Panama continued to distrust Bogotá.

However, the accession of Rafael Núñez to the presidency in 1884 marked the beginning of an attack on state power by those favoring centralism. While Conservatives under the Núñez presidency successfully concentrated power in Bogotá through the Constitution of 1886, they did not eradicate federalist support, either in Panama or in other Colombian departments. It was the discontent of those federalists which contributed to the bloody civil war between 1899 and 1902. It was also this traditional distrust of central authority and history of resistance to Bogotá's rule that motivated Panama's revolutionary leaders in 1903. Regional and departmental distrust of Bogotá, anger at the Marroquín administration's failure to secure passage of the Hay-Herrán Treaty, and fear that a canal may be built in Nicaragua, rather than on the isthmus, underlay the November revolution.

Aware of these factors and building upon them, two of the most influential Washington lobbyists for the Panama route, William Nelson Cromwell and Philippe Bunau-Varilla, by early autumn 1903 had urged Panamanian secession. While acting independently of one another and pursuing their own goals, they were closely associated with U.S. administration leaders in both the executive and congressional branches.[39] Only after his meetings with President Roosevelt and Secretary Hay on 9 and 16 October, respectively, did Bunau-Varilla promise potential Panamanian revolutionaries that their uprising would be protected by the United States within forty-eight hours of its initiation. Although Roosevelt had made no secret pact with Bunau-Varilla regarding support, the astute Frenchman correctly surmised the administration's response to an actual revolution. The correlation between those meetings and Bunau-Varilla's assurance to the revolutionaries, however, would later appear highly suspicious.[40]

By late summer and early fall of 1903, Roosevelt had become exasperated. Writing to Hay on 19 August, two weeks after the Colombian committee proposed its modifications to the Hay-Herrán document, the president fumed: "If under the treaty of 1846 we have a color of right to start in and build the canal, my offhand judgment would favor such proceeding. . . . I do not think that the Bogota lot of jack rabbits should be allowed permanently to bar one of the future highways of civilization." One month later he observed that either Nicaragua be reconsidered, which he had no intention of doing, or "in some shape or way we interfere when it becomes necessary so as to secure the Panama route without further dealing with the foolish and homicidal corruptionists in Bogota. I am not inclined to have any further dealings whatever with those Bogota people." Despite his frustration and anger, Roosevelt informed Albert Shaw, one of the members of his "kitchen cabinet," that the United States could not acquire the canal by direct military seizure of Panama. "Privately, I freely say to you," Roosevelt quickly added, "that I should be delighted if Panama were an independent state, or if it made itself so at this moment; but for me to say so publicly would amount to an instigation of a revolt, and therefore I cannot say it." Although he did not publicly reveal his position, his attitudes were sufficiently clear that it is not surprising that Bunau-Varilla correctly assessed the stance the president would take if a Panamanian revolution occurred.[41]

Orders transmitted to ships of the American Caribbean and Pacific fleets also showed Roosevelt's intention to support a possible revolution.[42] The day prior to the insurrection—2 November—the gunboat USS *Nashville*, anchored at Colón, Panama, received the following orders: "Maintain free and uninterrupted transit on the isthmus. If interruption threatened by armed force, occupy the line of railroad. Prevent landing of any armed force with hostile intent, either Government or insurgent, either at Colón, Porto Bello, or other point[s]."[43] On the same day the cruisers *Boston* and *Marblehead*, the monitor *Wyoming*, and the gunboat *Concord* were ordered to proceed to the Pacific coast of Panama. To the Caribbean side of the isthmus, the Navy Department had dispatched the cruiser *Dixie* on 2 November and the cruiser *Atlanta* the following day.[44]

Roosevelt, frustrated by what he believed to be Colombian duplicity, wanted the canal issue finally settled. The uprising seemed to provide that opportunity, and on 4 November the president commented:

> Just at present I am attending to the Panama business. For half a century we have policed that Isthmus in the interest of the little wildcat republic of Colombia. Colombia has behaved infamously about the treaty for the building of the Panama Canal; and I do not intend in the police work that I will have to do in connection with the new insurrection any longer to do for her work which is not merely profitless but brings no gratitude. Any interference I undertake now will be in the interest of the United States and of the people of the Panama Isthmus themselves. There will be some lively times in carrying out this policy.[45]

Angered by Colombian intransigence and convinced of the vital need for a canal, Roosevelt liberally interpreted that Article 35 of the 1846 treaty permitted the United States to ensure the complete neutrality of the proposed canal region and its railroad. As the dispatch to the *Nashville* on 2 November had indicated, this could entail stopping armed Colombian forces from crossing the isthmus to put down the revolution.

Actually, 400 Colombian troops, ordered to suppress any revolt, had landed at Colón the next day before the *Nashville* received its orders to intercept. The Panamanians, however, reacted quickly to that threat. Luring the Colombian military leaders to Panama City where they were arrested, they temporarily neutralized the Colombian force. With his superiors under arrest, Colonel Eliseo Torres commanded the 400 soldiers at Colón, where he faced a revolutionary government, a hostile U.S. naval presence, and an inability to use the Panama Railroad to transport his men. Realizing that no reinforcements from Colombia would be forthcoming and observing the arrival of the USS *Dixie*, Torres agreed to depart. Panama gave him $8,000 (U.S.) to pay for the passage of his soldiers and equipment on the steamer *Orinoco*. Once the steamer departed on 6 November, no ship could approach the isthmus without American acquiescence.[46]

Roosevelt was in sympathy with the revolutionaries, who had broken the impasse that had arisen between the United States and Colombia and had given the president a rather pleasant alternative. In fact, by 6 November, the date Colombian leaders in Bogotá first learned of the revolution, Roosevelt had determined his course of action. "Colombia," he wrote, "signed [its] death warrant when [it] acted in such infamous bad faith about the signing of the treaty. Unless Congress overrides me, which I do not think probable, Colombia's grip on Panama is gone forever."[47] That same day the United States recognized the independence of Panama. Fifteen days after the beginning of the revolution, Secretary of State Hay and newly appointed Panamanian Minister Philippe Bunau-Varilla signed a convention in Washington ending any chance of Colombia regaining sovereignty over its errant department. Article 1 of the treaty was short and to the point: "The United States guarantees and will maintain the independence of the Republic of Panama." Panama in return agreed to grant the United States perpetual use and control over a ten-mile-wide corridor extending the entire width of the isthmus and through which the canal would be constructed. In addition, it gave "to the United States all the rights, power and authority within the zone . . . which the United States would possess and exercise if it were the sovereign of the territory." For those and other considerations the United States consented to pay Panama $10 million in gold upon ratification and $250,000 annually in perpetuity, beginning in 1913.[48]

American proponents of a Panama canal could not have been more pleased. Panama, while accepting the same amount of money offered Colombia, had conceded in all but name its sovereignty over the canal zone, something Colombia had refused to do. These extremely favorable concessions by Panama, as well as Colombia's intransigence, affected Roosevelt's perception of the entire affair. On 30 November the president wrote Otto Gresham, a Chicago lawyer, that

> the Colombians need not come here to ask justice from me. They have received exact justice, after I had in vain endeavored to persuade them to accept generosity. In their silly efforts to damage us they cut their own throats. They tried to hold us up; and too late they have discovered their criminal error.
>
> By the way, on the score of morality it seems to me that nothing could be more wicked than to ask us to surrender the Panama people, who are our friends, to the Colombian people, who have shown themselves our foes.[49]

In view of Roosevelt's determination, Colombian chances of regaining sovereignty over Panama seemed remote.

Upon learning of the isthmian rebellion on 6 November, Vice President Marroquín and his top advisers faced a major decision: What would be the Colombian response to the revolution and to U.S. interference? Orders could have been given to the Colombian navy to sail to Panama and attempt to disperse the American vessels lying offshore, thereby enabling Colombian troops to land, but the "fighting fleet" of Colombia consisted of only one seagoing vessel and two stern-wheel river gunboats. The two 4.7-inch guns, the four 4-inch guns, and the four 14-inch torpedo tubes of the *Almirante Lego* were hardly a match for even the oldest and slowest American cruiser, let alone the combined American Caribbean and Pacific fleets.[50] Therefore, naval operations against U.S. fleets would be an unacceptable, indeed a suicidal, solution. Observers unfamiliar with Colombian terrain might have expected Colombia to send its army overland to retake Panama. Nature, however, had created an almost impenetrable barrier between Panama and Colombia, a barrier through which no Colombian army could march.[51] Since military maneuvers by land were totally impractical and since maneuvers by sea would have to cope with the seven American ships already anchored near Panama, Colombian leaders had little choice except to negotiate in order to retain national sovereignty over Panama.[52]

First, Bogotá probed U.S. intentions. Unofficially, General Rafael Reyes, the politically influential former minister to France and soon-to-be president of Colombia, met with Minister Beaupré on 6 November. Quickly summarizing the conversation, Beaupré telegraphed it to the State Department, where it was received two days later. The American minister reported:

> Knowing that the revolution has already commenced in Panama General Reyes says that if the Government of the United States will land troops to preserve Colombian sovereignty, and the transit,

> if requested by the Colombian Chargé d'Affaires, this government will declare martial law and by virtue of vested constitutional authority, when public order is disturbed, will approve by decree the ratification of the canal treaty as signed; or if the Government of the United States prefers will call extra session of Congress with new and friendly members next May to approve the treaty. General Reyes has the perfect confidence of the Vice President, he says, and if it becomes necessary will go to the isthmus or send representatives there to adjust matters along above lines to the satisfaction of the people there. . . . This is the personal opinion of Reyes and he will advise this government to act accordingly.[53]

Whether Reyes acted with official encouragement, or whether the idea was his alone, Beaupré could not elicit confirmation of the Reyes statement from Minister for Foreign Affairs Rico when they met on 9 November. However, neither did the foreign minister denounce the Reyes proposals. Rather than commenting on such declarations, he merely inquired whether the United States would permit Colombian troops to land in Panama and if, adhering to Article 35, would guarantee Colombian sovereignty over the isthmus.[54] Bogotá was in an embarrassing position. Unless the United States voluntarily yielded, Colombia would not be able to regain control over one of its departments. Yet, if its officials did not express outrage and attempt to regain, at least by strenuous diplomatic measures, the lost department, they would come under increasing attack for yielding to the "colossus of the North." The early official Colombian response was thus cautious and controlled as officials probed American intentions in order to find an acceptable solution.

Faced with an empty treasury, fearful of another major internal political shift, tired after three years of civil war, and matched against the power of the United States, Colombian leaders sought a peaceful solution to the Panamanian secession. Hoping to entice Panama to return voluntarily, Bogotá dispatched to the isthmus a four-man delegation headed by Reyes. On 20 November they met with Panamanian representatives aboard the Colombian steamer *Canadá* at Colón. Colombia's desire for voluntary reintegration evaporated as the Panamanian officials insisted that the separation was irrevocable, sanctioned as it was by the Panamanians and recognized by governments in both America and Europe.[55] The Panama delegation added, however, that it hoped Colombia would recognize its independence so that the two nations could reestablish friendly relations.[56]

On the day of the meeting aboard the *Canadá*, Reyes received a letter from Vice Admiral J. B. Coghlan, commanding officer of the U.S. Caribbean Squadron. If there were any lingering doubts in the minds of the Reyes contingent about military action against Panama, the Coghlan letter dispelled them. The admiral informed Reyes that his orders required him to prevent the landing of hostile forces in Panama, the implication clearly being that Colombian forces would fall within the "hostile forces" category. The four Colombians recognized, after reading the letter, that military action was totally impossible, and that Colombia must seek settlement by further diplomatic measures. Bogotá agreed, and, as a result, Reyes left Panama for Washington.[57] Upon his arrival on 28 November, he would represent his government in discussions with the United States to seek the judicious resolution of the Panama crisis.

Awaiting the Colombian emissary was a vigorous and self-confident administration, eager to play a major role in international affairs. American intervention on the isthmus in 1903 had been no aberration; it merely exemplified the nation's new international awareness. During the closing decade of the nineteenth century, the United States had emerged from a large domestically oriented republic into a powerful internationally active state. Concentrating on internal development, on the creation of a transportation and communications network, on the establishment of successful industry, and on the growing conflict between state and federal authority, the United States, during most of the nineteenth century, had frequently relegated international diplomacy to secondary importance. Its preoccupation with internal growth and development had not altered dramatically, with either the purchase of Alaska in 1867, or with the acquisition of naval rights in Samoa in 1879. By the 1890s, however, many Americans had realized the importance of foreign areas such as the Caribbean and South America, or at least had realized their potential danger if these countries should fall into the hands of a major European power. President Grover Cleveland's warning to Great Britain in 1895 to arbitrate its dispute with Venezuela, for example, had signified a transition which would elevate that particular region's importance in U.S. policymaking. But American interest was not limited to the Caribbean. Within four years the United States not only had annexed Hawaii but also, after a short war with Spain, had acquired control over Cuba, Puerto Rico, Guam, and the Philippines. Those acquisitions had thrust the United States into the world political arena. Americans no longer chose to ignore developments in Latin America or Asia while focusing their undivided attention on domestic issues.

Not surprisingly, America's coming of age internationally created new difficulties. Great Britain's decision in 1897 to upgrade its American legation to an embassy, for example, set the stage for a notable social crisis.[58] Prior to that year no ambassador had ever resided in Washington. What would be an ambassador's status in relation to American leaders? Who would pay courtesy calls first? Who would occupy the place of honor at diplomatic dinners and receptions? American leaders never before had worried about such considerations. The problem of the old-world powers had all seemed remote, not of their own nation. With the growing American role in international affairs, however, U.S. officials had to react to such minor new problems and circumstances as well as try to formulate major policies to guide the nation in its foreign activities.

The general mood of American leaders in 1903 toward foreign involvement can be characterized by briefly examining the actions and rhetoric of Roosevelt and William Howard Taft between 1901 and 1913. They both articulated, through their conduct, the prevailing national temperament at the turn of the century. Their actions demonstrated the difficulties that Colombian leaders faced in pressing their Panamanian claims in the fall of 1903 and thereafter.

Roosevelt and Taft welcomed America's growing international role,[59] which would enhance the nation's influence not only in Europe and Asia but also in Latin America, an area that since 1895 increasingly has attracted U.S. attention. By carefully using political, economic, and moral power, the two Republicans hoped that the United States could both restore order in chronically unstable Caribbean nations and lessen European influence throughout the region. Elihu Root, adviser, colleague, and friend to both men, explained in 1908 the basis for such a policy: "The United States must exercise a predominant influence [over the Caribbean states]. . . . We must control the route to the Panama Canal. . . . We cannot permit an un-American power to obtain possession of any of these countries." On the other hand, he continued, "we do not wish to take them into the American Union. To prevent the possibility of the one and the necessity of the other we wish to help all these peoples to build up and maintain peaceable, orderly and free governments of their own."[60] Agreeing with that evaluation, neither Roosevelt nor Taft viewed such a policy as selfish economic exploitation, or as narrow imperialistic aggression.

American intervention in the Caribbean during the first decade of the twentieth century was a duty, a duty to the citizens of the United States, a duty to neighboring states, and a duty to the world. One method of fulfilling all facets of that obligation was by increasing America's economic preponderance throughout the region.[61] That would satisfy U.S. economic and strategic requirements, raise the standard of life in the southern republics, and foster stable internationally responsible governments. As Secretary of State Philander C. Knox informed the National Civic Federation in 1911, the United States had a moral obligation to assist economically its less fortunate neighbors.

> If the American dollar [he asserted] can aid suffering humanity and lift the burden of financial difficulty from States with which we live on terms of intimate intercourse and earnest friendship, and replace insecurity and devastation by stability and peaceful self-development, all I can say is that it would be hard to find better employment. Anyhow, the Department of State will always be glad to take advantage of the American dollar in furtherance of peace on earth and good will to fellow men.[62]

Taft also viewed American assistance in humanitarian and religious terms. "The policy of isolation," he declared in January 1908,

> which would prevent us from exercising our influence or our direct control in matters where we are capable of doing good and advancing the world's progress, is a narrow, selfish, and altogether unjustifiable policy. . . . We must regard and have an interest in what our neighbors are doing, and when we can assist them, we cannot pass by on the other side as the Levite did, but we must take them up as the Good Samaritan did and bind up their wounds and prepare to send them on their way rejoicing.[63]

If small-minded individuals or selfishly motivated leaders misconstrued U.S. action in the Caribbean, American leaders believed, it was their lack of perception that should be condemned and not the policies of an internationally aware U.S. government.

Confident that the United States pursued a righteous course, Washington blurred the distinction between American goals and hemispheric interests. When vital issues were perceived as being at stake, as during the Panama incident in 1903, what was good for the United States seemed good for the entire hemisphere. Since an interoceanic route would benefit both the United States and the world, intervention or influence to ensure its security was justifiable. When Costa Rica appeared economically unstable in 1905, for example, Secretary Root noted: "It does seem to me so important to have the next door neighbor of Panama under the financial control of Americans, with a power of ultimate control of the United States rather than have it vested in a foreign power."[64] Three years later then Secretary of War Taft carried that logic even further. In a new treaty to be negotiated with the Panamanian government, he wrote the president,

> we should be given direct control over the elections, so as to permit us, should we desire, to intervene and determine who is fairly elected. This I agree detracts from the independence of the

> "Republic" but as the Republic has not shown itself competent in this regard, we are justified in insisting that we be given greater control to protect our own interests which are so closely involved with the peaceful continuance of the Panamanian government.[65]

Convinced that they pursued the right course relating to Panama, Colombia, and the Caribbean, American leaders between 1901 and 1913 were determined to "guide" less confident or potentially disruptive Latin American states.

The actions and rhetoric of these two administrations exemplified the general mood of Washington as General Reyes traveled north in November 1903. While Latin American leaders, especially those in Colombia, might question the propriety of recent U.S. actions on the isthmus, administration officials in Washington, emitting an aura of self-assurance and confidence, knew they had acted correctly. They personally realized, even if neighboring states had not, that the United States had come of age. It was ready and willing to assume its "destined" role as guardian of the Caribbean, as builder of an isthmian canal, and as arbiter of hemispheric conduct.

Notes

[1]*Statutes at Large and Treaties of the United States of America* 9 (December 1845–March 1851), "Treaty with New Granada," 12 December 1846, pp. 881–901. New Granada in 1846 would consist roughly of present-day Colombia and Panama.

[2]Ibid., 898–99.

[3]U.S. Congress, Senate, *Use by the United States of a Military Force in the Internal Affairs of Colombia*, Sen. Doc. 143, 58th Cong., 2d sess., 1904. Also see E. Taylor Parks, *Colombia and the United States, 1765–1934* (Durham: Duke University Press, 1935), 219–61.

[4]After a canal commission, appointed by President Ulysses S. Grant, had investigated alternative routes in 1876, sites in Panama and Nicaragua appeared to be the most suitable for a canal.

[5]For a general discussion of U.S. efforts to secure a canal in the nineteenth century see Parks, *Colombia*, 338–91.

[6]U.S. Congress, Senate, S. Res. 43, 46th Cong., 1st sess., 1879, *Congressional Record* 9:2312. Also see Parks, *Colombia*, 378. In 1861, New Granada was renamed the United States of Colombia; in 1886 the name was changed to the Republic of Colombia, the form still in use. The official title of the Türr syndicate in 1878 was the Société Civile Internationale du Canal Interocéanique de Darien, later reorganized and renamed Compagnie Universelle du Canal Interocéanique de Panama.

[7]For a full discussion of French activities see McCullough, *Path between the Seas*, 45–241; Philippe Bunau-Varilla, *Panama: The Creation, Destruction and*

Resurrection (London: Constable & Company, 1913); and Lemaitre Román, *Panamá y su Separación de Colombia.*

[8]For a fuller discussion see Parks, *Colombia*, 362–77; McCullough, *Path between the Seas*, 260–328; Graeme S. Mount, "American Imperialism in Panama" (Ph.D. diss., University of Toronto, 1969), 72–92; and Alfred Charles Richard, Jr., "The Panama Canal in American National Consciousness, 1870–1922" (Ph.D. diss., Boston University, 1969), 106–40.

[9]Charles E. Clarke, *My Fifty Years in the Navy* (Boston: Little, Brown & Company, 1917), 258–81. Clarke was the captain of the *Oregon* on this voyage.

[10]*Statutes at Large* 32, pt. 2 (1901–03), "Ship Canal Treaty," 18 November 1901, pp. 1903–5. For a discussion of British-U.S. negotiations see Bradford Perkins, *The Great Rapprochement: England and the United States, 1895–1914* (New York: Atheneum, 1968), 174–85; and Charles Campbell, Jr., *Anglo-American Understanding, 1898–1903* (Baltimore: Johns Hopkins, 1957), 186–239.

[11]The New Panama Canal Company had been organized in October 1894; it gave Colombia 50,000 of its 650,000 shares of stock. For information regarding the Walker Commission see Miner, *The Fight for the Panama Route*, 90–121. Also see U.S. Congress, Senate, *Report of the Isthmian Canal Commission, 1899–1901*, Sen. Doc. 222, 58th Cong., 2d sess., 1903–04, esp. pp. 171–75.

[12]As early as December 1901, Walker had indicated that $40 million might be sufficient. Walker to Alfred Noble, 30 December 1901, box 2, John Walker Papers, Library of Congress Manuscripts Division, Washington, DC (hereafter cited as Walker Papers).

[13]Address to U.S. Congress, 3 December 1901, Theodore Roosevelt, *Presidential Addresses and State Papers* (New York: Review of Reviews Company, 1910), 2:573.

[14]Haupt to Morgan, 14 September 1903, box 18, John Tyler Morgan Papers, Library of Congress Manuscripts Division, Washington, DC (hereafter cited as Morgan Papers). McCullough, on the other hand, believes that Roosevelt was crucial in shifting the committee's decision. For Walker's views see his letters to George Higbee (19 December 1900), Rufus Lane (18 February 1901), Alfred Noble (9 September and 30 December 1901), Henry Higginson (4 January 1902), and Lewis Haupt (1 February 1902), box 2, Walker Papers.

[15]*Statutes at Large* 32, "Spooner Act," 28 June 1902, chap. 1302, 481–84. For a more detailed examination of events surrounding passage of this act see Miner, *Fight for the Panama Route*, 116–56.

[16]For discussion of the actions of the Colombian ministers between 1901 and 1903 see José Joaquín Caicedo Castilla, *Historia Diplomática* (Bogotá: Ediciones Lerner, 1974), 1:319–28.

[17]Herrán to Felipe Paúl (minister for foreign affairs), 19 December 1902, in Cámara de Representantes, *Investigación sobre la Rebelión del Istmo de Panama* (Bogotá: Imprenta Nacional, 1913), 19–20.

[18]Paúl to Herrán, 10 January 1903, ibid., 21; Marroquín to Herrán, 10 January 1903, box 3, folder 57, Tomás Herrán Papers, Georgetown University, Washington, DC (hereafter cited as Herrán Papers).

[19]See Lemaitre Román, *Panamá y su Separación de Colombia*, 325–466 for information on the Hay-Herrán negotiations. Also see Marroquín to Herrán, 24 January 1903, in Antonio José Uribe, *Anales Diplomáticos y Consulares de*

Colombia (Bogotá: Imprenta Nacional, 1914), 4:840–41; Raimundo Rivas, *Historia Diplomática de Colombia, 1810–1934* (Bogotá: Imprenta Nacional, 1961), 589–91; Miner, *Fight for the Panama Route*, 188–96; Parks, *Colombia*, 390–91; and Tyler Dennett, *John Hay: From Poetry to Politics* (New York: Dodd, Mead & Company, 1934), 372–73.

[20]Herrán to "My Very Dear Friend," 1 February 1903, box 4, letterbook 2, p. 412, Herrán Papers.

[21]An excellent examination of the Liberal-Conservative struggle is found in Charles W. Bergquist, *Coffee and Conflict in Colombia, 1886–1910* (Durham: Duke University Press, 1978). Also see Helen Delpar, "The Liberal Party of Colombia, 1863–1903" (Ph.D. diss., Colombia University, 1967); Helen Delpar, *Red against Blue: The Liberal Party in Colombian Politics, 1863–1899* (University, AL: University of Alabama Press, 1981); William Paul McGreevey, *An Economic History of Colombia, 1845–1930* (Cambridge: Cambridge University Press, 1971), pt. 2; J. Fred Rippy, *The Capitalists and Colombia* (New York: Vanguard Press, 1931); Miner, *Fight for the Panama Route*, chap. 2; William M. Gibson, *The Constitutions of Colombia* (Durham: Duke University Press, 1948); and Thomas Royden Favell, "The Antecedents of Panama's Separation from Colombia: A Study in Colombian Politics" (Ph.D. diss., Fletcher School of Law and Diplomacy, 1950). For a discussion of Rafael Núñez see Gerardo Molina's *Las Ideas Liberales en Colombia, 1849–1914* (Bogotá: Universidad Nacional de Colombia, 1974), chap. 4.

[22]For a discussion of the impact of the war see, in addition to the above sources, Jesús María Henao and Gerardo Arrubla, *History of Colombia*, trans. J. Fred Rippy (Port Washington: Kennikat Press, 1972 [1938]); Joseph Arbena, "The Panama Problem in Colombian History" (Ph.D. diss., University of Virginia, 1970); Eduardo Lemaitre Román, *Reyes* (Bogotá: Editorial Iqueima, 1953); and Alex Perez-Venero, *Before the Five Frontiers* (New York: AMS Press, 1978).

[23]Quoted in Lemaitre Román, *Panamá y su Separación de Colombia*, 381. The letter was dated 26 July.

[24]Mallet to Marquess of Lansdowne, 12 February 1903, F.O. 55: General Correspondence to 1905: Colombia, 55/420-p. 298, Public Record Office, Kew (hereafter cited as PRO).

[25]Article 76, subsection 20, 1886 constitution, in Gibson, *Constitutions*, 325. For a detailed examination of the problems facing Marroquín see Miner, *Fight for the Panama Route*, 157–334; Arbena, "Panama," chaps. 7, 8; Rivas, *Historia Diplomática*, 584–91; Uribe, *Anales* 4:801–67; U.S. Department of State, *Papers Relating to the Foreign Relations of the United States, 1903* (hereafter cited as *FRUS*), 152–54; German Cavelier, *La Política Internacional de Colombia* (Bogotá: Editorial Iqueima, 1959), chap. 10; Cámara de Representantes, *Investigación*; and Bergquist, *Coffee and Conflict.*

[26]Marroquín to National Congress, 20 June 1903, in Uribe, *Anales* 4:794.

[27]Rivas, *Historia Diplomática*, 591; Miner, *Fight for the Panama Route*, 300–301.

[28]See the correspondence between the State Department and the American legation in Bogotá (ALB) from March to June 1903, *FRUS, 1903*, 132–55.

[29]Beaupré to Secretary of State John Hay, 30 March 1903, ibid., 133–34.

[30]Beaupré to Hay, 15 April 1903, ibid., 135.

[31]George Welby to Lansdowne, 14 March 1902, and Mallet to Lansdowne, 30 September 1902 and 26 March 1903, F.O. 55/420-pp. 167, 215, 311, PRO.

[32]Hay to Beaupré, 9 June 1903, *FRUS, 1903*, 146. Although Colombia initiated discussions, such a step did not commit its government to any treaty. A treaty negotiated and signed by the executive was not binding until it was ratified by the Colombian Congress. Hay also distorted the eagerness with which Colombia had pursued the negotiations.

[33]Beaupré to Hay, 18 September 1903, ibid., 196–97. For an extended examination of the Senate struggle see Lemaitre Román, *Panamá y su Separación de Colombia*, 325–466; Miner, *Fight for the Panama Route*, chap. 9; *FRUS, 1903*, 154–222; Rivas, *Historia Diplomática*, 591–94; Arbena, "Panama," chap. 8; and Cavelier, *La Política* 2:chap. 10.

[34]Beaupré to Rico, 5 August 1903, *FRUS, 1903*, 175–76.

[35]Ibid., 176–77.

[36]Beaupré to Hay, 12 August 1903, ibid., 179; Miner, *Fight for the Panama Route*, 326.

[37]Rico to Herrán, 13 August 1903, box 2, folder 48, and Rico to Herrán, 16 August 1903, box 3, folder 59, both in Herrán Papers.

[38]Beaupré to Hay, 2 November 1903, *FRUS, 1903*, 219–22. For the British view of the U.S.-Colombian disagreement from August through October see F.O. 288: Embassy and Consular Archives: Panama, 288/77, and F.O. 135: Embassy and Consular Archives: Colombia, 135/271, 272, PRO.

[39]Cromwell, an influential New York lawyer, had acted as the U.S. representative of the New Panama Canal Company since 1896; Bunau-Varilla had been in charge of the de Lessups engineering efforts at Panama in the 1880s. For a fuller treatment of the two and their activities in support of the Panama route see Miner, *Fight for the Panama Route*, 75–116, 354–58.

[40]Ibid., 354–58; Bunau-Varilla, *Panama*, 310–19.

[41]Roosevelt to Hay, 19 August 1903, Roosevelt to Marcus Hanna, 5 October 1903, Roosevelt to Hay, 15 September 1903, and Roosevelt to Albert Shaw, 10 October 1903, in Elting E. Morison, ed., *The Letters of Theodore Roosevelt* (Cambridge: Harvard University Press, 1951), 3:566–67, 625, 599, 628.

[42]The United States, just as the British, had forewarnings of a possible uprising. On 24 and 26 October, British diplomats alerted London that there was a "very probable eventuality" for revolution. See F.O. 55/418-p. 59, and F.O. 135/272-#68, PRO.

[43]Acting secretary of the navy to USS *Nashville*, 2 November 1903, *FRUS, 1903*, 247. The *Nashville* originally had been ordered to Colón on 30 October.

[44]Acting secretary of the navy to *Marblehead* and *Atlanta*, 2 November 1903, ibid., 247. The *Boston* was at San Juan del Sur; the *Marblehead*, *Wyoming*, and *Concord* at Acapulco, Mexico; and the *Dixie* and *Atlanta* at Kingston, Jamaica.

[45]Theodore Roosevelt to Kermit Roosevelt, 4 November 1903, Morison, *Letters of Roosevelt* 3:644. Also see Frederick W. Marks III, "Morality as a Drive

Wheel in the Diplomacy of Theodore Roosevelt," *Diplomatic History* 2 (Winter 1978): 43–62.

[46]Captain John Hubbard to Secretary of the Navy William H. Moody, 3 November 1903, *FRUS, 1903*, 249; Commander F. H. Delano to Moody, 6 November 1903, ibid., 251; Parks, *Colombia*, 401; Lemaitre Román, *Panamá y su Separación de Colombia*, 537–45; Rubén Carles, *Reminiscencias de los Primeros Años de la República de Panamá, 1903–1912* (Panamá: La Estrella de Panamá, 1968).

[47]Roosevelt to Albert Shaw, 6 November 1903, Morison, *Letters of Roosevelt* 3:649.

[48]*Statutes at Large* 33, pt. 2, "Hay-Bunau-Varilla Treaty," 18 November 1903, pp. 2234–41.

[49]Roosevelt to Gresham, 30 November 1903, Morison, *Letters of Roosevelt* 3:663.

[50]Fred T. Jane, *Jane's Fighting Ships, 1905–1906* (London: David & Charles Reprints, 1970 [1905]), 358.

[51]Even today this zone blocks completion of the Pan-American highway.

[52]For Colombia's reaction to the revolt see Arbena, "Panama"; Joseph Arbena, "Colombian Reactions to the Independence of Panama, 1903–1904," *The Americas* 33 (July 1976): 130–48; and Castilla, *Historia* 1:345–66.

[53]Beaupré to Hay, 6 November 1903, U.S. Department of State, Despatches from U.S. Ministers to Colombia, 1820–1906 on microfilm, Record Group 59, T-33, roll 60, National Archives. The foreign minister, writing to the ALB, said Reyes's proposal "never took the shape of a government act."

[54]Beaupré to Hay, 7 November 1903, ibid.

[55]By March 1904, Argentina, Brazil, Chile, and Mexico, along with a number of less powerful Latin American nations, had recognized Panama. For a discussion of Latin America's reaction to the revolution see E. Bradford Burns, "The Recognition of Panama by the Major Latin American States," *The Americas* 26 (1969–70): 3–14; John Patterson, "Latin American Reactions to the Panama Revolution of 1903," *Hispanic American Historical Review* 24 (1944): 342–51; and Lawrence O. Ealy, *The Republic of Panama in World Affairs, 1903–1950* (Westport, CT: Greenwood Press, 1970 [1951]).

[56]Rafael Reyes, *Misión Diplomática y Militar, 1903–1904* (Bogotá: Imprenta Nacional, 1904), 41–42; Lemaitre Román, *Panamá y su Separación de Colombia*, 587–599; Ernesto Castillero Reyes, *Panamá y Colombia* (Panamá: Instituto Nacional de Cultura, 1974), 52–77; Ernesto Castillero Reyes, *Historia de Panamá* (Panamá: Editor Panamá América, 1962), 52–67; Emilio Robledo, *La Vida del General Pedro Nel Ospina* (Medellín: n.p., 1959), 64–65; Lemaitre Román, *Reyes*. In addition to Reyes, the delegates were Pedro Nel Ospina, Jorge Holguín, and Lucas Caballero.

[57]Reyes, *Misión Diplomática*, 9–10, 44; Antonio José Uribe, *Colombia y los Estados Unidos de América* (Bogotá: Imprenta Nacional, 1931), 126.

[58]British Ambassador Sir Julian Pauncefote's arrival created a major social crisis in Washington. Britain claimed that its ambassador took precedence over America's Vice President Garret Hobart, who disagreed. During the spring of 1897 a diplomatic war raged on the social scene to decide who

would be proven right. In May the British finally conceded that the vice president outranked their ambassador.

[59]Theodore Roosevelt: 1898–1900, governor of New York; 1900–01, vice president; 1901–09, president. William Howard Taft: 1900, president of the Philippine Commission; 1901–03, civil governor of the Philippines; 1904–08, secretary of war; 1909–13, president.

[60]Root to Lyman Abbott of the *Outlook*, 24 December 1908, vol. 1, 189/2, Elihu Root Papers, Library of Congress Manuscripts Division (hereafter cited as Root Papers).

[61]The political and economic importance of trade is reflected in Root address to Trans Mississippi Commercial Congress, 20 November 1906, in Robert Bacon and James Brown Scott, eds., *Latin America and the United States: Addresses by Elihu Root* (Cambridge: Harvard University Press, 1917), 246–47, 253; Root to National Convention for Extension of Foreign Commerce, 14 January 1907, ibid., 271; Roosevelt to Congress, 8 December 1908, in Roosevelt, *Addresses* 8:1955; Taft address, Baltimore, Maryland, 26 October 1906, in series 10, reel 603, William Howard Taft Papers, Library of Congress Manuscripts Division (hereafter cited as Taft Papers); Taft to Board of Trade, Columbus, Ohio, 2 April 1908, in William H. Taft, *Present Day Problems* (New York: Dodd, Mead & Company, 1908), 80–81; Taft inaugural address, 4 March 1909, series 10, reel 606, Taft Papers; Taft to Congress, 7 December 1909, in William Howard Taft, *Presidential Addresses and State Papers* (New York: Doubleday, Page & Company, 1910), 1:455–56; Taft to Americus Club, 2 May 1910, in vol. 10, Philander C. Knox Papers, Library of Congress Manuscripts Division (hereafter cited as Knox Papers); and Knox, undelivered speech, 1912, in box 45, Knox Papers.

[62]11 December 1911, box 45, Knox Papers. Also see Knox commencement address at University of Pennsylvania, 15 June 1910, in vol. 10, Knox Papers; Francis M. Huntington-Wilson, *Memoirs of an Ex-Diplomat* (Boston: Bruce Humphries, 1945), 216; Taft remarks in Washington on 22 January 1910, in Taft, *Presidential Addresses* 1:564; Huntington-Wilson address, Baltimore, Maryland, 4 May 1911, in vol. 14, Knox Papers; and Knox interview, 1912, in box 29, Knox Papers.

[63]Address entitled "McKinley and Expansionism," 29 January 1908, Tippecanoe Club, Cleveland, Ohio, series 10, reel 604, Taft Papers. Also see William Howard Taft, *The United States and Peace* (New York: Charles Scribner's Sons, 1914), 39.

[64]Root to Hay, 7 January 1905, vol. 185/1, Root Papers. Also see Root to H. M. Flagler, 3 January 1905, ibid.

[65]Taft to Roosevelt, 16 May 1908, series 3, reel 80, Taft Papers.

Chapter II

Internal Pressures for Settlement: The United States and Colombia

As Minister Rafael Reyes sailed toward Washington in late November 1903, the informed Bogotá public, shocked and sullen, fumed over the loss of Panama and over U.S. intervention on the isthmus. The initial decision to seek a peaceful settlement—reached during a six-hour meeting of the Council of Ministers on 9 November—had not been unanimous. As an outcome of that meeting, Reyes had been named minister to the United States and had embarked quickly on his mission to Panama and to Washington.[1] A possibility still remained that Colombian officials might change their minds and attempt a more forceful resolution of the problem. While Minister Beaupré did not expect such a reversal, he warned of a growing anti-American sentiment in Bogotá, reporting that an influential group within the government, backed by public opinion, sought a declaration of war.[2]

Neither Roosevelt nor Hay wanted to use force against Colombia. Both hoped that the difficulties existing between that republic and its newly independent department might be resolved peacefully by negotiation. However, the Joint Board of the Army and Navy recommended that American troops be stationed on the isthmus to prevent any potential military action by Colombia. Roosevelt, fearing that such a move might trigger an unwanted Colombian military response, vetoed the idea. If there was to be fighting, Colombia must bear the blame, not the United States. "Would it not be well," the president wrote his secretary of the navy, William H. Moody, "to issue instructions down at and around Panama that under no circumstances must . . . [American forces] fire unless fired upon. If there should come a brush with Colombia I want to be dead sure that Colombia fires first."[3] The administration certainly would not have backed away from a fight but much preferred a peaceful solution. On that, Roosevelt, Hay, and the Colombian minister agreed.

Upon arrival in the United States, Reyes, who had been given broad discretionary powers in approaching the U.S. government, postponed delivery of the official Colombian position regarding the recent events on the isthmus. Instead, trying informally to probe the depth of American support for an independent Panama, he delayed for over three weeks the formal presentation of his government's arguments. Finally, on 23 December, he transmitted to the State Department a ten-page "statement of grievances," charging that the Roosevelt administration had deeply injured Colombia by its actions on the isthmus.[4] Adopting a moderate tone, Reyes noted that the United States had no reason to be angered by Colombian rejection of the Hay-Herrán Treaty. During the negotiations, he argued, the United States had been aware that final approval ultimately lay in the Colombian Congress and not in the executive.

A modified treaty, according to Reyes, would have passed the Colombian Senate had not Beaupré, by veiled threats and refusal to accept any modifications, "forced" that body to defeat the unamended convention. Even in rejecting the treaty, the Senate had voted unanimously to resume negotiations and reach a compromise by which the United States could construct a canal at Panama. At the very worst, Colombian officials had expected that the canal might possibly be built through Nicaragua and not through its own territory.[5]

Reyes contended that Colombian leaders had misjudged and underestimated the difficulties that would arise with the defeat of the Hay-Herrán Treaty. The situation was further complicated by U.S. action on the isthmus. "In the midst of profound peace between the two countries," the minister wrote, "the United States prevented by force the landing of troops where they were necessary to re-establish order, in a few hours, in the insurgent province."[6] Colombia, Reyes added, had possessed the capability to suppress the revolution effectively. The United States not only prevented action by Colombian forces, but it also prematurely recognized the revolutionary government of Panama, a recognition given only three days after the initial uprising. While sovereign states have the right to extend recognition to new stable governments, that right carries with it responsibility. To emphasize his argument, Reyes quoted former U.S. Secretary of State William Seward: "We insist that a nation that recognizes a revolutionary State, with a view to aid its effecting its sovereignty and independence, commits a great wrong against the nation whose integrity is thus invaded, and makes itself responsible for a just and ample redress."[7] In this instance, from a Colombian perspective, the United States, by military force and premature recognition, had assured the sovereignty and independence of Panama.

Arguments that the United States simply had acted under the 1846 treaty to guarantee "the perfect neutrality" of the isthmus to the extent of preventing Colombian troops from moving freely in their own department were, in Reyes's opinion, misinterpretations of the original treaty. In fact, accurately reflecting his government's attitude, he believed that the United States had violated Article 35 by erroneously interpreting "perfect neutrality" and by forcefully preventing Colombia from exercising its sovereign rights over the rebellious department.

> The United States has not respected our rights in that strip of land which Colombia considers as a divine bequest for the innocent use of the American family of States . . . and the Government of the United States, invoking and putting into practice the right of might, has taken from us by bloodless conquest—but by conquest, nevertheless—the most important part of the national territory.[8]

Since Colombia had not yet recovered from its devastating civil war, it had to rely for satisfaction on "the sentiments of justice" of the United States. "I propose," Reyes concluded, "that the claims . . . made in connection with the events of Panama be submitted to the Arbitration Tribunal of the Hague."[9] That eminent body could adjudicate the dispute and pave the way for the reestablishment of friendly relations between Colombia and the United States.

The ultimate fate of the Reyes mission rested upon the energetic, self-confident, and forceful Theodore Roosevelt. Since his elevation to the presidency in 1901, the former Rough Rider envisioned himself as an activist leader of the nation, whether in internal reform or in international affairs. As the occupant of the White House, he expected to use every legitimate power available to achieve American greatness. In that quest, he firmly believed that difficulties, crises, and uncertainties would arise. Only one year before the Panama insurrection, he had argued:

> Normally, the nation that achieves greatness, like the individual who achieves greatness, can do so only at the cost of anxiety and bewilderment and heartwearing effort. Timid people, people scant of faith and hope, and good people who are not accustomed to the roughness of the life of effort are almost sure to be disheartened and dismayed by the work and the worry, and overmuch cast down by the shortcomings, actual or seeming, which in real life always accompany the first stages even of what eventually turn out to be the most brilliant victories.[10]

Once convinced of the right course, however, Roosevelt would not hesitate or retreat during those times of difficulty, crisis, or uncertainty, but would persevere.

President Roosevelt was convinced that the Reyes letter of 23 December was a gross misrepresentation of recent events. Since at least 1898, he had sought construction of an interoceanic canal and by the spring of 1902 had favored the Panama route. The president had watched carefully the unfolding drama in Bogotá throughout the summer of 1903 as the Colombian Senate deliberated over the Hay-Herrán Treaty. What he observed had made him angry. The Marroquín administration, which had negotiated and signed the proposed treaty, seemed, in Roosevelt's view, to be breaking faith with the United States. Not only had the vice president refused to sign the agreement, but also his administration had refused to urge its immediate approval without modification. It had been those actions that had prompted Roosevelt to label Marroquín and his officials as "the Bogota lot of jack rabbits,"[11] and to write in October: "I feel we are certainly justified in morals, and . . . justified in law, under the treaty of 1846, in intervening summarily and saying that the canal is to be built and that they shall not stop it."[12] Given his personal awareness of the recent negotiations, the president believed that Reyes, by acting as if Colombia was an innocent injured party and by charging the United States with unjustifiable interference in Panama, distorted the actual facts.

Colombia's actions in the months following the revolution convinced Roosevelt that he had gauged correctly that republic's motives in defeating the Hay-Herrán Treaty. He interpreted the unofficial Reyes proposal of 6 November as an admission of bad faith on the part of the Marroquín administration, declaring that

> its offer of immediately guaranteeing the treaty to us [if we landed troops in Panama to protect Colombian sovereignty] is in sharp contrast with the positive and contemptuous refusal of the Congress which has just closed its sessions to consider favorably such a treaty; it shows that the government which made the treaty really had absolute control over the situation, but did not choose to exercise this control.[13]

Colombian leaders failed to realize such an offer would be so interpreted by Roosevelt. The Colombian minister of war simply reinforced the U.S. president's conclusions by making a remarkably similar offer to Beaupré on 27 November, the day before Reyes arrived in Washington from Panama.[14]

In his State of the Union message to Congress on 7 December 1903 and in a report to Congress detailing government actions initiated in compliance with the Spooner Act on 4 January, Roosevelt responded to the accusations contained in the Reyes letter.[15] He argued that Colombia had been offered exceedingly favorable terms in the Hay-Herrán Treaty, and that the United States could not build and protect a canal without all of the controls granted in that document. The president reasoned that, once canal construction had proved beyond the means of private enterprise and once Washington had determined to permit no other world power to undertake that formidable and expensive task, only the United States could build the canal. Therefore, when Colombia rejected the treaty, it torpedoed any chance of constructing an interoceanic passage at Panama. Such a rejection, Roosevelt informed the assembled congressmen, "squarely raised the question whether Colombia was entitled to bar the transit of the world's traffic across the Isthmus."[16]

There was no doubt in the president's mind about the correct answer. By refusing to grant the necessary controls freely and quickly, Colombia blocked "a mandate from civilization" to construct an interoceanic canal. The more reasonable Panamanians perceived the folly of ignoring the interests of mankind while pursuing selfish, nationalistic goals and, from Roosevelt's perspective, rightfully rebelled. The president firmly maintained that no one in his administration had helped prepare or incite the insurrection. Once the revolution succeeded, however, the United States had decided to extend recognition and protection to the new government. Those individuals in Colombia, who either because of a whim or sinister motivations had defeated the treaty, simply had to accept the just consequences of their action. The issues seemed clear-cut, and Roosevelt had no doubts or reservations about his government's policy toward Panama. His self-assurance also was reinforced by the "substantial support" for his Panamanian policies from all sections of the United States.[17]

Roosevelt used the two congressional messages not only to justify his Panama decisions but also to enunciate clearly America's position regarding Panamanian independence. "Failure to act," he declared, "as the Administration acted in Panama would have meant great waste of life, great suffering, great destruction of property; all of which was avoided. . . . Our action was for the peace both of Colombia and of Panama." Since the United States had acted correctly in guaranteeing Panamanian independence, it therefore would continue to stand behind that guarantee even if it meant war. To Roosevelt, American support was not even predicated on the passage by the U.S. Senate of the Hay-Bunau-Varilla Treaty. "It is to be remembered," he said, "that a failure to ratify the treaty will not undo what has been done, will not restore Panama to Colombia, and will not alter our obligations to keep the transit open across the Isthmus, and to prevent any outside power from menacing this transit."[18] Panama would remain independent.

Reiterating the major points made by the president to Congress on 4 January, Secretary Hay formally replied to the Reyes letter the next day.[19] He refuted the charges that the United States had acted improperly and asserted that the responsibility for the events in early November lay at Colombia's feet and not those of the United States. As a result, the United States could perceive no reason to lay before The Hague tribunal the differences of opinion existing between it and Colombia. The United States, Hay added, would be willing to assist Colombia and Panama to settle their differences so that those two nations could recognize each other diplomatically and live side by side in tranquility.

Although President Roosevelt believed Colombia combined "the worst forms of despotism and of anarchy, of violence and of fatuous weakness, of dismal ignorance, cruelty, treachery, greed, and utter vanity," since November 1903 he and his secretary of state had adopted a friendly tone in their communications with its leaders.[20] Despite the enormous power disparity between the two nations, American officials were uneasy about an irritated, sulking Colombia that not only bordered Panama but also was within easy reach of the major sea-lanes leading to the proposed canal. Since the United States would construct as well as protect the canal, any easing of tension would be beneficial, and that could be best achieved by friendly negotiations rather than belligerent confrontation.

American leaders therefore had welcomed the Reyes mission as an opportunity to settle this unfortunate isthmian tangle amicably. They also were pleased that the negotiations would take place in Washington and not Bogotá. Actually, Secretary Hay had cabled the American legation in Bogotá twice, informing the minister that he was free to take a leave of absence.[21] As a result, on 19 December, Beaupré had left Colombia for a vacation.[22] His departure assured Hay, as planned, that discussions between the nations over the next two months would be concentrated almost entirely in Washington.

In addition to the formal and strictly official talks directed toward reaching an equitable resolution of the whole episode, Reyes met informally with Washington leaders. During one of these meetings, on 20 December, he indicated a willingness to agree to the terms of the Hay-Bunau-Varilla Treaty, if the United States would use its offices to obtain a plebiscite in Panama which would allow the Panamanians to determine whether they wanted to rejoin Colombia voluntarily. Reyes also suggested that the United States pay Colombia $10 million to be used to build a railway from Buenaventura to Bogotá.[23] Discussing these proposals, Senator Henry Cabot Lodge wrote the president:

> In short his memo offer[s] a reasonable basis for negotiation. It may lead to nothing. But it is worth trying for if on the lines we discussed we can bring Colombia in, the whole thing will go through [Congress] at once and be greatly approved by [the] country. If [the] attempt fails we have additional proof of our own good dealing and strengthen our position.[24]

In a meeting with Secretary of War Elihu Root on 2 January, Reyes again proposed the payment of $10 million for railroad construction,[25] thereby suggesting that Colombia might be more flexible in settling the issues than its formal statement of grievances had indicated.

Since decisions relating to Panama—tied as they were to the U.S. Senate's canal deliberations—required thoughtful and coordinated consideration, neither Lodge, Hay, Roosevelt, nor Root immediately responded to Reyes's informal suggestions. Hearing nothing, Reyes, already dissatisfied with the tenor of the president's 4 January message to Congress and Hay's letter of 5 January, hinted that he might soon sail for Europe.

Roosevelt's messages to Congress and the Hay letter to Reyes had outlined the official American response to the Colombian arguments, leaving absolutely no doubt that Colombia could not regain sovereignty over its errant department. Furthermore, the United States seemingly had rejected all Colombian protests, arguments, and suggestions for settlement. Even Reyes's informal proposals for a plebiscite and monetary payment apparently were ignored. Therefore, believing that his mission could accomplish nothing further, he called on Hay on 11 January to inform the secretary that he definitely would be sailing for Europe on the sixteenth but was leaving Washington that very afternoon. Before departing, Reyes suggested two possible criteria for settlement. As in his earlier proposals, he urged that a plebiscite be held in Panama, but, instead of asking for $10 million outright, he proposed "an arbitration at Washington to determine whether Colombia [was] entitled to an indemnity and if so how much." Again, as in earlier discussions, the Colombian minister indicated that any funds received by his nation would be used in a railroad project to benefit the Colombian people.[26] After listening to these proposals, Hay then told the minister that they would receive careful consideration. Soon after the meeting concluded, Reyes left for New York where he would board ship for Europe.

Had Reyes delayed by one or two days his meeting with Hay, or simply restated without modification the informal proposals for both a plebiscite and a $10-million indemnity, his mission might have ended successfully. Meeting on 10 January, Roosevelt, Secretary Hay, and Senator Lodge had discussed the Colombian case as well as opposition to the Hay-Bunau-Varilla Treaty in the U.S. Senate. The president had argued consistently, in the months after the revolution, that the United States owed Colombia nothing "in law or in morals," but he never completely had rejected the idea of some monetary payment to settle the affair. In fact, both he and Lodge had indicated at this meeting that the United States might give Colombia $5 million.[27]

Rather than debate this vague possibility with the Colombian minister, Hay again listened to the modified terms presented by Reyes at the next day's meeting but said nothing, politely dismissing the minister and informing Roosevelt of the changed situation. The Reyes proposals were then discussed fully at a cabinet meeting on 12 January. Before any final decision was made, Hay suggested consulting Panama about a plebiscite; the president agreed. Therefore, Hay met with the Panamanian minister and after one hour finally obtained his assent to a settlement formula, which the secretary stuffed in his pocket before going to dinner at Attorney General Philander Knox's house. There he conferred with Roosevelt and Secretary of War Root and received their approval of the formula.[28]

Early the next day Hay wrote Reyes in New York, declining to change the American position regarding the submission of the entire problem to The Hague. However, the secretary noted,

> this Government is now, as it always has been . . . most desirous to lend its good offices for the establishment of friendly relations between the Republic of Colombia and that of Panama. We think that they might be exercised with a hope of a favorable result if Colombia . . . should consider that the conditions necessary to its recognition of the existing state of things are: First. To submit to a plebiscite the question whether the people of the Isthmus prefer allegiance to the Republic of Panama or to the Republic of Colombia. Second. To submit to a special court of arbitration the settlement of those claims of a material order which either Colombia or Panama by mutual agreement may reasonably bring forward against the other, as a consequence of facts preceding or following the declaration of independence of Panama.[29]

These proposals were for Colombia's careful consideration. The secretary did not expect, or even want, Reyes to return to Washington immediately.

Having responded to both the formal and informal Colombian suggestions, President Roosevelt and Secretary Hay focused their attention on the U.S. Senate, where a heated debate raged over ratification of the Hay-Bunau-Varilla Treaty with Panama.[30] Although the president believed the United States had acted honorably toward Colombia, not all senators agreed. The ranking Democratic member of the Senate Foreign Relations Committee, Senator John T. Morgan, led the attack against Roosevelt, arguing that the president had violated the 1846 treaty with Colombia and thus had unjustly secured the present canal treaty with Panama now pending in the Senate.[31] At least seventeen senators shared Morgan's appraisal.

Privately, Morgan was more vicious in his denunciation of the president, stating that the presidency had become too powerful, and that Roosevelt in particular had been motivated in this Panama case by personal ambition and arrogance. Senator Henry M. Teller, rather than Morgan, probably best summarized the sentiment of most of those who opposed American actions relating to the Panamanian revolution when he said:

> I only desire that when we build the canal we shall be able to stand before the world and say, "Here is a great enterprise; no other people could have done it without distress. We give it to the commerce and civilization of mankind, and we give it to them with clean hands."
>
> I am more anxious . . . that the Government of the United States should go before the world as an honest, law-abiding, justice-loving nation than I am that it should glory in the greatest work of human needs. It will not do to say it is in the interest of civilization, and thus acquit ourselves of a violation of international law. You have no right to take Colombia's land in the interest of civilization. That . . . is the robber's claim. It is the doctrine that might makes right. We want it, and therefore we take it.[32]

To remove this blot on American honor, Morgan and Teller had to convert at least thirty-one senators to their way of thinking, but they were unsuccessful. A resolution, acknowledging Colombian claims for redress and authorizing the United States to determine in negotiations with its weak sister republic the amount of money it should receive "in full compensation" for the loss of Panama and for any claims it might have against Panama, failed by a vote of 49 to 24. Immediately upon the defeat of this resolution, the Senate voted 66 to 14 to ratify the Hay-Bunau-Varilla Treaty.[33] When Roosevelt signed the treaty two days later on 25 February, he removed the last major obstacle preventing the immediate construction of an interoceanic canal across the Isthmus of Panama. Had the Roosevelt administration so desired, it could have considered the entire Panama affair now closed and could have viewed further Colombian protests as mere babble.

While the U.S. government acknowledged no moral or legal responsibility for the loss of Panama, it did express deep concern about the perpetual state of tension and ill feeling over the incident. American leaders were still unsure of future Colombian actions. When Reyes left the country, the State Department had urged the legation in Bogotá to monitor and report Colombia's attitudes and intentions toward both Panama and the United States. Chargé Alban G. Snyder noted that the anti-American feeling in Bogotá was bitter yet restrained, and that a divergence of both public opinion and private governmental opinion existed. Vocal Bogotá residents continued to demand a response against the United States, either going to war or breaking relations. On the other hand, such ideas had found little support in government circles. In fact, by 2 March 1904, Snyder believed the danger of an armed Colombian response had passed. Eight days later his feeling was confirmed when the Bogotá government reduced the standing army from 11,000 to 5,000 men.[34]

While angered by the actions of both Panama and the United States, the majority of Colombians in 1904 opposed war as a means to reassert sovereignty; three years of civil war had instilled a desire for peace. Additionally, the obvious power disparity between the United States and Colombia, as well as personal and party rivalries within Colombia, further undercut a strong movement in favor of a military response. Finally, Colombian leaders feared that a war over Panama could lead to the separation from Colombia of other political departments, particularly in the Cauca and northern coastal regions. For these reasons, war did not appear as a viable alternative to government leaders.[35]

By reducing its standing army, Colombian officials simply had accepted reality. With the U.S. Senate's approval of the Hay-Bunau-Varilla Treaty in late February, no Colombian military contingent could retake Panama. The reduction in troop strength, however, did not imply that Colombia planned to acquiesce quietly in the loss of its isthmian department. Governmental leaders in Bogotá had read Roosevelt's justification of the Panamanian rebellion and the American response given to the U.S. Congress in December 1903 and January 1904. They also were aware of Hay's rebuttal to the Reyes letter of 23 December as well as the other diplomatic correspondence passing between the State Department and the Colombian legation in Washington. For administration officials, such justifications and explanations were distortions of the truth, requiring rebuttal. Beginning in early February the Colombian cabinet considered an appropriate response, both to the American arguments and to Hay's letter to Reyes of 13 January.[36] News that the U.S. Senate had approved the Hay-Bunau-Varilla Treaty reached those officials during their deliberations. In Washington both the executive and the legislative branches now had committed themselves formally to the maintenance of Panamanian independence. The last rays of hope that a plebiscite might return Panama to Colombia faded. The cabinet ministers, therefore, desired to construct one last comprehensive document protesting the entire

Panama episode and stating their arguments and position to the world. They worked through February and March, and on 12 April 1904 the minister for foreign affairs presented the final product of that effort to the American legation at Bogotá.[37]

The nineteen-page memorandum, closely paralleling Reyes's 23 December argument, urged "both parties to adopt an equitable and conciliatory way for the solution of their differences." No suggestion was made as to the method or procedure for such a settlement. In fact, the memorandum did not reflect any mellowing of Colombia's attitude toward the United States or Panama. Colombian officials still thought the United States was solemnly bound by the 1846 treaty to restore their country's sovereignty over Panama, and that anything less would not be in the best interests of their nation.

Such a declaration by top administrative officials seems to be a retrenchment from the informal Reyes negotiations when Colombian leaders apparently had been ready to consider a settlement based on the holding of a plebiscite and of receiving a $10-million indemnity. A combination of factors probably influenced the Colombian cabinet's deliberations as it prepared its official position paper. Colombians considered the Roosevelt and Hay speeches to be misinterpretations of historical fact and misrepresentation of their motives. In addition, Senate action guaranteeing Panamanian independence and granting the United States absolute control of the future canal zone, simply added humiliation to injury. To concede the actual loss of Panama not only would mar national honor but also could jeopardize Colombia's efforts to establish a strong central government. If the Marroquín government acquiesced in the loss of Panama, it might discover other Colombian departments gravitating toward either partial or complete independence from Bogotá, a situation the politically powerful conservative Colombian aristocracy opposed. (The attitude of those conservatives carried special weight in early 1904 since presidential elections were to be held in mid-February.) Under the Colombian constitution, only those citizens who could both read and write, and who received an annual income of 500 pesos or owned property valued at 1,500 pesos, could vote for presidential electors. Therefore, although it would knowingly continue the strained relations with the United States, a reassertion of the 23 December position provided a more viable option to the Colombian government than adding to the present internal unrest and discord, or acerbating the already strained relationship between those who favored more power at the central level and those who favored more power at the departmental level.

The renewed Colombian arguments had little impact in Washington. While Bogotá's continued obstinance would be irritating, it would not be critical. The Roosevelt administration's desire to reach a settlement in January had hinged on the Senate's opposition to the Panama treaty. If it could have convinced Colombia to recognize Panama, opponents of the treaty would have relented, thereby assuring its quick passage. The offer of as much as $5 million to Colombia seemed a small amount to pay to bring the whole episode to a prompt and satisfactory conclusion. Once the Hay-Bunau-Varilla Treaty passed the Senate, however, the immediate need or desire for a settlement with Colombia lessened. The construction of the canal was assured and, if Colombia wanted to wax eloquent about supposed wrongs, that was fine. Senator Lodge, who together with the president had considered in January the payment of $5 million, believed the entire issue was dead. Writing to a friend, he added that, given Colombia's foolish behavior, "there seems no reason now for [the United States] doing anything for her."[38] The United States, having achieved its primary purpose, could afford to wait before effecting a final diplomatic agreement with Colombia.

Tension between the two nations appeared to relax by July 1904 as the newly elected Colombian president, Rafael Reyes, moved closer to his 7 August inauguration. Thoroughly familiar with the parameters of the isthmian problem, former Minister Reyes was anxious to assume the full powers of the presidency. Calling on the American legation in early July, he had expressed hope that the historic friendship between the two nations could be rapidly restored by a satisfactory settlement of the Panamanian problem.[39] Two weeks after the inauguration, the new minister for foreign affairs, Enrique Cortés, informed Congress that Bogotá, rather than continuing to irritate the United States, now hoped to gain its goodwill and esteem so that Colombia "might in the future be able to save something from the wreck."[40]

Reyes assumed office, seeking to reform the Colombian economy, improve transportation, industrialize, create a national bank, extend equal justice and civil rights to all citizens regardless of political affiliation, and reorganize the governmental bureaucracy. To accomplish these reforms, his administration needed a sound and friendly commercial and financial relationship with the United States. Practical considerations aside, however, Reyes realized that many Colombians still strongly resented U.S. actions in 1903. He and Cortés, therefore, were initially cautious in deviating from past Colombian arguments presented to the United States. While the tone of his administration was more friendly, the content of its proposals remained basically the same.[41]

Not until March 1905 did Reyes appoint Diego Mendoza as the new minister to the United States for the special purpose of settling the canal problem in conformance with national honor and dignity as well as in the nation's best economic and material interests. Mendoza's instructions revealed that, since Colombia must focus on the future and not the past, the independence of Panama should be regarded as a "completed action."[42] His job, therefore, would be to reestablish friendly relations with the United States.

Not content to work within normal diplomatic channels, Reyes also dispatched Cortés (a confidential agent and his former minister for foreign affairs) to Washington to represent him personally in completing "in the shortest time possible and under conditions of justice and equality" treaties with the United States and Panama.[43] Before his arrival at Capitol Hill, Cortés stopped at Colón in late March to discuss briefly with Panamanian President Manuel Amador Guerrero the future relations of Panama and Colombia, urging him to allow the Panamanians to vote as to whether they favored independence or realignment with Colombia. Thus, the Colombian government would be offered an honorable way to resolve the Panamanian question. The Reyes administration, Cortés assured Amador Guerrero, would accept an adverse plebiscite decision, thereby opening the door for diplomatic recognition, provided, he added, certain other issues could be resolved, including Panama's acceptance of its fair share of the Colombian internal and external debt contracted prior to the November revolution, the granting to Colombia of certain advantages in return for the use of a canal at Panama, and the resolution of each nation's joint boundary.

Within one week of Cortés's visit the Panamanian minister in Washington received instructions to initiate negotiations with Colombian diplomats. While Panama considered itself already independent and would not consider a plebiscite, it was willing to discuss some of the other issues raised by Cortés. But, as Panama and Colombia both recognized in 1905, the complete resolution of all questions arising from the 1903 revolution would require active negotiations not only with each other but also with the United States. Such negotiations, however, did not begin immediately.[44]

A change in secretaries of state, as well as Roosevelt's preoccupation with another international crisis, delayed the opening of discussions. Secretary of State Hay had been in poor health since January 1905. Hoping to recuperate on a vacation, he had sailed for Europe on 18 March. Rather than improve though his health continued to deteriorate, and on 1 July, shortly after returning to the United States, he died. President Roosevelt quickly named, as Hay's replacement, Elihu Root, a highly successful and influential New York corporate lawyer and former secretary of war from 1899 to early 1904. Despite his rapid appointment, Colombian negotiations were postponed to allow the new secretary time for a prolonged vacation as well as time to adjust to his position and familiarize himself with departmental policies and procedures.[45] Roosevelt, having taken a deep personal interest in the case, could have personally conducted negotiations with the Colombian representatives. However, in the late summer and early autumn of 1905, the president had no time for Colombia; he was preoccupied with peace negotiations between Russia and Japan, hoping to conclude the war initiated by Japan in February 1904.

By October 1905, Secretary Root was ready to consider the Colombian question. While Roosevelt intended to leave formal negotiations in the competent hands of his secretary, he did want to be informed of all important proposals and of any significant progress. Root, no stranger to the Colombian discussions, would exercise day-to-day control. As secretary of war, he had participated in top-level meetings concerning American policy toward Colombia and Panama. Visiting in France, he had not been involved in the events surrounding the November revolution, but he had approved Roosevelt's action. Writing his host in Paris in mid-December 1903, Root had characterized the Colombian dilemma: "They are now in the position of a girl who keeps refusing a fellow, with the idea that she will marry him sometime or other when she gets ready, and who wakes up some fine morning to find that he has married another girl."[46] By delaying the construction of an isthmian canal, Root reasoned, Colombia should not have been surprised by the Panamanian revolution or by the U.S. reaction. By its response, Colombia acted as if it considered its ownership of Panama as absolute. Root disagreed. To him, Colombia was being arbitrary and selfish, ignoring basic international responsibilities. In an address to a prominent Chicago audience in February 1904, he presented his own unique interpretation of international law:

> By the rules of might and justice universally recognized among men and which are the law of nations, the sovereignty of Colombia over the isthmus of Panama was qualified and limited by the right of the other civilized nations of the earth to have the canal constructed across the Isthmus and to have it maintained for their free and undisturbed passage.[47]

Root's conviction that the United States rightfully had assumed the responsibility of constructing and maintaining a canal for the use of the civilized world and rightfully had concluded a canal treaty with the new Panamanian government had been formed, therefore, before his appointment as secretary of state.

Following the unexpected four-month delay, the Colombian legation in Washington on 21 October presented Root with its government's interpretation of the situation and possible alternative solution.[48] The letter appeared paradoxical. The Reyes administration already had stated publicly its desire for closer ties with the United States and for an expeditious solution to the problems existing between the two nations. But the letter went further than any previous official correspondence in accusing the United States of fostering and then guaranteeing the Panamanian revolution. After reviewing in some detail U.S. actions relating to Panama and Colombia during late 1903, the document charged the United States with repeated violations of the solemn 1846 treaty. Its overall tone, however, was that of a "weak Republic" petitioning a great power for justice, not as an equal, brusquely threatening to act unless it received complete satisfaction. In the opening paragraph Colombia had suggested that settlement could be achieved by one of two methods: direct negotiation or arbitration. In preparing this letter, Minister Mendoza had evidently decided the best chance for an honorable and advantageous settlement lay in arbitration. Therefore, while giving the United States two choices, he weighted the arguments so that arbitration seemed the only viable option. Having levied his government's charges against the United States, including the charge that the United States actively participated in initiating and maintaining the insurrection on the isthmus, the Colombian minister noted:

> The undersigned does not flatter himself that you will be disposed to admit the justice of these [claims]. On the contrary, he supposed that they will be denied by you. If this should be the case, it appears evident that the only practicable means of adjustment, honorable for both countries, would bc to submit them to the decision of an impartial court of arbitration. On the other hand if your Government were disposed to admit the justice of Colombia's claims, a path would be happily opened toward a prompt and satisfactory adjustment by direct diplomacy.[49]

Mendoza was quick to add that the international image of the United States would be enhanced and its traditional sense of justice reaffirmed if it consented to arbitrate this case with a weak sister republic. In fact, he argued, the United States had little to lose. If the American position was correct then it would be completely vindicated. If, on the other hand, Colombia had the better case, the worst consequence facing the United States would be to acknowledge committing an injury "while seeking what [it] thought was of universal benefit," and to admit that Colombia rightfully could claim an indemnity. While noting that in reestablishing friendly relations between the three countries an indemnity should appear insignificant, Mendoza believed that an impartial arbitration would eventually allow Colombia to seek compensation.[50]

The Colombian minister had assumed correctly that the United

States would not accept as legitimate the charges levied against it in the letter. Indeed, the American response, when it was finally delivered on 10 February 1906, was unenthusiastic about the Colombian proposals.[51] Root charged that the October document contained little new information or opinion not expressed earlier by the Reyes mission; that Colombia had eliminated, by its presentation, the possibility of a diplomatic settlement in favor of settlement by arbitration; and that it again had failed to enumerate the specific nature of a settlement that would satisfy its national interests. In addition, Root viewed the Colombian assertion that the United States played a major role in fomenting the Panamanian rebellion as "an aspersion upon the honor and good faith of the United States." Roosevelt and his advisers, the secretary informed Mendoza, after having carefully studied the letter, could find no compelling reason to change their present policy toward settlement.

Negotiations had come to an impasse. The positions of the two governments had changed little since December 1903. To help reestablish economic stability, to put to rest this gnawing problem so Bogotá could concentrate on pressing internal problems, and to settle outstanding differences before the Panama Canal opened, Reyes reconsidered the Colombian position.

Given the disastrous financial status of Colombia, such a reevaluation seemed essential. Three years of civil war had created a spiraling inflation requiring immediate attention. From 1886 to October 1899, the federal government had emitted only 40,083,806 pesos. However, during the next four years the government issued an average of 19,341,769 pesos per month, totaling 870,379,622 by June 1903.[52] The value of these paper pesos depended upon confidence in the government since they were not backed by either gold or silver. As a result, the real value of the peso fell dramatically. In 1886 one paper peso was worth $2.50 in U.S. gold currency; by 1899 that value had dropped to $.297; by 1900, to $.104; by 1901, to $.038; by 1902, to $.014; by 1903, to $.011; and during both 1904 and 1905, to $.010.[53] In addition, the Reyes administration faced a total national debt calculated at $19,541,567 (U.S.) by 1905–06.[54] In view of such dismal financial realities, Reyes hoped an arrangement with the United States over Panama would offer a cash indemnity and the prospect of increased trade in the future. Both would not only strengthen his government but also would assist its struggle to alleviate pressing financial, economic, social, and political problems.

One of the greatest economic hurdles facing President Reyes and his successors in the opening decades of the twentieth century was the lack of an integrated, efficient transportation network. If those leaders ever hoped to unify the nation into a single coherent political and economic unit, they had to undertake major expansion of that system. But without funds—funds expected in a treaty settlement with the United States—no administration could bridge the three fingers of the mighty Andean Mountains which divided the republic into three sections.[55] Until new cart paths and railroads could be built, populous interior cities and departments, including the national capital at Bogotá, had to rely upon the Magdalena River, flowing between the Eastern and Central Cordilleras, as their major artery to the Caribbean. Unfortunately, that river was not ideally suited to a growing international trade which could assist Colombia's economic recovery.

To demonstrate the state of travel in Colombia in the early twentieth century, and to emphasize the pressure on its leaders to obtain funds to improve internal transit, one need only describe a normal journey from the coast to one or two interior cities.[56] A passenger landing at the coastal city of Barranquilla near the mouth of the Magdalena could expect a rather uncomfortable and unpredictable transit to the national capital 880 miles inland. After transferring to a sternwheel river steamer at Barranquilla, the traveler could expect an uneventful voyage for sixty or seventy miles up the Magdalena. Past the town of Calamar, however, the river became more onerous, the channel constantly shifting and creating new uncharted sandbars and mud banks, not to mention unseen snags just below the surface. Should the steamer lodge on one of these obstacles, hours, even days, might pass before the wayfarer could proceed farther. Any delay would magnify the rather scant and uncomfortable conditions for all passengers on board.

While the local companies may have provided a bare stateroom, containing only a cot, washbowl, and water pitcher, each passenger had to supply his own sheets, pillow, towels, soap, and the all-important mosquito nets. Even those small cabins would become intolerable after 9 or 10 A.M. as the tropical temperature soared. If the passenger selected one of the express steamers in Barranquilla, he would stop only at the most important river towns to take on wood and mail. However, if he chose an intermediate steamer, he would have the "opportunity" of leisurely seeing numerous small towns all along the Magdalena. Had he arrived during the rainy season, May to November, he could expect, without any encounters with sandbars, mud banks, or snags, to complete the first leg of his journey—the 613 miles to La Dorada—within five to ten days. If conditions were not so ideal, if he arrived, for example, during the dry season after the river had dropped, he might discover the same trip would take three to five weeks.

Arriving in La Dorada, the sojourner must transfer to the Dorada Railway for a seven-hour journey to Beltrán, where he then would have to transfer onto a second steamer for a twenty-six-hour trip—in ideal conditions—to Girardot. There he would board another train to travel the seventy-eight miles to Facatativá. During the rainy season he might unexpectedly discover that mud slides had temporarily disrupted all traffic for several days between the two towns. Upon finally reaching Facatativá, he would learn that, since the Girardot Railroad was only 3′ wide and the gauge of the Facatativá Railway 3′ 6″, he would have to transfer one final time before reaching Bogotá. Recounting the 880-mile trip from the coast to Bogotá, the traveler would realize that he and his luggage had embarked and disembarked no less than ten times.

Relatively modern harbor facilities at Barranquilla generally assured that incoming products could be rapidly loaded into the river steamers for the trip up the Magdalena to a city such as Medellín, the capital of the department of Antioquia. However, compared to obstacles facing imported freight destined for interior cities, passenger travel inland was quick and uncomplicated. Once loaded, the riverboat chugged up the Magdalena, stopping frequently at small towns and villages to pick up local produce or to unload part of its cargo. Upon reaching Puerto Berrío 500 miles from the coast, after a journey of ten days under ideal conditions, the freight must be transferred by hand from the steamer to the Puerto Berrío Railroad for its delivery to Medellín. Once loaded, the train began its journey toward the Antioquian capital. Lying between Puerto Berrío and Medellín, however, was the 5,000-foot Central Cordillera. Therefore, the train stopped at the small town of Cisneros on the western slope and unloaded its cargo onto mule wagons, which immediately began the nine-mile trek to Santiago on the other side of the mountain range.[57] The sturdiest two-wheel wagons could carry a maximum weight of only 1,140 pounds. Pack mules, which also were used to transport merchandise, could carry only 250-pound loads, 125 pounds evenly strapped on either side. Any items weighing over 1,140 pounds posed a major difficulty and might well sit for a long time at Cisneros. Once over the La Quiebra Pass, the freight was transferred from the wagons and mules onto the second half of the Puerto Berrío Railway for the last leg of the Medellín trip.

Farther south, the Central Cordillera posed an even greater problem to Colombian transportation and communications. If a merchant in Bogotá desired to ship an order to Cali, the capital of the department of Valle de Cauca, that product must cross the central Andean chain at the Quindío Pass near Ibagué. The trip from Bogotá to Ibagué would be uneventful, although a traveler would have to shift trains once. Arriving at Ibagué, passengers and packages would be transferred to mules for the ascent over the 12,000-foot mountains. Since the Quindío Pass abruptly rises, at times to a 45° angle, and at other times

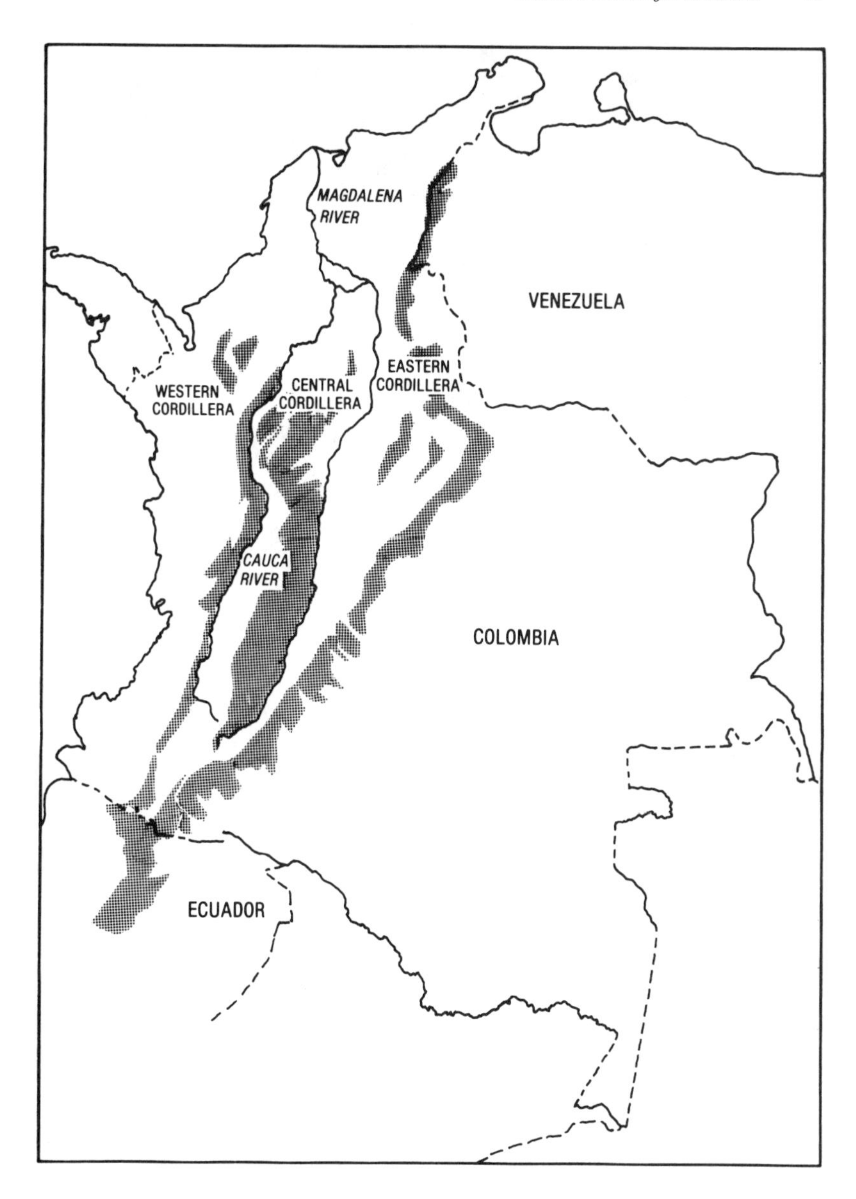
MAGDALENA
RIVER
VENEZUELA
EASTERN
CORDILLERA
CENTRAL
CORDILLERA
WESTERN
CORDILLERA
CAUCA
RIVER
COLOMBIA
ECUADOR

Map 1

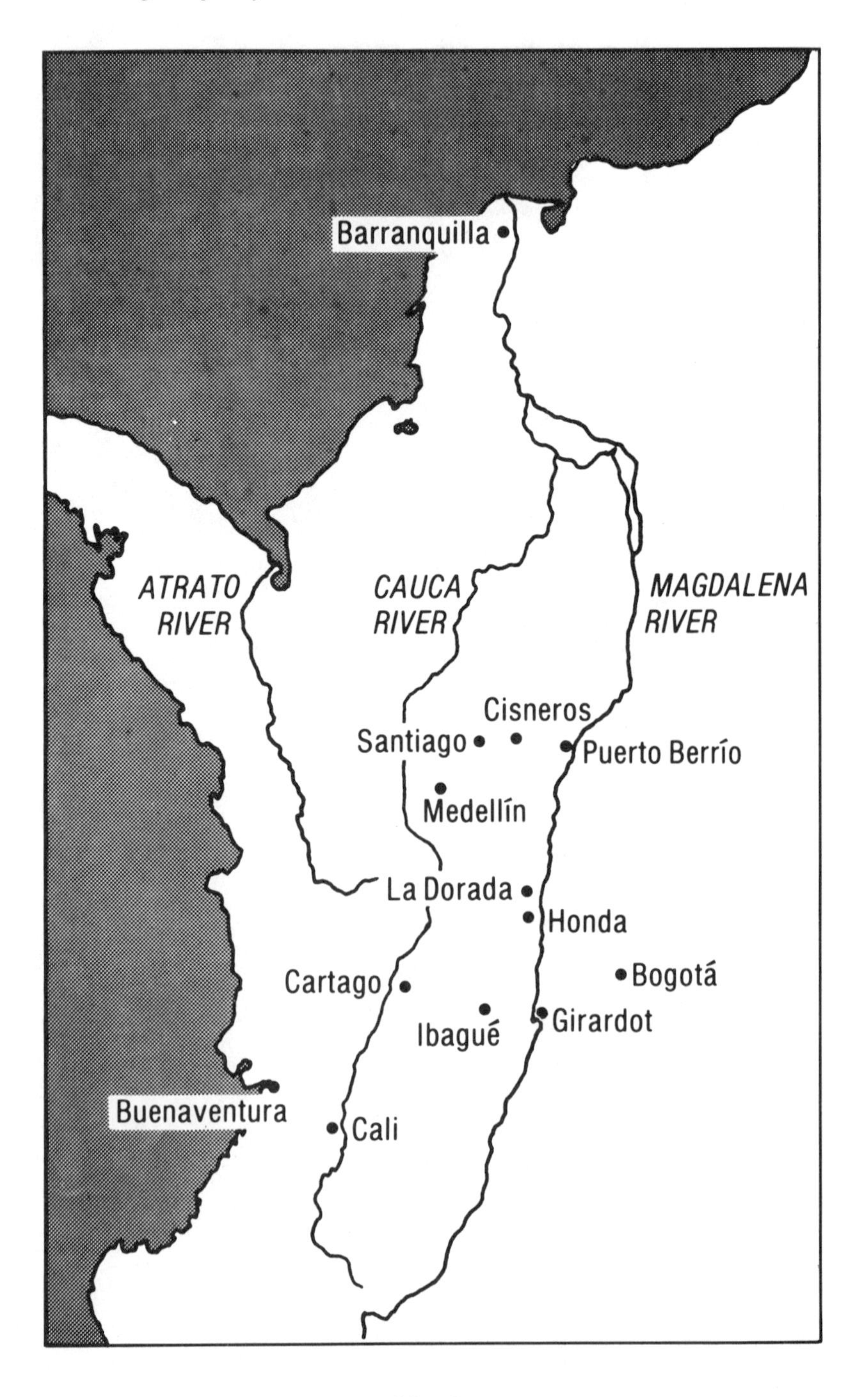
Barranquilla
ATRATO
RIVER
CAUCA
RIVER
MAGDALENA
RIVER
Cisneros
Santiago
Puerto Berrío
Medellín
La Dorada
Honda
Bogotá
Cartago
Ibagué
Girardot
Buenaventura
Cali

Map 2

narrows to a width of only one or two yards, heavy freight could not reach Cali from Bogotá. Once across the mountains, the traveler would continue his journey by muleback for three additional days until he reached Zarzal in the Cauca Valley. After resting, he would complete the next sixty miles on muleback until he arrived at the railroad in Palmira which connected with Cali. From there, a train could be boarded for the ride to the coastal city of Buenaventura. However, if he desired to travel south to the departmental capitals of Popayán or Pasto, this meant another four to seven days on muleback. If, upon arriving at Pasto, he desired to reach the Pacific port of Tumaco, he would rely on mules and canoes to complete the 120-mile journey.

If a settlement with the United States could aid in overcoming the transportation handicap, if it could enable unification of the three disparate sections of Colombia into an economic and political whole, and if it could assist Colombia's economic recovery, then Reyes could justify his reconsideration of a Panamanian agreement. But the astute president also realized more was at stake than either potential commercial advantages on the isthmus or a possible monetary indemnity. Even if those two advantages never materialized, Colombia still could not afford to antagonize the United States. After all, it was Colombia's largest customer. As Tables 1 and 2 indicate, the United States between 1900 and 1911 received far more Colombian merchandise than any other major power. Between 1906 and 1911, for which accurate comparable data is available, the United States received an average of 46 percent of Colombian exports each year. Although similar data is unavailable for the corresponding 1900–05 period, there is no reason to believe that the 1906 and 1907 statistical ratios were abnormal. Trade with the United States during those earlier five years was sufficiently large, no doubt to impress further upon President Reyes the necessity of maintaining cordial relations with a nation that had assisted the Panamanian revolutionaries. The official Colombian response to the United States regarding Panama, therefore, had to balance national honor with pragmatic economics.

Considering these factors, President Reyes, by late May 1906, indicated to the new American minister in Bogotá, John Barrett, that he realized the "impracticality" of discussing further the questions of arbitration and indemnity. Instead, he expressed the desire to seek a more realistic and practical solution.[58] To attain that goal, Reyes could have found no more willing minister than Barrett. Having achieved a close working relationship with the Colombian president and minister for foreign affairs, he was frequently consulted by them during the fragile initial stages of the reformulation of the Colombian position. Barrett's role increased in importance when, in the summer of 1906,

Table 1. Colombian Exports Including Gold, FOB, 1900–05 (Based on Data from the Receiving Nations)

	1900		*1901*	
	1[a]	*2*[b]	*1*[a]	*2*[b]
United States	8.777.518	48.77%	6.567.757	35.86%
Great Britain	2.805.621	15.59%	4.990.654	27.25%
France	2.971.897	16.51%	2.981.308	16.28%
Germany	3.442.623	19.13%	3.775.701	20.61%
	1902		*1903*	
United States	7.414.062	41.73%	10.160.664	41.13%
Great Britain	3.968.750	22.34%	6.592.798	26.68%
France	3.036.458	17.09%	3.761.773	15.23%
Germany	3.346.354	18.84%	4.191.136	16.96%
	1904		*1905*	
United States	16.311.320	49.20%	13.779.644	51.20%
Great Britain	7.674.528	23.15%	4.535.573	16.85%
France	2.962.264	9.94%	2.351.779	8.74%
Germany	6.205.189	18.72%	6.245.059	23.21%

Source: Based on Miguel M. Urrutia and Mario Arrubla, eds., *Compendio de Estadísticas Históricas de Colombia* (Bogotá: Direccíon de Divulgación Cultural Publicaciones, 1970), 158, 184, 185.
[a]Exports in pesos.
[b]Percentage of exports in relation to the four nations listed. Lacking Colombian data on total exports, it is not possible to determine accurately a nation's percentage of Colombian trade.

President Reyes and Mendoza split over the shifting Colombian position.[59]

Mendoza still strongly supported an arbitrated solution, fearing that any treaty negotiated by Colombian agents with the United States and Panama would face the same fate as the Hay-Herrán Treaty. To him, once the agreement was signed, the United States would view it as accepted, thereby undercutting any substantive review of that document by the Colombian Congress. Reyes's comments to Barrett in late May further angered Mendoza since he believed the Colombian

Table 2. Colombian Exports Including Gold, FOB, 1906–11 (Based on Colombian Data)

	1906		1907	
	1[a]	2[b]	1[a]	2[b]
United States	4.708	32.51%	4.809	32.06%
Great Britain	723	5.00%	827	5.51%
France	210	1.45%	133	.89%
Germany	716	4.94%	631	4.21%
Total	14.481		14.999	
	1908		1909	
United States	8.621	58.35%	8.588	54.25%
Great Britain	2.553	17.30%	3.651	23.07%
France	568	3.84%	483	3.05%
Germany	1.456	9.85%	1.549	9.79%
Total	14.775		15.829	
	1910		1911	
United States	7.833	44.04%	12.250	54.75%
Great Britain	NA[c]		4.596	20.54%
France	NA		769	3.44%
Germany	NA		1.910	8.54%
Total	17.787		22.376	

Source: Based on Urrutia and Arrubla, eds., *Estadísticas*, 133, 134; and Boletin Numero 3, *Comercio Internacional de Colombia, 1898–1922* (Bogotá: Dirección General de Estadística, 1924), 1.
[a]Exports in thousands in pesos.
[b]Percentage of total Colombian exports.
[c]NA = not available.

president had sabotaged his efforts to resolve the crisis by arbitration. In a scathing critique of Reyes, Mendoza dispatched a six-page letter to fellow Colombians outlining how Reyes had bypassed and undercut the embassy when he sent Cortés to Panama and to Washington, how Cortés had not shared his diplomatic discussions with Mendoza, and how Reyes planned to reap personal economic rewards by achieving a solution to the Panama crisis. Mendoza argued that, since Reyes's actions smacked of "high treason," Liberal members of the Colombian legislature should resign in protest.[60]

By ignoring orders to return home and by openly attacking the Reyes administration, Mendoza totally alienated Reyes. On 11 August 1906 the Colombian cabinet declared its Washington diplomat a traitor. This furor effectively eliminated any possibility of positive discussions in Washington until a new minister could assume control of the legation. Therefore, Barrett became the official American spokesman in the early treaty deliberations extending from May until August 1906.

Notes

[1]Uribe, *Colombia*, 126.

[2]Beaupré to Hay, 17 November 1903 (two messages), 20 and 25 November 1903, Department of State, Despatches, T-33, rolls 60, 61. Also see Welby to Lansdowne, 12 and 23 November 1903, F.O. 135/272-#76, #77, PRO; and Lemaitre, *Reyes*.

[3]Roosevelt to Moody, 21 December 1903, in Morison, *Letters of Roosevelt* 3:674. For Roosevelt's reaction to the Joint Board's recommendation see Roosevelt to Secretary of the Treasury Leslie M. Shaw, 24 December 1903, ibid., 678.

[4]Reyes to Hay, 23 December 1903, *FRUS, 1903*, 284–94. For a discussion of the Reyes mission see Reyes, *Misión Diplomática*; Robledo, *Ospina*, 64–65; and Castillero Reyes, *Panamá y Colombia*, 52–67.

[5]*FRUS, 1903*, 284–94.

[6]Ibid., 288.

[7]Ibid., 289.

[8]Ibid., 292.

[9]Ibid., 293.

[10]Address at the Coliseum, Hartford, Connecticut, 22 August 1902, in Roosevelt, *Addresses* 1:91–92. Also see address at Augusta, Maine, 26 August 1902, ibid., 126; and Roosevelt to Henry Cabot Lodge, 19 July 1908, in Henry Cabot Lodge, *Selections from the Correspondence of Theodore Roosevelt and Henry Cabot Lodge, 1884–1918* (New York: Charles Scribner's Sons, 1925), 2:304.

[11]Roosevelt to Hay, 19 August 1903, Morison, *Letters of Roosevelt* 3:566–67.

[12]Roosevelt to Senator Marcus A. Hanna, 5 October 1903, ibid., 625.

[13]Roosevelt to Congress, 7 December 1903, in Roosevelt, *Addresses* 2:704; Roosevelt to Otto Gresham, 30 November 1903, in Morison, *Letters of Roosevelt* 2:663. For information relating to the 6 November proposal see chap. 1 in this volume.

[14]Beaupré to Hay, 27 November 1903, Department of State, Despatches, T-33, roll 61.

[15]Message of 7 December 1903, in Roosevelt, *Addresses* 2:648–709; message of 4 January 1904, in *Congressional Record*, 58th Cong., 2d sess., 38, pt. 1:418–25.

[16]Roosevelt to Congress, 4 January 1904, ibid., 419.

[17]Roosevelt to Congress, 7 December 1903, ibid., 706–7. Also see Roosevelt to Cecil Spring Rice, 9 December 1903; and Roosevelt to Gresham, 30 November 1903, in Morison, *Letters of Roosevelt* 3:651, 662. A. C. Richard, in his "Panama Canal," studies over one hundred daily U.S. newspapers and discusses the support for the president.

[18]4 January 1904, ibid., 423, 425.

[19]Hay to Reyes, 5 January 1904, *FRUS, 1903*, 294–306.

[20]Roosevelt to Charles Fletcher Lummis, 4 January 1904, in Morison, *Letters of Roosevelt* 3:688.

[21]Hay to Beaupré, 13 and 18 November 1903, in U.S. Department of State, Diplomatic Instructions of the Department of State, 1901–1906: Colombia (on microfilm), RG 59, M-77, roll 48, National Archives.

[22]Alban G. Snyder to Hay, 19 December 1903, Department of State, Despatches, T-33, roll 61. During the absence of the American minister, Snyder, as chargé, assumed control of the legation.

[23]Lodge to Roosevelt, 20 December 1903, Henry Cabot Lodge Papers, Lodge to TR Series, 1912–1918, Massachusetts Historical Society (hereafter cited as Lodge Papers).

[24]Ibid.

[25]Hay Diary, 2 January 1904, Library of Congress Manuscripts Division.

[26]Ibid., 11 January 1904.

[27]Ibid., 10 January 1904.

[28]Ibid., 12 January 1904.

[29]Hay to Reyes, 13 January 1904, *FRUS, 1903*, 313–14. Also see Hay Diary, 13 January 1904.

[30]The Senate debate lasted from 4 January to 23 February 1904.

[31]Morgan address to U.S. Senate, 23 November 1903, *Congressional Record*, 58th Cong., 1st sess., 37, pt. 1:428.

[32]Teller address to U.S. Senate, 18 January 1904, ibid., 58th Cong., 2d sess., 38, pt. 1:835. For Morgan's fears see Morgan to H. Watterson, undated but probably February 1904, and Morgan to Alton Parker, 29 February 1904, book 19, Morgan Papers.

[33]Both roll call votes are found in *Congressional Record*, 58th Cong., 2d sess., 38, pt. 3:2260–61.

[34]See Francis B. Loomis (acting secretary of state) to Snyder, 16 January 1904, Snyder to Hay, 18, 21, and 30 January, 13 and 28 February, and 2, 10, and 26 March 1904, in Department of State, Despatches, T-33, roll 61. Beaupré had informed the State Department on 11 January that Colombia was bankrupt, and that there was no money to buy new weapons or to pay the troops.

[35]For a fuller discussion of Colombian opinion see Arbena, "Panama"; and Arbena, "Colombian Reactions," 130–48. The fear of secession was perhaps more imagined than real. Nevertheless, since Colombia had just concluded

a civil war to determine whether ultimate power lay in Bogotá or in the departments, the central government's anxiety is understandable.

[36]Snyder to Hay, 19 April 1904, *FRUS, 1904*, 206.

[37]Rico to Snyder, 12 April 1904, ibid., 206–24.

[38]Lodge to Henry White, 1 April 1904, Lodge Papers.

[39]Snyder to Hay, 4 July 1904, Department of State, Despatches, T-33, roll 62.

[40]Snyder to Hay, 22 and 27 August 1904, ibid.

[41]Reyes suggested to Roosevelt that a plebiscite be held in Panama, not to return Panama to Colombia but as a "salve to [our] national honor." Roosevelt replied that he did not oppose the idea and would recommend that Panama hold such a vote. William Russell (U.S. minister to Colombia) to Hay, 13 January 1905, U.S. Department of State, Despatches from U.S. Ministers to Colombia (DFMTC), RG 59, T-33, roll 62, National Archives; Hay Diary, 19 February 1905; Roosevelt to Reyes, 20 February 1905, series 2, reel 337, Theodore Roosevelt Papers, Library of Congress Manuscripts Division.

[42]Mendoza's instructions are quoted in Castillero Reyes, *Panamá y Colombia*, 77–78.

[43]After only a few months in the Reyes government, Cortés resigned as foreign minister to pursue his substantial business interests. Clímaco Calderón replaced him in the cabinet.

[44]For a fuller discussion of the Cortés mission to Panama and Panama's response see Castillero Reyes, *Panamá y Colombia*, 73–92.

[45]Root left Washington in early July for a vacation and did not return to work at the State Department until late September or early October. Philip C. Jessup, *Elihu Root* (New York: Dodd, Mead & Company, 1938), 1:453–55.

[46]Root to General Horace Porter, 15 December 1903, vol. 181/1, Root Papers.

[47]Root address to Union League Club, Chicago, 22 February 1904, in Robert Bacon and James Brown Scott, eds., *Addresses on International Subjects by Elihu Root* (Cambridge: Harvard University Press, 1916), 181. Also see Root to James C. Carter, 25 February 1904, in vol. 184/2, Root Papers.

[48]Diego Mendoza to Root, 21 October 1905, Notes from the Colombian Legation in the United States to the Department of State, 1810–1906 (NFCL), RG 59, T-51, roll T-11, National Archives.

[49]Ibid.

[50]Ibid.

[51]Root to Mendoza, 10 February 1906, *FRUS, 1906*, 419–21.

[52]Guillermo Torres Garcia, *Historia de la Moneda en Colombia* (Bogotá: Imprenta del Banco de la República, 1945), 275.

[53]Ibid., 276. Also see James R. Mood, "Handbook of Foreign Currency and Exchange," in U.S. Bureau of Foreign and Domestic Commerce (BFDC), *Trade Promotion Series* 102 (Washington, DC: Government Printing Office, 1930), 51.

[54]U.S. Bureau of Statistics, *Statistical Abstracts of the United States, 1907*, 734.

[55]The Western, Central, and Eastern Cordilleras of the Andes extend from Ecuador northward toward the Caribbean.

[56]The following description of travel inside Colombia is based on accounts in P. L. Bell, "Colombia: A Commercial and Industrial Handbook," in BFDC, *Special Agent Series* 206 (Washington, DC: Government Printing Office, 1921), 393–412; Phanor James Eder, *Colombia* (London: T. Fisher Unwin, 1913), 88–100; W. Duval Brown, "Caribbean Markets for American Goods: Colombia," BFDC, *Trade Information Bulletin* 342, 1925; Ernst B. Filsinger, "Commercial Traveler's Guide to Latin America," BFDC, *Miscellaneous Series* 89, 1922; and F. Loraine Petre, *The Republic of Colombia: An Account of the Country, Its People, Its Institutions, and Its Resources* (London: Edward Stanford, 1906). The following mythical traveler will use railroads as they existed between 1914 and 1919.

[57]Cisneros lies at an altitude of 3400′; Santiago, at 3750′.

[58]Barrett to Secretary of State Elihu Root, 26 May 1906. U.S. Congress, Senate, Sen. Doc. 542, 60th Cong., 2d sess., 1908–09, p. 24.

[59]Legal adviser Hayne Davis had informed Mendoza on 7 June 1906 that, if Colombia maintained its present position on arbitration, it would win its case. Mendoza evidently also believed that Colombia could compromise no further and must maintain unchanged its present position. Hayne Davis Papers, Southern Historical Collection, No. A-878, University of North Carolina, Chapel Hill.

[60]A copy of Mendoza's letter may be found in F.O. 371: General Correspondence: Political, 1906–1941, 371/43-p. 190ff., PRO. For a discussion of Mendoza's actions see Castillero Reyes, *Panamá y Colombia*, 77–92.

Chapter III

Republican Settlement: The Root-Cortés-Arosemena Treaties

After two years of bluster, tension, and confrontation, 1906 seemed auspicious for the final resolution of the isthmian problem. Internal pressure appeared to be relaxing on Reyes as departmental commissioners of agriculture, commerce, and industry, meeting at the National Commercial Congress in July, unanimously resolved to "hereby make known to the Government the necessity of promptly settling, in a manner honorable and convenient to Colombia, all questions pending with the United States and Panama."[1] Likewise, the United States also seemed to be pursuing a course of friendship and settlement. Learning from Bogotá that certain Colombian departments might be planning to secede and join Panama "under alleged secret approval of the United States," Secretary Root quickly had informed the American legation that the Roosevelt administration did not sanction such a move. He further emphasized that relations with Colombia were friendly, and that the United States sought to work with, not against, President Reyes in establishing a prosperous, stable Colombia.[2] Indeed, such action seemed to mesh smoothly into the overall American policy for Latin America, as enunciated by Secretary Root on 31 July at Rio de Janeiro. The American people and its government, he asserted,

> wish for no victories but those of peace; for no territory except our own; for no sovereignty except sovereignty over ourselves. We deem the independence and equal rights of the smallest and weakest member of the family of nations entitled to as much respect as those of the greatest empire; and we deem the observance of that respect the chief guaranty of the weak against the oppression of the strong. We neither claim nor desire any rights or privileges or powers that we do not freely concede to every American republic. We wish to increase our prosperity, to expand our trade, to

> grow in wealth, in wisdom, and in spirit; but our conception of the true way to accomplish this is not to pull down others and profit by their ruin, but to help all friends to a common prosperity and a common growth, that we may all become greater and stronger together.

Addressing the Trans-Mississippi Commercial Congress in Kansas City on 20 November, Root was enthusiastic about future commercial relations with Latin America. "Immediately before us, at exactly the right time, just as we are ready for it, great opportunities to the south are presented."[3] As he realized, to take full advantage of those opportunities, Washington needed to reduce the fear and suspicion of the United States in this hemisphere. What better way of doing so than by resolving the three-year dispute with Colombia?

During this apparent mutual relaxation of hostility, President Reyes and his administration worked toward a new accord with both the United States and Panama. An optimistic John Barrett wrote Secretary Root that "excellent progress has been made in the Colombia-United States-Panama matter. . . . A regular campaign has been skillfully started over Colombia by President Reyes, along lines blocked out by him and me, to educate the people in favor of making treaties without fail this fall or winter with the United States and Panama."[4] Within one week of this communiqué, Barrett began his forty-day, 1,000-mile journey on muleback to meet Root and familiarize him with the latest treaty developments.[5] Armed with up-to-date information, the secretary and a saddle-sore Barrett then met with Foreign Minister A. Vásquez Cobo on 24 September at Cartagena.

Publicly, Root and Vásquez Cobo appeared cordial but gave no indication as to the status of their private talks in which the two leaders discussed in detail the new Colombian proposals as an acceptable basis for a treaty. At the conclusion of their lengthy conference, Root verbally agreed to the general thrust of the Colombian document and signified his willingness to enter into formal treaty negotiations with the Colombian envoy in Washington.[6]

As a basis for formal negotiations, Vásquez Cobo had urged a seven-part proposal, thus marking a major reversal in his government's position toward the United States.[7] Based on the previous three-month reevaluation, the Colombian propositions asked neither for an indemnity from the United States nor for the arbitration of points of dispute between the two nations. Instead, Vásquez Cobo proposed that Bogotá negotiate two treaties, one with the United States and one with Panama, with the direct object of settling once and for all the gnawing isthmian dilemma. Formally acknowledging the irreparable separation of Panama, Vásquez Cobo and Reyes hoped to regain some of the advantages their government may have won had it retained possession of that territory. Under their terms the United States would guarantee the free passage of Colombian ships, troops, and war materials through the canal at all times; levy a duty on Colombian merchandise and mails no higher than that levied on similar U.S. items; and charge Colombia rates for its use of the isthmian railroad, not to exceed more than it had paid before the 1903 revolution. In addition, Colombia requested the establishment of a differential tariff allowing its molasses and sugar to enter the United States at a much lower rate. Since the United States had strong influence over Panama, the Colombian plan urged the American government to use its good offices to effect a Panamanian-Colombian agreement. Such a settlement should include Panama's acceptance of its rightful share of the Colombian external and internal debt up to November 1903. Furthermore, Panama also should permit Colombia's national products to enter duty free, a concession the Colombians would gladly reciprocate.[8]

Should these terms be incorporated into a series of three interrelated treaties, Colombian officials believed any major obstacles existing between the parties would be largely eradicated. Secretary Root agreed, but, while generally approving the proposed terms, he informed Vásquez Cobo that the Roosevelt administration could not accept a differential tariff that would almost certainly cause hostile Senate reaction to any treaty settlement. Furthermore, the status of Colombian and Panamanian trade lay outside American jurisdiction; therefore, the United States could only recommend that Panama agree to the free-trade concept.[9] Aside from these two major reservations, Root envisioned just minor modifications to effect a mutually acceptable solution.

With their interests integrally entwined in these negotiations, the three governments decided that each of the proposed treaties—the ones between the United States and Panama, the United States and Colombia, and Colombia and Panama—must stand or fall together. If any one of the three failed ratification, none would go into effect. Had the United States exercised absolute sovereignty over Panama, acceptable treaties with Colombia would have been quickly signed. However, the United States would not dictate terms to the Panamanian government but would only advise and recommend. Ideally, under the gentle persuasion of Secretary Root and President Roosevelt, Panamanian leaders would approve those general terms already discussed by the United States and Colombia.

Negotiations between the three governments fell into two distinct phases: September 1906 to July 1907 and August 1907 to January 1909. During the initial phase, discussions were, for the most part, friendly and cooperative. An overoptimistic Secretary Root had even indicated that agreement should be reached by mid-June 1907 at the latest.[10] However, he had misjudged the difficulties of reaching an acceptable solution to the financial terms by which Panama would assume from Colombia a just and equitable share of the old external and internal debt.

At his meeting with Root in Cartagena, Foreign Minister Vásquez Cobo had suggested that Panama pay $5 million as its legitimate share of Colombian debt contracted prior to its secession. Unfamiliar with the exact peculiarities of the case, Root, while not objecting, declined to admit that as a justifiable figure.[11] Upon reflection, Colombian leaders indeed thought the sum might be incorrect. Therefore, in early December, Colombian Minister Enrique Cortés, writing to William Buchanan, former U.S. minister to Panama, argued for an additional $1 million.[12] Reaction to such an amount was unfavorable in both the United States and Panama. Since the Panama-Colombia talks were essentially coordinated by the United States, Root engaged Cortés in a prolonged series of informal discussions seeking modification of the $6 million figure. His efforts were successful when, in early March 1907, the Colombian minister revised the demands. In return for Colombian recognition, Panama must now pay $3 million in gold, acknowledge Colombian control of 50,000 shares of the New Panama Canal Company, enter into a reciprocal, duty-free trade agreement, and suppress within its territory any revolutionaries who conspired to overthrow the Colombian government.[13] Writing to Panamanian Minister José Domingo de Obaldía in New York, Root noted: "It appears to this Government that the proposals of Colombia, as thus modified, are reasonable, and that it is clearly for the interest of Panama to accept them."[14]

Uneasy about the future ramifications of a reciprocal trade agreement, Panamanian leaders opposed inclusion of duty-free provisions relating to natural products. Similarly, they objected to any clause concerning revolutionaries as unnecessary. Despite Colombia's reduction of its indemnity demand by $3 million, they also believed that figure was still too high. In addition, Panama favored paying its fair share of Colombia's old external and internal debt in Colombian bonds, not in gold. By purchasing those bonds on the open market at approximately 40 percent of their face value—the current going rate—and then by transferring them to Colombia at face value, Panama could greatly lighten its financial burden. Until these issues could be resolved, Panama's leaders, despite Root's support of Bogotá's position, indicated they would not approve any agreement. Their refusal to accept

Colombia's terms without modification pushed a settlement beyond Root's anticipated 15 June deadline.[15]

At this inauspicious moment, a portentous new development aroused consternation and apprehension in Washington. Secretary Root learned that Colombia had just opened a first-class legation at Tokyo, which, according to rumor in Bogotá, was to negotiate a treaty with Japan, a treaty that would include "the cession . . . of a coaling station on the east and west coast of Colombia in the event of a war . . . between Japan and the United States."[16] What made such a cession truly ominous in the summer of 1907 was that American-Japanese relations already were under strain. Arguments over U.S. immigration, naturalization, and segregation practices that discriminated against the Japanese had even led to rumors of war. Since negotiations were under way to resolve that tension diplomatically, Secretary Root did not expect the outbreak of hostilities in the Pacific. Nevertheless, even the hint of such a Japanese-Colombian treaty, with its startling coaling provisions, was extremely distressing. In forwarding this explosive information to Roosevelt, Root warned that "Colombia as our enemy is a source of vital danger if we have any other enemy."[17] Militarily, Colombia could never threaten the United States, yet its border with Panama, as well as its strategic location astride the entrances to the canal, made its friendship or neutrality vital to the United States.

Perhaps this surprising development was a Colombian effort to force a breakthrough in the negotiations that had stalled unexpectedly. Or perhaps President Reyes hoped to use Japanese friendship to offset the power of the United States in the Caribbean region, although this explanation seems less likely. Whatever his original intention, Reyes wanted the United States to know about Colombia's discussions with Japan. He even urged the American chargé, William Heimke, in September 1907, to translate a newspaper article by the subsecretary for foreign affairs which praised the Japanese, noted the possibility of war between Japan and the United States, and concluded that "the Japanese may be our future great friends."[18] Reyes was not trying to antagonize the United States. Quite the contrary was true, as Heimke wrote when he sent his information to Washington

> in order, as [Reyes] suggested, that my Government might realize and become impressed with the importance of being the first to cultivate and continue to enlarge relations of friendship and commerce with Colombia, and thus be moved to expedite the completion of the proposed new treaty between that country and the United States.[19]

Perhaps the threat of international competition would increase American pressure on Panama, thereby resulting in its acceptance of Colombia's latest terms of settlement.

Despite this new Colombian pressure, Secretary Root was in no mood to rehash textual arguments with Panama. Having labored so diligently on an agreement it had rejected, he was now willing to allow his good friend and colleague, Secretary of War William Howard Taft, to handle the next stage in the delicate diplomatic discussions.[20]

Secretary Taft was the ideal choice to assume control over the important day-to-day wrangling between Colombia, Panama, and the United States. In his role as president of the Philippine Commission from 1900 to 1903 and as secretary of war since 1904, he had formed an ideal working relationship with both Roosevelt and Root. Their mutual respect and trust already had developed into genuine friendship. When Root joined Secretary Taft in Roosevelt's cabinet in July 1905, these three powerful national leaders called themselves the three musketeers, even going so far as to sign their correspondence with the appropriate names of D'Artagnan (Roosevelt), Athos (Root), and Porthos (Taft). In addition, President Roosevelt had frequently utilized Taft's skills as a conciliator in both domestic and foreign crises between 1904 and 1907.[21] In dealing with Panama, Taft, as the American in charge of canal construction, had the additional advantage of already having established a working relationship with its leaders.

It was hoped that Taft, with his easygoing manner, infectious laugh, and previous experience, could resolve the Panamanian objections to the proposed treaties. Although he would manage the discussions, he was to keep both Roosevelt and Root informed of any developments. Although Secretary Root had withdrawn temporarily from the actual deliberations, he indicated to his colleague his displeasure with Panamanian tactics, especially relating to the proposed monetary payment. "It seems quite clear," he argued, "that these [Panamanian leaders] are simply playing with us, and I think they should be made to understand that we do not like it."[22] Taft, well aware of Root's disgust and anxiety, worked diligently throughout June and early July 1907 to effect an acceptable compromise.

By 1 July, Panama, however, still objected to paying Colombia $3 million in gold. Its representative in these tripartite discussions, William Nelson Cromwell, admitted to Taft that Panama might be willing to pay $900,000 in cash if the rest of the debt could be paid in Colombian bonds. But a plan more likely of approval by his client, Cromwell added, would be one in which the United States, as virtual sovereign in the canal zone, assumed liability for one-half of Colombia's claims. Cromwell then alerted Taft to a new problem that now threatened the tripartite negotiations and that must be addressed simultaneously with the debt question: Panama would not accept Colombia's borders as defined by an 1855 law. Rather, the correct demarcation, according to the Panamanian government, was that set forth in an 1847 Colombian statute.[23]

To resolve these two vital issues, Taft, Cromwell, and Cortés met in New York on 3 July. Compromising on the money question, Cortés and Cromwell approved a new arrangement, whereby Colombia would lower its financial demands from $3 million to $2.5 million in gold. Ten days later Panamanian officials tentatively agreed to pay an initial installment of $1 million in gold, followed by the transfer to Bogotá of the first six annual payments of $250,000 each owed Panama by the United States under the terms of the Hay-Bunau-Varilla Treaty. Nor did Taft, Cromwell, and Cortés ignore the boundary question. Acting on his own initiative, Cortés defused that potential crisis by consenting to submit the dispute to an arbitration tribunal of one Panamanian, one Colombian, and Secretary Root.[24] Success seemed at hand.

No sooner had the good news reached Washington than discouraging reports began to arrive. Cortés had evidently exceeded his instructions when he agreed to arbitration and, after careful reflection, informed Taft on 4 July that Cromwell had misled him. As a result, Cortés now decided to withdraw his approval of arbitration and to await official word from Bogotá.[25] By late July instructions arrived from President Reyes, who refused to budge on the Colombian boundary proposal; it was not subject to arbitration.[26]

In an ironic reversal of roles, Colombia, which off and on for three years had argued for arbitration with the United States, now had to refute the logic of arbitration. Cromwell, using almost the identical logic Colombian officials had tried against the United States, wrote Cortés:

> You must allow me to say that the refusal of your Government to submit the boundary question to arbitration does not seem to be tenable. If Colombia is right in its boundary contention then it will be sustained by arbitration. If it be in error then its present claim will not be sustained and the propriety of arbitration will be justified. As to Colombia, no harm can come from arbitration if she is right. As to Panama, irreparable harm would come if the proposition were surrendered without honorable and authoritative determination.[27]

With the situation reversed, Colombia adopted the same position as had the United States earlier, a position which held that arbitration was out of the question.

While Panama protested the Colombian boundary claims, the United States remained silent. With an agreement within grasp, Root, reclaiming direction of the negotiations, hoped to postpone any boundary problem until after the treaties had been signed, but these hopes were dashed when Minister Cortés insisted that a boundary settlement must be reached before any treaty was signed. Root's displeasure over these events, however, was not directed against Cortés or Colombia but against Panama, for he believed that the Colombian boundary claims were justifiable and that Panama was being unnecessarily difficult.[28] The secretary also was slightly distraught with Taft, who had not conducted the negotiations with a sufficiently firm grasp. Writing to Cromwell, Taft noted: "Root is impatient with me and much disappointed that the boundary question has been injected into the negotiation, and does not understand quite how the question can be raised now by Panama in good faith."[29] To Taft, significant compromise by both Panama and Colombia was in order, but Root disagreed. While no records exist, this conflict evidently was resolved as a result of a conference held by Root and Taft with President Roosevelt at Oyster Bay on 13 August. Three days later Root verbally—and eventually in writing—affirmed the Colombian boundary claims as proper and just.[30]

Despite American support of Colombia's boundary claims, the Panamanians initially refused to modify their attitude and voluntarily surrender any territory they thought should belong to Panama, especially the Atrato River and the Gulf of Cupica. Deliberations dragged on throughout the summer, autumn, and winter of 1907 with no breakthrough, although Cromwell offered in July to relinquish his client's claims to two thirds of the disputed territory, provided Bogotá recognize Panama's claims to the river and the gulf. When Cortés rejected the proposal, Cromwell countered in mid-August, urging that the boundary question be left out of the tripartite agreements altogether and resolved at a future date. That proposal Cortés found more agreeable, especially since Root promised that he would confirm in writing the U.S. position that Colombia's claims were valid while Panama's were "without merit." Upon further reflection and discussion, Cortés, Taft, Cromwell, and Minister José Arango of Panama signed a preliminary protocol on 17 August. In that document, Panama agreed to pay Colombia $2.5 million in gold, forfeit its claims to the 50,000 shares of the New Panama Canal Company, and not harbor Colombian revolutionaries. Colombia, in return, would recognize Panama's independence and strive to establish normalized relations with its former department.[31]

The Reyes administration had no objection to the terms actually written into the protocol Cortés had signed; rather, it was deeply disturbed with the omission of the boundary question. Unlike Cortés, Foreign Minister Vásquez Cobo insisted that Panama must officially recognize Colombia's territory as defined by the 1855 law. When it became apparent that Panama had no immediate intention of doing so, Bogotá in December repudiated Cortés's actions. Therefore, a nervous Cortés wrote Root in late January 1908: "The situation is such that unless our line is accepted, no alternative would be left to me but to suspend negotiations. This lame conclusion would be a source of great mortification to me personally, and [I] would be compelled to adopt it with the deepest regret."[32] Panama as well as Colombia, however, remained obstinate, and the August protocol remained tabled.

In Bogotá, President Reyes also felt the pressure of continued delay and postponement. If Colombia were to reestablish a peaceful relationship with Panama and the United States, secure important concessions in the use of the canal, and quiet dissent in its coastal departments by assuring, through peaceful settlement, benefits of commerce and shipping, it must resolve the isthmian mess peacefully and quickly. Yet, despite the many benefits that would accrue to the nation upon ratification of the treaties, Reyes faced a suspicious population and Colombian legislature. If he relented and even partially accepted Panama's boundary claims, existing internal unrest could rapidly magnify and create a severe crisis, imperiling his administration as well as future ratification of the proposed treaties.[33] If, however, he refused to modify in any way Colombia's claims, the work of the last few months would be wasted, conditions would revert back to their status shortly after the rebellion, and the coastal departments, anxious for the increased trade and profit normalized relations with Panama would bring, might grow increasingly belligerent toward his government.

Forced to act, Reyes, through Cortés, finally informed Secretary Root in late March that Bogotá would proceed in the discussions, agreeing to eliminate any mention of the boundary dispute.[34] The Colombian president could make such an offer because ten days earlier his armed forces had seized the most hotly contested region along the Panama-Colombia border. Evidently, Root had prior knowledge of the maneuver and not only did not oppose but also "recognized that [Colombia was] fully justified in so doing it."[35] Not surprisingly, Panamanian officials immediately requested that the U.S. government guarantee its territorial integrity as stipulated in Article 1 of the Hay-Bunau-Varilla Treaty, but the United States received this proposal coolly. Second Assistant Secretary of State Alvey A. Adee saw no need for action by the United States. "I do not see that Article I . . . obligates us to land force[s at] Panama to settle a boundary dispute in Panama's way. We guarantee Panamanian independence, and one of the sacred rights of Spanish American independence is the privilege of scrapping with neighboring states."[36] Although the official American response was phrased more diplomatically, it retained Adee's basic assessment.

While not complying with Panama's request, the secretary of state was still concerned with retaining its goodwill. Possibly to give the new republic a means of saving face, Root suggested that Bogotá arbitrate the westernmost section of the boundary known as the Jurado. To Reyes and Cortés such a proposal made sense. Under Root's plan, Panama would accept as valid all Colombia's boundary claims, with the single exception of the limits of Jurado.[37] Since these claims would have been upheld for the most part and since Colombian forces already occupied much of the Jurado, Reyes believed he could agree to this minor arbitration. The positive results of settlement seemed worth such a small concession, and Colombia had a good chance of gaining its Jurado claims. However, the diplomatic machinery moved slowly among the three governments, and not until December 1908 did Panamanian leaders finally agree to the arbitration of the Jurado district, realizing that Bogotá, not they, had the moral and diplomatic support of the United States, and that, given the presence of a Colombian military force in the Jurado, coupled with the absence of a Panamanian army, they would be unable either to extract further concessions from Bogotá or to wrest the disputed territory from Colombia's grasp.

Once Colombian officials acknowledged the need for close cooperation with the United States in the spring of 1908 in order to resolve the boundary dispute with Panama, the threatened Japanese coal concessions evaporated. While Colombia did sign a treaty with Japan in late May, it allowed only for the exchange of diplomatic and consular officials and for mutual trading privileges, privileges already held by the United States and most of Europe. A few months later an informant in the Ministry for Foreign Affairs reassured the American chargé that no secret agreement existed with Japan: President Reyes "is depending much more upon the national prosperity which it is hoped will result to Colombia from the completion of the negotiations for the Panama and United States treaties . . . than upon any arrangement with Japan."[38] A potentially explosive situation had died quietly. Neither Colombia nor Japan would challenge American hegemony in the Caribbean.

Following the breakthrough in December 1908, the treaties could be molded into final form. On 3 January 1909 the major participants gathered at Root's Washington residence to resolve last-minute details and to formulate the exact wording of the three agreements. Shortly after midnight, when all had finally expressed satisfaction over their labors, Root, Minister Cortés, and Minister Carlos Arosemena of Panama, affixed their signatures to the appropriate treaties.[39] Now, after months of strenuous effort, these men could only wait to determine how accurately they had read their nations' feelings and how these documents would be received by their various legislative bodies. Initial legislative response seemed good. By late January, Panama had approved both the treaty with the United States and the one with Colombia. By the first week in March the U.S. Senate had approved the treaties with Panama and with Colombia. In Washington, Roosevelt and Root, according to the British ambassador, were "extremely anxious" to see all the treaties accepted before they attended William Howard Taft's presidential inauguration. The ultimate fate of the three treaties, however, lay not in their hands but in those of the Colombian legislature.[40]

Since his inauguration in 1904, Colombian President Reyes had been one of the firmest advocates of a peaceful settlement with both the United States and Panama. Wracked by major economic problems, his nation needed to focus its attention toward internal reform rather than toward a prolonged confrontation with either the United States or Panama. If Colombia could resolve its differences with those two nations, Reyes realized the Panama Canal could rejuvenate economic prosperity in Colombian Atlantic and Pacific coastal areas.[41] If his country accepted these treaties and recognized Panama, Colombian ships, merchandise, and mails also would receive unique privileges in the canal zone. Not only would such benefits assist reestablishing stable economies in coastal provinces but also would defuse a potentially explosive political situation in the same region, a situation created by Bogotá's delay in resolving the Panamanian question. The coastal departments of Narino, Cauca, Antioquia, Bolívar, Atlántico, and Magdalena realized that normalized political relations were tied directly to normalized trade relations, about which they were most concerned. Therefore, from the standpoint of practicality, President Reyes earnestly desired approval of the treaties.

Although five years had passed since the revolution, many Colombians still resented American actions on the isthmus. In 1903 and 1904, Colombia, pitted against the power of the United States, had been helpless. Now, with the Root-Cortés-Arosemena treaties, Colombia held a decisive position in which its vote meant life or death for these documents. Some Colombians may have thought this was an ideal chance to demonstrate, albeit belatedly, their nation's anger over the loss of its former department, even at the expense of continued strained relations with both the United States and Panama.

Coupled with this smoldering resentment of American actions in 1903, and more significant in terms of possible ratification, was the growing unrest with the rule of Rafael Reyes.[42] Shortly after assuming office, the fifty-nine-year-old president adopted the theme "peace and concord." Colombia was in disastrous shape, and the only viable means of escape, the popular charismatic leader argued, was to join as a unified force seeking the revitalization of national life. Party factionalism, which characterized earlier recovery efforts, must cease. The new executive offered hope to Colombians, provided they placed their confidence in him.

The initial enthusiasm of Reyes soon crashed on congressional shoals. The Colombian Senate chose Reyes's major political foe as its presiding officer. Unperturbed, Reyes submitted to Congress, during the summer of 1904, a program that would alleviate the economic crisis. He proposed that Congress grant him broad authority to increase customs tariffs up to 80 percent; establish new taxes on tobacco, timber, paper, and the exportation of hides; fix the price of salt; create a central bank that would have exclusive control over the issuance of new bank notes; modify existing territorial divisions; and reorganize the federal bureaucracy. Congressmen in both houses of the legislature were hesitant, and their debates extended from days to weeks to months without granting the president the powers he had requested. Meanwhile, the nation suffered the agonies of economic and fiscal collapse.

When the regular session of Congress adjourned without approving his recovery program, Reyes convened a special session on 30 November, but it adjourned two weeks later still unable to reach an agreement. An impatient Reyes then sought action. Less than two months later, on 1 February 1905, he announced that a new extralegal congressional body—the National Assembly—would convene on 15 March, its purpose to save "the public administration from anarchy and the nation from the grave dangers to which it has been exposed by the last Congress."[43] The future of Colombia required immediate programs, not prolonged delays.

Reaction to the announcement was mixed. Reyes, his hands tied by the recalcitrant Congress, had gained the sympathy of the people as well as the support of some members of the legislature who were willing to give him an opportunity to test his reforms. However, other Colombians, both Liberal and Conservative, objected to the new body. One Reyes critic, writing four years later, sarcastically summarized the opposition viewpoint:

> [Reyes] has eliminated even the faintest shadow of popular representation, replacing the popularly elected bodies by what he calls a National Assembly, which he might have called, had he so desired, by any other name; for instance, National Corps de Ballet, National Acrobatic Troupe, or Colombian Sistine Chapel Choir.[44]

Critics argued that, while each department was guaranteed one Liberal and two Conservative representatives in the new organization, Reyes's cronies carefully controlled the selection process. Members of the legislative body were chosen by municipal councils, which were greatly influenced by departmental governors who had been appointed by President Reyes.[45]

As soon as the National Assembly convened in March, Reyes pushed through a number of new constitutional changes. One such measure abolished the vice presidency and reserved for the president the right to name his own successor from the cabinet. Another granted the assembly the power to redefine and rearrange departmental and municipal boundaries at its own discretion. A third major modification of the constitution revised the president's term of office. In the 1904 election, Reyes had been chosen to serve for six years; by the new provision his term was to run from 1 January 1905 to 31 December 1914. The constitutional amendment noted that this was indeed an aberration and was "only good during the administration of General Reyes." After 1914 presidents again would be limited to six-year terms.

In order to revitalize his nation, Reyes believed that he needed to focus his attention on reform, not politics. By abolishing the office of vice president and reserving the right to name his own successor, he eliminated the possibility of a coup similar to that by which his immediate predecessor, Vice President Marroquín, had seized power in 1900 from the legitimate president. Additionally, with the power to rearrange departmental and municipal boundaries, Reyes could exercise great leverage in gaining support for his reform programs. Finally, the extension of his term to 1914 provided ten uninterrupted years, during which he could refashion Colombia into a viable economic state.

Along with the constitutional modifications, the National Assembly granted President Reyes the authority to reorganize his nation's fiscal and economic system by instituting new taxes, creating governmental liquor and salt monopolies, and establishing a central bank. Each of these powers, however, alienated some sector of Colombian society. In reorganizing the revenue system, Reyes removed from departmental governments the lucrative tobacco and liquor taxes, and in introducing the central bank, he alienated political leaders who had established the Board of Conversion in 1903 to withdraw paper pesos from circulation. The new bank replaced that board with a body more responsive to the president's control.[46] And, in tightening his grip on power, Reyes created growing apprehension that he sought to transform Colombia into a dictatorship.

Measures severely hampering Reyes's political opponents also disturbed many Colombians. By the end of his first year in office, the president not only had consolidated power and established his own legislative body but also had begun imprisoning political opponents. At the same time, the Colombian press faced intensified censorship by the administration which would continue until 1909. By April 1907,

Reyes clearly enunciated the role he expected of political parties within Colombia. Addressing the National Assembly, he declared:

> This will be the principal object of the political groups: they will either change into coincident forces for doing good or they will have to disappear, for the nation can no longer tolerate within its strong organism any disrupting and opposing forces to its progress and well being under the name of political entities.[47]

Since his government directed the method of Colombian reform, any opposition undermined his regime as well as the nation's progress.

If Reyes successfully had utilized this new power to accomplish an economic recovery, his position might have remained firmly grounded. Indeed, despite his policies he had solid bipartisan support during his first year or two in office, but recovery did not come quickly even with the reorganization, new taxes, and new construction programs. The alleged favoritism and corruption of the Reyes administration, as well as the president's failure to alleviate the economic unrest, made him more vulnerable to increasing political attacks. With his rigid control of the press, the president could obstruct, but not eradicate, the spread of such criticism. Although no major movement developed to overthrow his regime, discontent was evident. In December 1905 the government broke up a revolutionary conspiracy, while two months later Reyes barely escaped death at the hands of assassins. Discontent and dissatisfaction continued to increase with each passing year, and in 1908, when Reyes finally utilized his power to realign departmental and municipal boundaries along arbitrary political lines, opposition further intensified.[48]

Despite the existence of this political unrest within Colombia, neither high Colombian nor American administrative leaders expected a problem over ratification of the Root-Cortés-Arosemena treaties. In fact, as early as January 1909 reports from U.S. diplomatic and consular personnel were unduly optimistic. Consul Isaac Manning at Cartagena reported that local businessmen were pleased with the settlement and had wired their support to Reyes.[49] Chargé Paxton Hibben informed the secretary of state that the foreign minister "assured me that it was the hope and belief of General Reyes that there would not be the slightest difficulty in regard to the ratification of the treaties here."[50] American Minister Thomas Dawson, having just arrived in Bogotá, announced that the president said "he had no doubt that the National Assembly would ratify [the treaties] by an overwhelming or even a unanimous vote, and this by the end of next week."[51] While outwardly confident and optimistic, Reyes must have known his political situation was a bit shaky, but, so long as the National Assembly determined the fate of the treaties, his optimism appeared legitimate. The president had polled twenty-one of the forty-eight assembly delegates as they had arrived in Bogotá for the 22 February opening of the legislature, and all had expressed approval. Referring to that poll, both the president and the minister for foreign affairs expressed their complete confidence "of the unanimous ratification [as] soon as the assembly meets. The treaties [they maintained] are satisfactory in every detail." Dawson quickly relayed the good news to Washington.[52]

Amidst the general optimism regarding favorable passage in Colombia, Manning had interjected a possible disquieting note. In his 26 January report, he briefly mentioned that the constitution still invested in Congress the right to approve or reject treaties, and Reyes had planned to call for congressional elections so that a new body could make the necessary determination. On consulting his departmental governors, Reyes learned that, should elections be held, large numbers of antiadministration figures most likely would be chosen. Fourteen of the seventeen governors advised him to postpone any election and instead to reconvene the friendly National Assembly in order to improve chances for passage of the treaties. Reyes, Manning concluded, took his governors' advice.[53] Even though the consul cited this disturbing factor, he too closed his report optimistically. American leaders, therefore, did not believe this problem would disrupt the ratification process.

Addressing the National Assembly legislators, Foreign Minister Francisco José Urrutia urged passage of the Root-Cortés-Arosemena treaties. Emphasizing national interests, he proposed that they look to the future and not to the past:

> In order to arrive at the result now achieved, it has been necessary that the Chief of State and those of us who have been his collaborators . . . should, rather than complain over the cruel mutilation of our territory that wounded our patriotism and caused national grief, pay attention to the imperious and not-to-be neglected necessities of the future, and, accepting as irremediable facts that are so, should firmly confront the responsibility of putting an end to the terrible litigation which has stained and blackened so many pages of our contemporaneous history. . . . The abnormality of our relations of public and private international law with an entity bordering upon us and profoundly linked to our own, causes us continual difficulties. . . . [We] cannot remain impassive, inactive, silent, absorbed in our rancors, hoping for the promised day of vengeance which does not come, which will never come. Out of the excess of evil we should snatch a good, even if in doing it we are forced to restrain the expression of sentiments which, although they may be generous, nevertheless must be recast in the mold of present necessities and advantages.[54]

Convening on 23 February the National Assembly officially received the treaties and, after the traditional cursory first reading, sent them to committee.

On 4 March, while the Colombian committee discussed the documents, William Howard Taft became the twenty-sixth president of the United States. Unsuccessful in urging Elihu Root to remain in charge of the State Department, the new president then turned to the powerful Republican senator, Henry Cabot Lodge, who also refused the honor. As his third choice for secretary of state, Taft selected former Attorney General Philander Knox, who by mid-December 1908 had agreed to enter the cabinet. Since Taft firmly believed in delegating considerable power to his department heads, Knox, during the next four years, would control the Colombian negotiations with little presidential supervision.

As the Colombian committee examined the documents, Secretary Knox received a disturbing message from Dawson in Bogotá: "Opposition developing. The enemies of the President [are] attacking the assembly, demanding elected Congress and the amendment Jurado clause. . . . Ratification is certain unless Reyes weakens."[55] Adee wondered if, in light of such pressure, the United States should not try to stiffen Reyes's backbone. By that time, however, events in Bogotá were outrunning decisions in Washington.[56]

By late February, dissatisfaction with the Reyes regime and its treaties had become more vocal. On the twenty-fifth, one of the most powerful Liberal leaders, Nicolás Esguerra, addressed a memorial to the National Assembly, contesting that body's right to approve treaties or to carry out any legislative function since it had not been popularly elected.[57] Enemies of Reyes, regardless of party affiliation, echoed Esguerra's remarks during the following weeks. Once the president, facing this unexpected rising protest, agreed to summon an elected session of Congress in February 1910, the intensity of the outcry subsided. The protests, however, had badly shaken the heretofore self-assured Reyes. Emerging from a meeting with him on 7 March, Dawson was convinced that the president had lost his confidence and was "plainly nervous."[58]

The following day the assembly committee favorably reported the treaty: fourteen approved unconditional ratification, three approved ratification with amendments, and one rejected ratification. Once the report became public, students in Bogotá began anti-Reyes and anti-treaty demonstrations that continued throughout the daylight hours of 9 March.[59] On the heels of that demonstration came a letter from the military chiefs in the department of Santander—through which flowed the Magdalena River, Colombia's major commercial artery—expressing dislike of any treaty sanctioning "the iniquitous treason of November third."[60] Reyes then met with student leaders to discuss the treaty, but the talks degenerated into a wholesale attack on Reyes's policies since 1904. On 11 March students demonstrated in Bogotá, "shouting for liberty and for the rejection of the treaties." Faced with these renewed protests, legislators became cautious. As Dawson informed Secretary Knox, the assembly delayed consideration of the treaties and waited for Reyes to take decisive action. That body, however, rejected any formal postponement of consideration since it did expect the president to reassert control over the situation.[61]

Reyes's next move astounded Colombia. The man who up until now had exercised such widespread control throughout the nation, and who had established his own legislative body, abruptly resigned on 13 March. Crowds stoned the administration newspapers and the homes of government leaders, chanted "down with the tyrant" and "death to the traitors" in the streets, and harassed assembly members. The frustration and repressed anger of five years had been freely expressed. As the jubilant crowds drifted away, the Reyes rule seemed at an end. But the former president reconsidered his decision later that night and reassumed office. Dawson described the scene:

> Next morning, March fourteenth, Bogotá woke to find Reyes in the Presidency, a state of siege declared, machine guns placed commanding the central Plaza, the police and troops armed with Mausers, and . . . the three most dreaded Generals in the country, in command. . . . The malcontents were terrorized, and the city became as quiet as a graveyard.[62]

Until the state of siege was lifted three days later, no more than five Colombians could gather together in public.[63] The demise of the Reyes administration had been short-lived.

The reason for Reyes's surprising resignation and his abrupt reassumption of power is unclear. He may have hoped to determine his most vociferous opposition and then, upon reassuming power, deal with it accordingly. However, a one-day retirement would be too short to flush out hidden opponents, nor would such dramatics have been necessary to obtain that information. Most probably the recent events had cracked Reyes's self-confidence and revealed the growing strong feelings against his administration. Rather than leading his nation toward unity and prosperity, he watched it descend into turmoil over his leadership. Disillusioned and disgruntled, he may have decided to resign, but the sudden decision left his supporters in a precarious position and the nation without a popularly chosen leader. The raucous display in Bogotá celebrating his "retirement" probably convinced Reyes that intense fighting might occur between pro- and anti-Reyes forces over control of the government. By reassuming power, he could restore order, at least until the nation elected a new Congress on 30 May. When Acting President Jorge Holguín requested that he resume his duties, he agreed.[64]

Following his resumption of power, Reyes did not successfully quell opposition. He attempted to do so by not only deporting certain personages, including Luis Martínez Silva, who had been linked to the December 1905 conspiracy, but also by returning powers over certain governmental monopolies to departments. The carrot-and-stick approach did not succeed in ending anti-Reyes outbursts. On 16 March, Reyes once again submitted his resignation to the National Assembly, which then sought the opinion of Colombian municipal officials. Carlos Restrepo, a moderate critic of Reyes, explained what happened in his own municipality of Medellín. Privately, all but one of the Medellín officials had earlier claimed to be anti-Reyes. However, when faced with going formally on record favoring Reyes's resignation, they hesitated, unsure of the future impact on their lives of such a commitment. When Medellín's formal response to the National Assembly arrived at Bogotá, it revealed that city officials opposed the resignation.[65] Citing such responses as evidence of his support, Reyes decided to withdraw his resignation.

Despite his firm belief that the tripartite treaties were in Colombia's best interests, Reyes knew public and political opposition to the treaties was too strong. If he tried to ram them through the assembly, he could expect a renewal of antiadministration demonstrations. Within hours of reassuming office on 14 March, he recommended that the National Assembly suspend its treaty deliberations and instead submit the two documents to a Congress that he would convene in special session in July. When sentiment against the treaties did not subside, Reyes announced on 10 May the further postponement of the accords until the February 1910 session of Congress. Writing nine days later a pessimistic Hibben lamented: "There seems to be little hope of ratification of the treaties either now or in February. I think it unlikely that General Reyes will be in power in February, or even in July."[66] Hibben's intuition was sound. Reyes's cabinet ministers all had resigned on 26 May, and the president found it difficult to find replacements. Emboldened by Reyes's weakness, the opposition press intensified its attack. Finally, and most ominous for the embattled president, Liberals and Conservatives, creating the Union Republicana coalition, subordinated their normal rivalry and began working together to defeat Reyes's congressional delegates.[67]

Under the guise of an inspection tour, Reyes journeyed toward the coast shortly after the 30 May congressional election. British diplomat

V. H. Huckin immediately alerted London that Reyes may not be planning to return since he carried an unusually large amount of luggage and also had released from his employ all household servants. Huckin proved correct, and, on 7 June, Reyes announced his resignation once again. At Cartagena, on the evening of the thirteenth, he secretly boarded ship for England.[68] In this almost fugitive manner, Reyes, the man who had carefully orchestrated for five years Colombia's movement toward a negotiated settlement, surrendered forever his presidency.

Only two days prior to Reyes's unannounced departure, the United States adopted a more distant and reserved attitude toward Colombian ratification. "The Government of the United States," Assistant Secretary of State Francis M. Huntington-Wilson wrote the Bogotá legation,

> views with relative indifference the question of the ratification of our treaties by Colombia and Panama, whose interests are apparently much more concerned. This Government has felt sanguine of their ratification only owing to the general desirability of settling the question involved, and particularly as being beneficial to Colombia and Panama rather than to the United States. In view of the absurd distortion of this situation by public clamor the Legation should make the above attitude well known and for the rest should maintain an impassive and dignified attitude.[69]

This attitude of feigned unconcern and disinterest certainly marked a noticeable shift from the active pursuit of agreement throughout the Roosevelt administration. In fact, despite the obvious internal discord in Colombia, Secretary of State Knox had written Dawson as late as 15 March that "it would be deplorable if this outbreak [of 13 March] should disturb the ratification of the treaties." Two days later, Knox, acting on the advice of Adee, further sought to encourage Reyes to press for ratification.[70] But, as additional distressing reports flowed into the department from Hibben in Bogotá, Secretary Knox and Assistant Secretary Huntington-Wilson reanalyzed the American attitude during the closing days of May. On 19 May, the chargé informed the department that "opposition to the United States and to the treaties . . . grows daily more bitter and more open." Five days later he reiterated that "anti-American feeling is growing, daily," and that there exists "a very real sentiment of bitterness and hostility toward us." Finally, Hibben reported that Reyes, on whom the United States had placed its ratification hopes, faced an "extremely precarious" political future and was expected "to resign at any time."[71] Deciding on the basis of the pessimistic reports to await the resolution of the Colombian domestic upheaval before reinitiating discussion about treaty ratification, Huntington-Wilson dispatched the 11 June message to Bogotá.

Adopting a low profile in Colombia seemed a practical solution to the current crisis. Anti-American feeling in general, and hostility toward the treaties specifically, had not died with the resignation of Reyes. Indeed, the new interim president who would serve until 1910, Ramón González Valencia, in March had argued that approving the treaties would gravely affect the national honor and dignity of Colombia.[72] Although other Colombian leaders, such as Esguerra and Carlos Restrepo, opposed Reyes more than the agreements themselves, they did not actively support the Root-Cortés-Arosemena treaties after Reyes's fall. Perhaps Huckin best summed up the situation when he said that, since the treaties were regarded as the work of the Reyes administration and since that administration was being repudiated, "the actual merits or demerits of the treaties are hardly likely to be taken into consideration."[73] A more realistic evaluation of the merits and demerits would have to wait until popular passions cooled.

Faced with continuous public opposition to the treaties, the Colombian foreign minister, Carlos Calderón, in late September 1909 asked the United States to abandon completely the current treaties and enter into a new single agreement between the United States and Colombia, thereby avoiding the controversial issue of recognizing Panama.[74] The United States declined, pointing out that the major reason for American participation in the treaty process was to normalize relations between Panama and Colombia, a facet not covered in the new Colombian proposal.[75] Washington was perfectly willing to postpone any discussion until tension eased in Colombia.

Given its hostility toward the old administration and the United States, the boiling point of the politically aware Bogotá citizenry was dangerously low. By 7 March 1910 the assistant manager of the Bogotá City Railway Company (the largest American firm in Colombia) became involved in a disagreement with police about the questionable arrest of one of the company's Colombian conductors. As the argument grew hotter, a crowd gathered. Tempers quickly snapped, and a minor incident mushroomed into a massive anti-American rampage. Not only Americans but also any Colombian believed to be too sympathetic toward the United States was subject to harassment or attack. While actual violence was limited to 7 March, the verbal attack on the United States continued unchecked. For the first time since the Panamanian revolution, Americans in Bogotá feared for their safety. The U.S. minister, Elliott Northcott, wrote on 1 April: "The streets of Bogotá are today, and have been since March seventh unsafe for Americans." Two weeks later, fearing the possible outbreak of more violence, he sent his wife and child out of the country, but fortunately no further demonstrations occurred.[76]

Although the brief violent outburst against the United States had passed, a lingering resentment remained. That attitude, evidenced in both public and governmental circles, made future consideration of the tripartite agreements impolitic, if not impossible. Having replaced Reyes with General Ramón González Valencia, the new Colombian leaders could hardly adhere to his isthmian solution as reformulated in mid-1906. They themselves had attacked the former president's position. Chargé Arthur Frazier cited the peculiar dilemma of one of the new cabinet ministers—the minister for foreign affairs, Enrique Olaya Herrera—who in 1909 had violently opposed the tripartite agreements. "As a leader of the opposition to General Reyes," Frazier noted, "he found a certain policy [of attack] incumbent upon him; as a Minister of the Government conditions are altogether changed."[77] While Olaya Herrera may have recognized the importance of normalized relations with both Panama and the United States, he still could not, as foreign minister, publicly advocate ratification of the tripartite treaties. Still, the new administration realized that it was in Colombia's interests to resolve this seven-year dispute.[78]

Restrained by the current Colombian mood, Olaya Herrera reverted to the nation's pre-1906 position and urged the United States to arbitrate all differences. The foreign minister acknowledged that no matter how the arbitral tribunal ruled, his government would recognize those rights the United States already had acquired in the canal zone. It was hoped that Panama would be reunited to Colombia, but, should this fail, he expected the United States to grant Bogotá special privileges in the use of the canal, and that Panama would additionally agree to pay its share of the Colombian debt and to adhere to a boundary as defined by Colombia.[79]

Inadvertently, former President Theodore Roosevelt fortified the Colombian argument that arbitration provided the only acceptable solution. Speaking at the University of California on 23 March 1911, he proudly revealed his role in the initial acquisition of the canal. "If I had followed traditional methods," Roosevelt argued, "I would have submitted a dignified state paper to Congress and the debate would have been going on yet. But I took the Canal Zone and let Congress debate, and while the debate goes on the Canal does also." This surprising statement was not considered headline material in the United States, but Colombian officials certainly thought it of major importance.[80] They could cite Roosevelt's speech as an outright admission that the United States had been intimately involved in the secession and therefore had violated the 1846 treaty with Colombia. Under international law, different interpretations of treaties and their violation were considered arbitral matters.

Demands for arbitration fell on deaf ears in Washington. When Minister Pedro Nel Ospina made a formal appeal for arbitration in November 1911, the State Department simply failed to reply.[81] So long as the new Colombian leaders insisted on arbitration, U.S. officials were not interested in a settlement. Although this deadlock stretched through the summer of 1912, the unpleasant possibility of permanent disagreement worried leaders in both Washington and Bogotá.

At this juncture, American Minister James T. DuBois influenced Colombian leaders to reconsider their position. Since his arrival in Bogotá in November 1911, he had diligently worked toward relaxing tension. After examining Colombia's arguments carefully, DuBois outlined to Secretary Knox his own personal suggestions for a just settlement. In that memorandum he accepted as valid most of the arguments against the United States, including the need for an expression by the United States of sincere regret over events in 1903 and the payment of an indemnity.[82] Given these views, DuBois not surprisingly established a friendly rapport with Colombian leaders. Although he believed that nation had legitimate grievances, he also realized his government's aversion to arbitration. He therefore urged Colombia to abandon the arbitral method and enter into direct negotiations with the United States. Realizing that the United States would not consent to arbitration, Colombian officials finally relented in October and agreed to direct discussions. DuBois, in the United States on a leave of absence, met with his superiors in Washington on 20 October 1912 to discuss the new situation.[83]

After six weeks of debate on the nature of a direct settlement, Secretary Knox and his counselors agreed upon a specific plan. After examining these proposals on 29 November, President Taft gave his final approval. Within days, Minister DuBois was briefed on the American terms. Concerned that its minister had become too imbued with the Colombian viewpoint, the State Department vigorously urged that he totally familiarize himself with the U.S. position. Knox also warned DuBois that he must not deviate from his instructions whatsoever; any changes in the proposals must be approved first by the department. Before concluding, the secretary also noted the earnest desire of the Taft administration to reach a settlement with Colombia before leaving office in March 1913.[84]

In his oral and written instructions, DuBois was given a five-point plan to present to Colombian officials. He should first try to obtain their assent to the Root-Cortés-Arosemena treaties without any modifications. If, as expected, that request was refused, he was then to offer certain inducements to obtain that approval. For an option to construct a canal along the Atrato River in Colombia and for coaling privileges on two Colombian islands, the United States would agree to pay $10 million.[85] Although U.S. Army engineers already had discounted the Atrato as a practical canal route, such an offer would eliminate forever the outside possibility that some other power might buy the option and try to use it.[86] More importantly, it would permit the United States to pay Colombia $10 million without appearing to pay the indemnity for which Colombia long had argued. If Bogotá sought additional concessions, DuBois was to propose U.S. assistance in settling the boundary dispute with Panama as well as offer to submit the legal ownership of the Panama railroad, now under American control, to arbitration. If Colombia still refused to sign the tripartite agreements, DuBois, after receiving permission from Washington, could offer one final concession: the United States, in a separate accord, would remove all objectionable features in the Root-Cortés-Arosemena treaties. Knox cautioned that throughout his discussions DuBois was to remember that "the Government of the United States will not for a moment consider the use of any language which would impugn in any way the past attitude, acts, or motives of the United States in connection with this matter."[87] The Taft administration would not acknowledge any error in American policy toward the isthmus in 1903 and 1904. If Colombia insisted, negotiations again would be deadlocked.

Arriving in Bogotá on 15 January 1913, DuBois immediately talked with Olaya Herrera to arrange a meeting with President Carlos Restrepo, who had been elected to replace González Valencia in 1910. At that conference five days later, he urged the president to ratify the tripartite treaties, but Restrepo emphatically refused.[88] After conferring with Washington, DuBois received authorization to offer the agreed-upon concessions. Meeting again with the foreign minister on 25 January, DuBois outlined the American proposals concerning the Atrato, the boundary, the Panamanian railroad, and the amendatory treaty. After considering these proposals the Restrepo administration decided they were unacceptable, partly because Restrepo believed that the Taft administration seemed unlikely to meet Colombian objections, and partly because he thought that the incoming Democratic administration might be more flexible in resolving diplomatic events associated with a recently defeated Republican foe.[89] A disappointed DuBois on 15 February informed Colombia that the United States was therefore withdrawing its proposals for settlement.[90] Secretary Knox accurately reflected the opinion of the Taft administration when he wrote: "[I feel] that this Government has made every effort consistent with the honor, dignity and interests of the United States in its sincere aim to bring about a state of better feeling on the part of the Government of Colombia."[91] Despite those efforts the Taft administration had failed to attain the elusive Colombian settlement.

What had happened? Why had the optimism of mid-1906 turned into gloom by early 1913? The unexpected Panamanian resistance to the proposed terms between 1906 and 1908, and the anti-Reyes movement in Colombia in mid-1909, scuttled the best chance for success. Panama, while desiring Colombian recognition, sought to obtain it as painlessly as possible. Colombia calculated that Panama, as one of its former departments, owed $6 million as its share of the national debt. Panamanian officials refused to approve any treaty that demanded such an outrageous sum. Not until July 1907, one full year after negotiations had begun, did Panama agree to a monetary settlement, and then it relented only after Colombia had reduced its demands to $2.5 million. But troubles with Panama had only just begun. For the next eighteen months it refused to accept Colombia's demarcation of the line separating the two nations. Despite Colombian seizure of part of the contested territory, and despite Secretary Root's support of the Colombian line, Panama held out until December 1908 before agreeing to a settlement. Once that obstacle fell, the final treaties were quickly signed in early January 1909.

Panama had delayed the treaty a crucial thirty-one months. Had agreement been reached in late 1906 or even in 1907, President Reyes might have secured ratification. As it was, by early 1909 his control had begun to slip, and his political opponents would use the treaties to topple his regime. In addition, there remained in Colombia lingering resentment over Roosevelt's actions in November 1903. Colombians were still convinced that Panamanian traitors, together with U.S. assistance, had stripped Panama from their nation. To recognize Panama, therefore, would sanction those actions and besmirch national honor. Had the Reyes regime not become an issue in the ratification process, this antagonism and resentment might have been successfully overcome; it certainly would have taken a battle. The Colombian economic and fiscal plight, however, required normalized relations with both Panama as the future site of the interoceanic canal and with the United States as the most powerful American state. That was a persuasive argument. Contending that national stability and prosperity required approval of the treaties, Reyes, utilizing his broad political powers, would have had the best chance of securing ratification in 1906 or 1907.

In 1909 the resentment toward the United States and Panama fused with the growing dissatisfaction with the Reyes regime. Assuming broad authority in 1905, Reyes had promised to revitalize the nation but had failed. By 1909 critics, becoming more vocal, charged that he had usurped constitutional authority in Colombia as well as established a government of cronyism, corruption, and intimidation. His decision to recognize the secessionist state, Panama, enabled the political opposition to tap underlying Colombian resentment toward the United States and Panama as a means to undermine the current dictatorial administration. Since Reyes fled the country in March, these tactics proved highly successful.[92]

In closely associating Reyes with a U.S.-Panama-Colombia settlement, the new Colombian leadership limited its future options. Once in office, it realized the necessity of arranging an isthmian solution, but, in ousting Reyes, it had intensified anti-American and anti-Panamanian feelings in Colombia. As a result, the Restrepo administration could only renew demands for arbitration until the current tension again subsided, paving the way for direct negotiations, the same route former President Reyes had adopted. Not until late 1912 did the Colombian administration finally abandon its arbitration proposals. The Taft administration, upon learning that Colombia desired to negotiate directly, was anxious to reach an agreement before it left office. By early February 1913, however, Colombia had decided to postpone further negotiations until after the inauguration of Woodrow Wilson.

Notes

[1]Barrett to Robert Bacon (acting secretary of state), 13 July 1906, *FRUS, 1906*, 435; Uribe, *Anales* 5:33.

[2]Root to ALB, 2 June 1906, Diplomatic Instructions of the Department of State, 1901–1906: Colombia (DI), RG 59, M-77, roll 48, National Archives.

[3]Bacon and Scott, *Latin America*, 10 (Rio de Janerio), and 247 (Kansas City). For a fuller discussion of Elihu Root and his actions at the Rio Conference see Bacon and Scott, *Latin America*, 1–45; Lejeune Cummins, "The Origin and Development of Elihu Root's Latin American Diplomacy" (Ph.D. diss., University of California, Berkeley, 1964); and Donald J. Murphy, "Professors, Publicists, and Pan Americanism, 1905–1917: A Study in the Origins of the Use of 'Experts' in Shaping American Foreign Policy" (Ph.D. diss., Wisconsin, 1970). Panama's presence at the conference occurred because most Latin American nations had recognized its independence; Colombia still had not done so.

[4]Barrett to Root (in Lima, Peru), 30 July 1906, Numerical and Minor Files, 1906–1910, RG 59, M-862, roll 30, case 194, National Archives (hereafter cited as NMF). While Barrett no doubt conferred with Reyes, he probably overstated his role in "blocking out" the Colombian campaign. Barrett's view of his own importance, at least while in Bogotá, was quite high.

[5]Barrett's destination was Guayaquil, Ecuador, where he planned to join Secretary Root and fully brief him on the Colombian situation.

[6]Root's public remarks are found in Bacon and Scott, *Latin America*, 154–55. The agreements reached during the private talks are discussed in a

memorandum handed to Secretary Root by Minister Cortés, 8 November 1906, M-862, roll 166, 1502, NMF. For Root's response to the Cortés memorandum see 8 November 1906, ibid.

[7]Confidential memorandum from Foreign Minister Vásquez Cobo to Barrett to Root, 20 September 1906, M-862, roll 166, case 1502, NMF; Root on Vásquez Cobo memorandum, 20 September 1906, ibid.; Cortés to Root, 8 November 1906, ibid.; Barrett to Roosevelt, 2 August 1906, series 1, reel 66, Roosevelt Papers. For the initial Reyes proposals see Barrett to Root, 23 May 1906, Decimal File of the Department of State, RG 59, T-33, roll 64, National Archives (hereafter cited as DF).

[8]Ibid. National products would include cattle, sheep, pigs, eggs, fruit, vegetables, and other native-grown foods.

[9]Cortés to Root summarizing Root-Vásquez Cobo talks at Cartagena, 8 November 1906, ibid.

[10]John W. Foster to Enrique Cortés, 31 May 1907, NMF, vol. 166, 1502. For a discussion of the tripartite negotiations see Castillero Reyes, *Panamá y Colombia*, 69–123. For a fuller discussion of U.S.-Panama relations from 1903 until 1922 see Mount, "American Imperialism," 162–97; and Ralph Minger, "Panama, the Canal Zone, and Titular Sovereignty," *Western Political Quarterly* 14 (1961): 544–54.

[11]Root on Cortés memorandum, 8 November 1906, M-862, roll 166, 1502, NMF.

[12]5 December 1906, ibid. Buchanan, in late 1906 and early 1907, worked with the three governments to achieve settlement.

[13]Cortés to Root, 4 March 1907, ibid.

[14]24 April 1907, ibid.

[15]H. G. Squiers (U.S. minister to Panama) to Root, 16 May 1907, ibid.; Cromwell to Taft, 10 May 1907, series 3, reel 66, Taft Papers; Cromwell to Taft, 4 June 1907, reel 67, ibid.

[16]William Heimke to Root, 20 June 1907, vol. 582, 7804, NMF.

[17]Ibid.

[18]Heimke to Root, 26 September 1907, ibid.

[19]Ibid.

[20]Taft to his mother, 18 August 1907, series 1, reel 21, Taft Papers. Also see Taft to Root, 1 July 1907, box 166, Root Papers.

[21]The biographical information on Taft comes from Ralph Eldin Minger, *William Howard Taft and United States Foreign Policy: The Apprenticeship Years, 1900–1908* (Urbana: University of Illinois Press, 1975); and Henry F. Pringle, *The Life and Times of William Howard Taft* (New York: Farrar & Rinehart, 1939). Roosevelt, for example, used Taft in dealing with Panama, the Philippines, Cuba, China, and Japan.

[22]Root to Taft, 6 June 1907, M-862, roll 166, 1502, NMF.

[23]As a lobbyist for the Panama route, Cromwell had played a pivotal role on Capitol Hill in 1902 in securing passage of the Spooner Act. Roosevelt distrusted this crafty New York lawyer, but Taft, America's chief negotiator in the summer of 1907, placed great confidence in Cromwell's ability. For a discussion of Cromwell's and Panama's proposals see Taft to Root, 1 July 1907, box 166, Root Papers; and Cortés to Taft, 4 July 1907, series 3, reel 68, Taft Papers.

[24]Taft to Root, 7 July 1907, series 8, reel 491, Taft Papers.

[25]Correspondence related to this "misunderstanding" about the arbitration includes Cortés to Taft, 4 July 1907, series 3, reel 68, ibid.; Cortés to Root, 4 July 1907, vol. 166, 1502, NMF; Cromwell to Taft, 5 July 1907, series 3, reel 68, Taft Papers; Taft to Cromwell, 7 July 1907, and Cortés to Cromwell, 8 July 1907, ibid.; Robert Bacon to Root, 9 July 1907, box 49, Root Papers; and Cromwell to Taft, 12 July 1907, series 3, reel 68, Taft Papers.

[26]Cortés to Root, 16 and 27 July 1907, vol. 166, 1502, NMF.

[27]13 July 1907, series 3, reel 68, Taft Papers.

[28]Root to Taft, 16 August 1907, reel 69, ibid. Also see Bacon to Taft, 24 July 1907, reel 68, ibid.; and Root to Cortés (not sent) 20 July 1907, ibid.

[29]27 July 1907, series 10, reel 604, ibid.

[30]Root to Cortés, 26 August 1907, vol. 166, 1502, NMF. One month after the 13 August meeting, Taft departed for the Philippines, not to return until late December.

[31]For a review of these deliberations see Cromwell to Taft, 27 July and 2 August 1907 (reel 68), and 13 August 1907 (reel 69), series 3, Taft Papers; Taft Secretarial Notes, 15 August 1907, series 10, reel 604, ibid.; Taft to Root, 15 August 1907, series 8, reel 491, ibid.; Taft to Root, 17 August 1907, ibid. (includes text of the protocol); Root to Taft, 16 August 1907, series 3, reel 69, ibid.; Taft to Root, 17 August 1907, series 10, reel 604, ibid.; Taft to Roosevelt, 17 August 1907, series 8, reel 491, ibid.; Taft to his mother, 18 August 1907, series 1, reel 31, ibid.; Thomas Dawson to Root, 7 December 1907, vol. 166, 1502, NMF; and Vásquez Cobo to Cortés, 31 December 1907, and to Root, 26 January 1908, ibid.

Under the protocol, Panama would use none of its cash reserves to meet the $2.5 million debt. Instead, it would transfer to Colombia the first ten annual payments of $250,000 each owed it by the United States under the Hay-Bunau-Varilla Treaty. Those payments were to begin in 1908 and end in 1917.

[32]Cortés to Root, 26 January 1908, vol. 166, 1502, NMF.

[33]Dawson to Root, 7 December 1907, Vásquez Cobo to Cortés, 31 December 1907, Cortés to Root, 26 January 1908, and Dawson to Root, 6 March 1908, all in ibid.

[34]Cortés to Root, 31 March 1908, and Dawson to Root, 31 March 1908, ibid. Reyes's decision helped convince Vásquez Cobo, who had consistently argued that Panama must formally recognize Colombia's boundary claims, to resign his post.

[35]Cortés to Root, 25 April 1908, series 3, reel 79, Taft Papers.

[36]Memorandum, Adee to Root, 8 April 1908, vol. 673, 9271, NMF.

[37]Cortés to Root, 25 April 1908, ibid. Also see series 3, reel 79, Taft Papers.

[38]Paxton Hibben to Root, 27 October 1908, vol. 582, 7804, NMF.

[39]Cromwell to Taft, 5 January 1909, series 3, reel 116, Taft Papers; Root to Andrew Carnegie, 12 January 1909, vol. 189/2, Root Papers.

[40]Root-Cortés-Arosemena treaties in *FRUS, 1909*, 223–33; James Bryce to Edward Grey, 12 January 1909, F.O. 371/708-p. 75, and Root to Bryce, 16 January 1909, 371/708-p. 113, PRO.

[41]Dawson to Root, 16 September 1908, vol. 427, 5025, NMF; Reyes to Constituent and Legislative National Assembly, 20 July 1908, ibid.

[42]The following discussion of the Reyes administration from 1904 to 1909 and its political opposition is based on Lemaitre Román, *Reyes*, 233–326; Bergquist, *Coffee and Conflict*, 231–46; Cavelier, *La Política* 3; Robledo, *Pedro Nel Ospina*, 66–83; Castillero Reyes, *Panamá y Colombia*, 69–123; Eduardo Lemaitre Román, *Rafael Reyes: Biografía de un Gran Colombiano* (Bogotá: Espiral, 1967), 277–84; Abel Cruz Santos, *Economía y Hacienda Pública*, Tomo 2, vol. 15, in the series *Historia Extensa de Colombia* (Bogotá: Ediciones Lerner, 1966), 97–133; Baldomero Sanín-Cano, *Administración Reyes, 1904–1909* (Lausana: Imprenta Jorge Bridel & Company, 1909), 332–33; Henao and Arrubla, *History of Colombia*, 523–27; Carlos Restrepo, *Orientación Republicana* (Bogotá: Biblioteca Banco Popular, 1972), 1:343–400; and Luis Martínez Delgado, *Jorge Holguín o el Político* (Bogotá: Departamento de Divulgación y Publicidad de la Caja Agraria, 1980), 260–309.

[43]Cruz Santos, *Economía*, 104.

[44]Santiago Pérez Triana to Taft, 4 May 1909, vol. 167, 1502, NMF. Triana represented Colombia at the second Hague conference.

[45]Gibson, *Constitutions*, 354–55; Alban G. Snyder to Root, 22 July 1905, enclosing the Reformatory Acts, *FRUS, 1905*, 255; Henao and Arrubla, *History of Colombia*, 523.

[46]Antonio José Uribe, *La Reforma Administrativa en Colombia* (Bogotá: Libreria Colombiana, 1917), 398–400.

[47]*FRUS, 1907*, 285.

[48]The December 1905 conspiracy involved seventy men who hoped to install in Reyes's place a triumvirate of Luis Felipe Angulo, Luis Martinez Silva, and Moya Vásquez. All those found guilty were offered either exile or prison. The February 1906 assassination attempt resulted in the execution of the three assassins and the arrest of Conservative General Aristides Fernandez.

For comments on growing unrest see Martínez Delgado, *Jorge Holguín*, 260–309; Robledo, *Pedro Nel Ospina*, 66–83; and Lemaitre Román, *Reyes*, 333–42. Also see Snyder to Assistant Secretary of State Francis B. Loomis, 18 July 1905, DFMTC, T-33, T 63; Barrett to his mother, 25 January and 13 February 1906, box 9—Correspondence, John Barrett Papers, Library of Congress Manuscripts Division; Sam Koppel (ALB) to Root, 20 August 1906, *FRUS, 1906*, 436; Dawson to Root, 24 December 1907, vol. 427, 5025, NMF; Isaac Manning to Assistant Secretary of State Robert Bacon, 21 January 1908, ibid.; Dawson to Root, 21 March 1908, ibid.; Dawson to Root, 13 April 1908, vol. 673, 9271, ibid.; Dawson to Root, 18 April 1908, vol. 427, 5025, ibid.; and Hibben to Root, 25 January 1909, vol. 741, 10717, NMF.

[49]Manning to Bacon, 26 January 1909, RG 84: ALB—Correspondence from Consulates, October 1907 to July 1909, National Archives.

[50]12 February 1909, RG 84: ALB—Press Despatches to the Department of State (PDTS), National Archives.

[51]Dawson to Secretary of State Robert Bacon, 17 February 1909, ibid.

[52]Dawson to Bacon, 17 February 1909, *FRUS, 1910*, 363.

[53]Manning to Bacon, 26 January 1909, RG 84: ALB—Correspondence. Also see vol. 167, 1502, NMF.

[54]22 February 1909, vol. 167, 1502, NMF; Uribe, *Anales* 5:35–44.

[55]1 March 1909, *FRUS, 1910*, 376.

[56]Adee memorandums of 2 and 17 March 1909, vol. 167, 1502, NMF; Secretary of State Philander C. Knox to Dawson, 17 March 1909, ibid.

[57]Restrepo, *Orientacíon*, 397–98; Lemaitre Román, *Reyes*, 312–16; Dawson to Knox, 8 March 1909, vol. 427, 5025, NMF.

[58]Dawson to Knox, 29 March 1909, vol. 167, 1502, NMF. This communiqué summarizes events between 7 and 27 March.

[59]Ibid. Also see Martínez Delgado, *Jorge Holguín*, 265–67; and Restrepo, *Orientacíon*, 398–99.

[60]For the complete Santander letter see military chiefs in Santander to Reyes, 10 March 1909, vol. 167, 1502, NMF.

[61]Dawson to Knox, 29 March 1909, ibid. Also see Dawson to Knox, 10 March 1909, *FRUS, 1910*, 376.

[62]Dawson to Knox, 29 March 1909, vol. 167, 1502, NMF.

[63]Henao and Arrubla, *History of Colombia*, 526.

[64]Martínez Delgado, *Jorge Holguín*, 267. Holguín, who had served on the Reyes commission to Panama in November 1903, had been a longtime supporter of the president. When Reyes resigned, he exercised the power to name his own successor; he chose Holguín.

[65]Restrepo, *Orientación*, 399–400.

[66]Hibben to Knox, 19 May 1909, vol. 427, 5025, NMF. For Reyes's decision to postpone the treaties see Hibben to Knox, 10 and 12 May 1909, vol. 167, 1502, NMF; Hibben to Knox, 13 May 1909, RG 84: PDTS; Cortés to Knox, 16 March 1909, vol. 167, 1502, NMF; and Dawson to Knox, 27 March 1909, ibid. Also see V. H. Huckin to Grey, 31 March and 13 May 1909, F.O. 135/330-#29, 35, PRO.

[67]Cruz Santos, *Economía*, 131–33; Henao and Arrubla, *History of Colombia*, 525; Huckin to Grey, 1 June 1909, F.O. 135/330-#39, PRO.

[68]Consul Charles Latham to assistant secretary of state, 14 June 1909, vol. 427, 5025, NMF; Hibben to Knox, 16 June 1909, ibid.; Huckin to Grey, 4, 11, 18, and 28 June 1909, F.O. 135/330-#9, 42, 44, 49, PRO.

[69]11 June 1909, vol. 168, 1502, NMF. Also see Huntington-Wilson to Knox, 28 May 1909, vol. 167, 1502, ibid.

[70]Knox to Dawson, 15 March 1909, *FRUS, 1910*, 378; Adee memorandums, 2, 16, and 17 March 1909, vol. 167, 1502, NMF; Knox to Dawson, 17 March 1909, *FRUS, 1910*, 378. Also see Knox to Cortés, 22 March 1909, ibid., 381.

[71]Hibben to Knox, 19 and 26 May 1909, vol. 427, 5025, NMF; Hibben to Knox, 24 May 1909, vol. 428, 5025, ibid. Also see Hibben to Knox, 10 and 12 May 1909, vol. 167, 1502, NMF; and 13 and 19 May 1909, RG 84: DTS. Similar reports were being sent to London from the British legation. See Huckin to Grey, 19 and 31 March and 13 May 1909, F.O. 135/330-#26, 29, 35, PRO.

[72]R. G. Valencia and 800 others to Reyes, 10 March 1909, vol. 167, 1502, NMF.

[73]Huckin to Grey, 31 March 1909, F.O. 135/330-#29, PRO.

[74]Elliott Northcott (U.S. minister in Bogotá) to Knox, 29 September 1909, *FRUS, 1910*, 399.

[75]Adee to Northcott, 23 October 1909, vol. 168, 1502, NMF. On 21 October, Knox approved the contents of the Adee telegram before its despatch. For a discussion of the anti-American feeling and the reactions of the new Colombian government see Hibben to Knox, 24 July 1909, vol. 428, 5025, NMF; Northcott to Huntington-Wilson, 24 August 1909, vol. 540, 6958, ibid.; Northcott to Knox, 25 August 1909, vol. 428, 5025, ibid.; Northcott to Knox, 1 and 29 October 1909, vol. 168, 1502, ibid.; Northcott to Knox, 25 November 1909, RG 84: PDTS; Northcott to Knox, 5 January 1910, vol. 168, 1502, NMF; Northcott to Knox, 6 January 1910, vol. 428, 5025, NMF; and Northcott to Knox, 1 March 1910, box 8217, 5025, DF.

[76]Unfortunately, the railway company was not only a symbol of the United States in Bogotá but also had the dubious honor of gaining its concession from President Reyes. Events surrounding the initial outbreak are discussed in Northcott to Knox, 7 and 12 March 1910, box 8217, 5025, DF. Subsequent occurrences are found in Northcott to Knox, 8, 19, and 25 March and 1 April 1910, ibid.; Latham to assistant secretary of state, 11 March 1910, ibid.; and Huntington-Wilson to Senator Stephen Elkins, 16 April 1910, ibid. One of the Colombians who faced hostile crowds was Cortés, who, with his wife, had tried to return to Colombia on 26 May but had been driven immediately out of the country by a mob.

[77]Frazier to Knox, 25 January 1911, RG 84: PDTS.

[78]For the attitude of the new president, Carlos Restrepo, and his minister for foreign affairs, Olaya Herrera, in 1909 and 1910 see Restrepo, *Orientación*; Cavelier, *La Política* 3; Northcott to Knox, 15 July 1910, box 8217, 5025, DF; Northcott to Knox, 25 August 1910, Department of State Decimal File, RG 59, 711.21/22, National Archives; Frazier to Knox, 19 September and 12 November 1910, 25 January 1911, RG 84: DTS; Frazier to Knox, 31 December 1910, RG 59, SD 821.00/363-1/2; Frazier to Knox, 11 February 1911, RG 59, SD 711.21/34.

[79]Olaya Herrera to Frazier, 30 November 1911, RG 59, SD 711.21/27.

[80]Brief excerpts from Roosevelt's speech were found in regular print at the bottom of the front page of the *New York Times*, 24 March 1911, and on page four of the *Washington Post*, 24 March 1911. The Colombian minister in Washington quickly pointed out the significance of Roosevelt's comments in a letter to Knox, 28 March 1911, RG 59, SD 711.21/38. For a discussion of the debate over Roosevelt's actual words in his speech see James F. Vivian, "The 'Taking' of the Panama Canal Zone: Myth and Reality," *Diplomatic History* 4 (Winter 1980): 95–100. Alfred Richard, Jr., argues unconvincingly that, given popular U.S. support for the recognition of Panama, it is misleading to say Roosevelt "took Panama." See Richard, "Panama Canal."

[81]Ospina to Knox, 25 November 1911, RG 59, SD 711.21/64. Also see box 29, Knox Papers.

[82]DuBois to Knox, 30 September 1912, RG 59, SD 711.21/119.

[83]DuBois to Knox, 5 February 1913, *FRUS, 1913*, 289–91.

[84]For DuBois's summary of the instructions see DuBois to Knox, 5 February 1913, ibid., 289–91. A memorandum of the oral instructions to DuBois, dated 2 December 1912, is found in RG 84: Foreign Service Post

Records, 1912 (GC), National Archives. Written instructions followed on 6 December. See Knox to DuBois, RG 59, SD 711.21/119.

[85]President Taft had approved the $10 million offer on 30 November 1912. See Taft to Knox, series 6, reel 382, Taft Papers. "While I think the sum stipulated to be paid is a large one," he wrote, "I believe the advantage of settling the question is so great that I would not hesitate to recommend such a treaty to the Senate for its ratification."

[86]Major S. A. Cheney and Captain F. R. McCoy, "Memo on the Atrato River Route for a Canal," box 74, Frank McCoy Papers, Library of Congress Manuscripts Division.

[87]Knox to DuBois, 6 December 1912, RG 59, SD 711.21/119.

[88]DuBois to Knox, 20 January 1913, RG 59, SD 711.21/130.

[89]DuBois to Knox, 31 January 1913, RG 59, SD 711.21/132.

[90]DuBois to Knox, 17 February 1913, RG 59, SD 711.21/136.

[91]Knox to Taft, 20 February 1913 (a thirty-five-page report on the failure of the negotiations), RG 59, SD 711.21/138a.

[92]Reyes maintained that opposition to his domestic policies and powers convinced him to leave the country. That opposition was so strong, he believed, that civil war might have broken out had he remained. See Reyes's "Exposición," 20 August 1909, in Sanín-Cano, *Administración Reyes*, 330–36.

Chapter IV

Democratic Settlement: The Thomson-Urrutia Treaty

Within days of his inauguration on 4 March 1913, Woodrow Wilson pledged to guide the nation into a new age in hemispheric relations, an age that would witness the transformation of Latin American skepticism, doubt, and hostility into trust, confidence, and friendship. Disavowing Taft's Dollar Diplomacy, with its seemingly unquestioned support of American business abroad and its apparent disregard for foreign sensibilities, the new president declared:

> The United States has nothing to seek in Central and South America except the lasting interest of the peoples of the two continents, the security of Governments intended for the people and for no special group or interest, and the development of personal and trade relationships between the two continents which shall redound to the profit and advantage of both and interfere with the rights and liberties of neither.[1]

Unscrupulous businessmen who took unfair advantage of foreign markets, or who tried to secure monopolistic concessions, could expect brusque treatment from this Democratic administration. Only by encouraging the fair, equitable, and upright behavior of business abroad could Wilson emphasize his commitment to peaceful, mutually advantageous relations among sovereign nations.

However, in renouncing the method of foreign expansion used by his predecessors, Wilson had no intention of rejecting economic penetration per se, just the limited vision and the selfishness it exemplified under the two previous Republican administrations. Rather, he planned to enlarge, not curtail, U.S. international trade along lines more compatible with his own vision of America's world mission, which, according to Harley Notter, was

> to realize an ideal of liberty, provide a model of democracy, vindicate moral principles, give examples of action and ideals of government and righteousness to an inter-dependent world, uphold the rights of man, work for humanity and the happiness of men everywhere, lead the thinking of the world to promote peace—in sum, to serve mankind and progress. . . . Wilson thought that the fostering of America's material prosperity was also a part of her duty. We wished to be strong in order the better to show ourselves great and carry out our mission. The matter was not selfish except incidentally; service to mankind was the purpose to which our power was to be turned.[2]

From the beginning of his presidency, Wilson believed that American economic penetration throughout the world must actively reflect the ideals of that vision. Only after effecting the union of economics and morality could he and his administration enthusiastically welcome future penetration.

Colombian leaders, observing Wilson's attitudes during the months following his election, expected a more understanding group of Washington officials with whom to negotiate. The president-elect's emphasis on mutual respect, confidence, and friendship, as well as on moral obligations and political and economic cooperation, had raised Colombia's hopes. Since the Panama episode had stained American honor, perhaps this administration would prove more flexible in reaching an acceptable settlement with the injured Colombian people. After allowing the new administration time to settle in, Colombian Minister Julio Betancourt wrote Secretary of State William Jennings Bryan on 3 May urging arbitration of the problems existing between their two nations, an approach the Taft administration continually had rejected.[3] Finally, two months later, on 18 July, Bryan replied, urging direct negotiations rather than arbitration as the method of settlement. While not meeting the Colombian request, Bryan's message was friendly and full of hope for a solution:

> Our nation has its own honor at stake in all matters which involve fair dealing toward other nations, and I speak for the President and I am sure for the whole people, as well as for myself, when I express the earnest desire that we may be able to remove every obstacle that stands in the way of perfect confidence and free intercourse between [our] two nations.[4]

One month later Colombia scrapped its arbitration proposal and agreed to direct negotiations to be held in Bogotá, not Washington.[5]

Renewed negotiations with Colombia offered the Wilson administration an ideal opportunity to demonstrate its commitment to a new era in hemispheric relations. In light of recent American history, the president faced a difficult task in convincing Latin American nations that his administration pursued a different, more moral, more compassionate policy than either its domestic predecessors or its foreign counterparts. Removal of the long-standing Panamanian issue by direct negotiations with Colombia could well provide one highly visible method of bridging the distrust, misunderstanding, and past enmity of South America. The peaceful resolution of that problem, achieved in an atmosphere of friendship and cooperation, and formally ratified by both governments, could provide an irrevocable example of America's new attitude toward its sister republics. Further erosion of Latin American skepticism and hostility might follow.

Even before the new American minister, Thaddeus A. Thomson, arrived in Bogotá in late August to supervise negotiations, complications already had surfaced between the United States and Colombia. In mid-April, Chargé Leland Harrison had informed the State Department of the presence in Colombia of Lord Murray of Elibank, an influential representative of the British firm of S. Pearson and Son. Murray had informed the American legation that his immediate goal in Colombia was to secure petroleum grants, which he hoped would lead eventually to railroad concessions. In assuring the legation that such concessions would not undercut the American position in Colombia, Murray readily acknowledged the present and future political and commercial predominance of the United States in that nation.[6]

While S. Pearson and Son had no plans to undermine the political predominance of the United States in Colombia, it did want to secure the best petroleum lands. By claiming interest in railroad concessions, Murray deliberately misled both Harrison and Colombian officials. Such rhetoric was a ploy to convince Bogotá to grant potentially lucrative petroleum contracts in return for future Pearson railroad investments, which Colombians so desperately desired. As Murray clearly pointed out in instructions to his company's agent in Bogotá, "We are to make a most determined effort to get an effective oil concession in Colombia and are to use our full force in this direction. It may be well to also talk of railroad and harbour construction and other concessions, but I may say for your own information that our apparent activity in Colombia along the latter lines is more or less a blind."[7] Weetman Pearson, Murray's superior, reaffirmed such sentiments, writing that "of course we are not interested in any business in Colombia outside oil."[8]

Initially, the U.S. legation in Bogotá did not perceive Murray as a threat to American interests in Colombia. The British lord had been in the country over one month before Harrison had alerted the State Department of his presence. By that time, although Harrison was still unaware, Murray had signed a preliminary oil agreement with Colombian Minister of Public Works Simon Araujo, granting S. Pearson and Son the rights to exploit petroleum and hydrocarbons in a concession of over 3,800 square miles. President Restrepo and his Council of Ministers formally approved that document on 24 April.[9]

The Colombian venture was not the first undertaken by Pearson and Son in the Caribbean region. The driving force, as well as head of the company, Weetman Pearson, had agreed in 1889 to construct a drainage canal near Mexico City for 2 million pounds.[10] Impressed by his work the Mexican government between 1895 and 1911 granted Pearson at least twelve other contracts, totaling over 14 million pounds, ranging from the construction of modern harbor facilities at Veracruz to dredging operations, irrigation projects, and railway construction. While supervising these various projects, Pearson became interested in potential Mexican oil lands. In 1901 he bought oil options near San Cristóbal, and by 1906 he had obtained concessions from the Mexican federal and state governments for the right to explore for oil and, if found, to establish exclusive production facilities in the states of Veracruz, San Luis Potosí, Tamaulipas, Tabasco, and Chiapas. When finally in 1910 he had brought in several large strikes on his properties, he formed the Águila Oil Company, which within three years had produced 60 percent of all oil in Mexico and was valued at 5 million pounds.[11] Not surprisingly, Pearson then turned his attention to oil development in other Caribbean states, including Colombia. Thus, he had dispatched Lord Murray in 1913 to explore Colombia, Ecuador, and Costa Rica and, if the explorations seemed encouraging, to discuss possible petroleum concessions with those respective governments.

In explaining his mission to Harrison after conducting his explorations, Lord Murray acknowledged the deep concern the United States had exhibited during the past twenty years over any significant European presence in the Caribbean. He maintained that his inquiries involved simply a business deal that would prove beneficial to both his company and to Colombia. From Pearson and Son's standpoint, the United States had no need to worry, and, for at least four months, Washington gave no indication of concern over the proposed contract.

By late September the State Department had begun to indicate interest in the proposed agreement. By 1 October officials were sufficiently concerned to direct the American legation in Bogotá to

> inform President Restrepo discreetly and verbally that the Government of the United States is not indifferent to the proposed concession to Pearson and Son by the Colombian Government and that the United States, in principle, does not feel in sympathy with concessions that give a monopoly and thus exclude all others.

> In this connection you will further inform the president that the United States is most anxious to speedily and satisfactorily arrange all contentious matters between the two governments and would regret to have so extensive a concession to another nation become a matter of discussion at this time.[12]

This was not a formal protest against the contract; it was only verbal and was to be given just to the president, not even to the foreign minister. Nevertheless, the implication was clear: the Restrepo administration should rethink its position carefully. Since the Colombian Congress had not approved the specific terms of the concession presented by Murray, there was ample time for reconsideration.[13] Such approval, the message hinted, might possibly delay the much sought-after settlement over Panama and therefore could endanger the indemnity of $15 or $20 million being discussed between the two nations' representatives in Bogotá.

If the United States had been so concerned about monopolistic concessions, or equally worried about the growing economic presence of British firms in Colombia, it is puzzling why no vigorous protest was sent in late April or early May when the State Department first received news of Murray's contract. What was the reason for the five-month delay? What had happened between April and October to change American perspective?

At least one U.S. corporation had certainly responded more quickly to the threat of British commercial competition than had Washington. On 6 June 1913, W. T. S. Doyle, recently ousted head of the U.S. State Department's Latin American Division, arrived in Bogotá to represent the General Asphalt Company of New York. His goal was to dissuade the Bogotá government from granting Murray a petroleum concession; his firm wanted the contract.

Doyle's arrival initiated a sharp economic rivalry between the General Asphalt Trust and S. Pearson and Son, both in Colombia and elsewhere.[14] The British firm immediately responded to Doyle by ordering an agent to Caracas, Venezuela, to help undercut petroleum concessions held there by General Asphalt. As yet, Pearson and Son had not decided whether to initiate full-scale war against its American foe or simply look sufficiently "ferocious and dangerous" to convince Asphalt's officials to reach some sort of economic agreement in Colombia.

In light of the Pearson and Son counterattack in Venezuela, the president of General Asphalt Trust decided to "try to come to terms" with his British rival. By mid-September 1913 the two firms opted for cooperation rather than conflict. Although Doyle's departure from Colombia quickly thereafter signaled a Pearson and Son victory, it did not indicate sanction of Murray's activities by the U.S. government.

In his earlier attacks on the British firm, Doyle had warned the American legation in Bogotá that both Murray and Pearson represented the British government and that, if their concession were granted, Britain would gain the right to construct an interoceanic canal by way of the Atrato River. This exaggerated charge rested on Article 2 of the proposed Pearson contract, which granted the company the right to construct all facilities necessary for the exploitation of petroleum resources, including the right to build railroads, pipelines, and canals. Such a provision, Doyle had argued, could provide Britain a lever to use in its current dispute with the United States over the exemption from tolls of American vessels using the Panama Canal.

The idea of Britain constructing a second interoceanic canal seemed rather preposterous, but there was indeed that remote chance. Officials in Washington had long been aware of the possibility of a canal by way of the Atrato, Mulata, and Cupica rivers in northern Colombia. After a study by U.S. Army engineers in February 1912, however, that route was considered quite improbable, although not impossible.[15] Earlier, in 1909, the Atrato route had attracted notice. Between August 1908 and August 1909, rumors had circulated in Colombia that a concession might be granted to construct a canal via the Atrato, and that the concessionaires might be associated with Britain. Noting the persistence and growing frequency of the rumor, the British chargé, acting on instructions from the Foreign Office, notified his American counterpart that London did not then have, nor would have in the future, anything to do with such a project. Chargé Paxton Hibben, transmitting the message to the State Department, summarized in one sentence the British position as outlined to him: "His Majesty's Government has no intention of risking embroiling itself with the Government of the United States by lending its support to any such enterprise."

In London the American embassy later confirmed Hibben's analysis of the British stand.[16] The U.S. position in the Caribbean had not deteriorated in the intervening four years, nor had the British indicated a new desire to confront the United States in its own backyard. Nevertheless, John Bassett Moore, speaking for the State Department in 1913, indicated that the "canal concession" feature in the Murray contract was "specially objectionable."[17] Had that canal clause been the only objectionable feature the U.S. government saw in the proposed contract, it perhaps could have been easily modified to satisfy all concerned.

American objections went deeper, however. There was a second, more important reason—indeed, the decisive reason—for urging Colombia on 1 October to consider carefully the proposed petroleum agreement. The Wilson administration specifically hoped to reduce the political impact of the Cowdray* firm on Caribbean states. Reflecting that goal, Secretary Bryan's October note originally stated that "the United States . . . does not feel in sympathy with concessions to companies whose close relations to European Governments seem to place their activities as much in a political as in a commercial field." Rather than directly emphasize its reservations about European firms, the State Department decided to rephrase its note in more generalized open-door rhetoric: "The United States . . . does not feel in sympathy with concessions that give a monopoly and thus exclude all others."[18] The decision to justify its veiled warning to Colombia solely in economic terms obscured its true position. After all, U.S. firms had been active in Colombia and already had obtained their own petroleum options. Furthermore, given the five-month delay before America's negative response, an economic explanation seems unsatisfactory. Even an explanation incorporating both economic and political fears of active European financial interests in the Caribbean seems unconvincing. The U.S. decision leading to the dispatch of the note cannot be adequately explained either in open-door or generalized anti-European rhetoric. While both attitudes helped shape its response, America's specific perception of S. Pearson and Son provided the critical factor that convinced Wilson and Bryan to dispatch the note in October and not in April.

Throughout his first year in office, Wilson's attention often shifted to internal Mexican affairs, specifically to what would be the American response toward the Mexican ruler, Victoriano Huerta, who had come to power in February 1913 and had been provisionally recognized by Great Britain on 31 March.[19] Wilson was not anxious to extend recognition to a man he thought had gained power by violent means, including the assassination of his predecessor, Francisco Madero. By August the president had ordered John Lind to Mexico as his special emissary to resolve existing differences between the Wilson and Huerta administrations. One prerequisite for settlement was the promise by Huerta not to run for a regular term as president in the scheduled October elections. If Lind could gain this key assurance, the way would be cleared for U.S. recognition of the next constitutionally elected president.

Wilson's antipathy toward the Mexican president had grown during the summer of 1913. Convinced that Huerta's illegal assumption of power and his dictatorial manner would hinder the extension of republican governments throughout the hemisphere, Wilson worked in August and September to achieve Huerta's voluntary removal from the

---

*Weetman Pearson was elevated in 1910 to the peerage of Baron Cowdray.

presidency. Lind, expressing concern over the activities of the Pearson petroleum interests in Mexico, dispatched a radiogram to Secretary of State Bryan on 13 September, reporting that "the head of [the] largest foreign interest in Mexico, not America, leads me to guess that the interest is deliberately urging Huerta to become a candidate."[20] If true, such action directly conflicted with America's Mexican policy. Only three weeks earlier the State Department had heard equally disturbing reports that the Pearson interests had secured the British recognition of Huerta in March, an action inconsistent with America's own aims.[21] Such reports emphasizing Cowdray's political activities within Mexico increased the skepticism and concern with which the United States watched Lord Murray's maneuvering for Colombian petroleum concessions. Faced with those alleged activities in Mexico, which appeared to undermine his anti-Huerta policy, Wilson, not surprisingly, used the October note to express his deep concern over another potential Cowdray foothold in the Caribbean.

Disquieting reports from Lind in Mexico during October reinforced the administration's doubts about Cowdray.[22] The emissary was convinced that Cowdray controlled the Huerta government, that he dictated British policy toward Mexico, and that he sought to monopolize the Mexican oil fields. Despite the fact that Lind's reports relating to Cowdray were the makings of a fertile imagination, generally without basis in fact, they were influential. His views deeply affected the perceptions of Wilson and Bryan, both of whom assumed he correctly interpreted events in Mexico. Wilson, for example, on 11 October complained that the British embassy in Mexico was "guided in action and opinion by representations of Lord Cowdray."[23] Since the opportunities for such a large and powerful firm to deal unfairly in an economically weak or politically divided American nation could be great, a strong U.S. response was necessary.

That response came on 27 October as President Wilson addressed the assembled delegates at the Southern Commercial Congress in Mobile, Alabama.[24] The United States, he declared, "must regard it as one of the duties of friendship to see that from no quarter are material interests made superior to human liberty and national opportunity." Writing to the president the next day, Secretary of State Bryan elaborated on Wilson's theme:

> The right of American republics to work out their own destiny along lines consistent with popular government, is just as much menaced today by foreign financial interests as it was a century ago by the political aspirations of foreign governments. If the people of an American republic are left free to attend to their own

> affairs, no despot can long keep them in subjection; but when a local despot is held in authority by powerful financial interests and is furnished money for the employment of soldiers, the people are as helpless as if a foreign army had landed on their shores. This, we have reason to believe, is the situation in Mexico, and I cannot see that our obligation is any less now than it was then. We must protect the people of these republics in their right to attend to their own business, free from external coercion, no matter what form that external coercion may take.
>
> We must be relieved of suspicion as to our motives. We must be bound in advance not to turn to our own advantage any power we employ. It will be impossible for us to win the confidence of the people of Latin America unless they know that we do not seek their territory or ourselves desire to exercise political authority over them. . . . Our only object must be to secure to the people an opportunity to vote, that they may themselves select their rulers and establish their government.[25]

In order to guard the economic and political liberty of neighboring peoples, the United States needed to resist this foreign financial domination and to control firms like Cowdray's, which seemed to seek special advantages and privileges as well as to thwart an American policy aimed at improving hemispheric life.

Committed to the establishment of republican institutions throughout Latin America, Wilson and Bryan renewed their efforts to obtain Huerta's voluntary resignation. Fearful that the Mexican dictator might obtain European support, the State Department dispatched a circular telegram to foreign embassies on 7 November, emphasizing that the American government "must now proceed to employ such means as may be necessary" to obtain Huerta's downfall. In achieving that goal the United States hoped it could rely on European assistance in persuading the general to relinquish his presidency.[26]

Interference from both the British government and corporations especially concerned the Wilson administration. Since late October it had increasingly emphasized to London its uneasiness over the British and Cowdray actions in Mexico. Simultaneously, it again had alerted the American legation in Bogotá that it disapproved of the Murray-Cowdray concession in Colombia.

Britain's response to Washington's disquiet in mid-November surprised the Wilson administration. Prime Minister Herbert H. Asquith, concerned over the growing threat to Anglo-American friendship, indicated that he had no intention of blocking this latest U.S. effort in Mexico.[27] American suspicion and misunderstanding of Britain's earlier attitude toward Huerta dissipated further as a result of meetings between President Wilson and Edward M. House with British representative Sir William Tyrrell between 12 and 14 November. According to House, Tyrrell not only satisfactorily explained Britain's past positions but also "assured the President that his government would work cordially with ours and that they would do all that they could to bring about joint pressure through Germany and France for the elimination of Huerta."[28] Nor were Tyrrell's reassurances mere rhetoric. Foreign Secretary Sir Edward Grey informed the British ambassador to Mexico on 11 November that London would not support Huerta "in any way against the United States."[29] The British, therefore, finally appeared willing to work harmoniously with the Wilson administration. However, despite statements of reassurance, Washington officials were still skeptical of British economic interests, especially those headed by Baron Cowdray in Mexico and other Caribbean states. Lind's reservations about Cowdray were still shared by both Wilson and Bryan.

On 19 November, less than one week after Tyrrell's meetings with Wilson, Secretary Bryan cabled the legation at Bogotá to "use its strongest efforts in a discreet and unofficial manner to secure the failure of [the Murray-Pearson] contract."[30] Success came four days later. Believing that the petroleum issue had become a pawn in U.S.-Colombian treaty discussions, Lord Murray formally withdrew the proffered agreement on 23 November. The immediate threat of a powerful "foreign financial menace" gaining a foothold in Colombia had passed.

In his attempt to obtain Colombian concessions in 1913, Murray and the Pearson interests had been caught in the middle. They had arrived in Colombia to begin their exploratory studies before Wilson's inauguration. By the time they had drawn up a contract and submitted it to the Colombian Congress, the new Wilson administration had reopened the isthmian negotiations with a Colombian administration whose officials were quite pleased to have Pearson and Son invest in their nation since they badly needed foreign investment to effect an economic upturn. Nor, at least in April, did the Colombian president foresee difficulty in passing the Murray contract.[31] Even after the 1 October note from the United States, President Restrepo still expected some sort of agreement with Murray, although he assured Thomson that it would contain no monopolistic features.[32] By late October, however, the Colombian government had begun to realize the extent of U.S. opposition to the contract. Since that document already had been signed by Minister of Public Works Araujo and approved by Restrepo and his Council of Ministers, the president did not want to withdraw it from congressional consideration. However, both he and Foreign Minister Urrutia expected it to die in Congress. If by some remote chance it appeared to be gaining approval, the Colombian administration had indicated to Thomson that it would take steps to obstruct its passage.[33] While such a promise might create a better atmosphere in which to resolve the old isthmian dilemma, it carried little political risk for President Restrepo. Although he and his political advisers had approved the Murray contract in April, they were having second thoughts by mid-October because of U.S. and British pressure.

When the Colombian chargé in London, Pedro Mario Carreno, alerted Bogotá in mid-October that the British government demanded arbitration of a dispute involving the Puerto Wilches Railroad, Colombian officials reacted in alarm.[34] Since contracts relating to that railroad had been negotiated and signed by the Reyes administration and had not been approved by Congress as required by law, they had been declared void by Reyes's successors. Reacting to the appeals of British investors hurt by the government's action, the British Foreign Office in 1912 urged Colombia to submit the dispute to arbitration at The Hague if the investors and the government could work out no mutually acceptable resolution. Colombia, however, resisted that suggestion. Therefore, the Foreign Office decided to adopt a more forceful policy, one that demanded arbitration.

The Restrepo administration found the Foreign Office's demand unacceptable since aggrieved British investors had not yet exhausted all legal options available to them within the Colombian judicial system. It also reminded British officials that foreign firms investing in Colombia as a matter of routine waived their rights to seek diplomatic intervention in economic disputes unless they were denied access to the Colombian judiciary. In this case, disgruntled British investors, if they so chose, could still freely pursue their cases in Colombian courts. Therefore, Araujo and the foreign minister stressed that the British demand for arbitration was both unwarranted and unacceptable. If the British government persists, Araujo informed Murray on 14 October, not only will the petroleum contract be scrapped but Colombia also will sign no contract with any British firm. While Murray quickly agreed to add a more precise stipulation in his contract firmly denying the right of the British government to intervene diplomatically in a future dispute between Colombia and Pearson and Son, Colombian leaders remained uneasy. The Restrepo administration decided to stall the Murray contract until the British Foreign Office stated its own position on future diplomatic intervention on behalf of British investors. This flurry of activity over intervention was but the prelude to a long British-Colombian discussion over the Puerto Wilches Railroad and the justification for British intervention. Lord Murray, realizing that his petroleum contract had become a pawn in the dispute between Colombia and Britain over intervention and between the United States and

Colombia over resolution of the Panama affair, formally withdrew his proposal on 24 November.[35]

In terms of U.S. policy the entire Murray episode reflected President Wilson's deep concern over the future of the Caribbean states, especially that foreign corporations might hinder the establishment of republican institutions throughout the hemisphere. He believed it was his duty to resist contracts such as the proffered petroleum agreement with Colombia. Experience with Cowdray interests in Mexico had convinced the president that such firms, by supporting morally or legally objectionable despots, could flaunt popular will as well as undermine American policy toward neighboring states. By hinting that the U.S.-Colombian negotiations might proceed more satisfactorily if the Murray contract were rejected, Washington hoped to derail any effort by Cowdray to become an important force in Colombian domestic politics. For the new Democratic administration, the subsequent withdrawal of the Colombian contract brought closer the realization of a new hemispheric age.

Secretary Bryan reinforced the president's desire to alter American policy toward neighboring states. He had run on an anti-imperialism platform when he sought the presidency in 1900, and later had indicated his displeasure with the tactics of the Republican administrations in foreign affairs. However, Bryan was chosen not for his policy opinions but for his political assistance to Wilson at the Democratic convention.[36] Having carried the presidential banner in 1896, 1900, and 1908, Bryan was expected to exercise considerable political influence with Congress and the public, in addition to his routine departmental duties. One official obligation the secretary relished was his control over departmental appointments. A firm believer in the patronage system, Bryan axed some of those most closely associated with previous Colombian negotiations in favor of the "more deserving" party faithful. Secretary of the Navy Josephus Daniels recorded one method by which Bryan filled vacant diplomatic posts. Seeking a position for the brother of the chairman of the National Democratic Committee, Bryan offered a trade to any willing cabinet colleague. "I will give a man a position at $4,000," he suggested, "if you will give me a $4,000 job in another Department." The attorney general replied: "All right, I will give him a place if you will let me name the Minister to Persia." Bryan agreed, informing his colleague to "send over your man."[37] Having selected the Persian minister, the secretary could now turn his attention to other pressing appointments, including the choice of a new minister to Colombia.

Given the strained relations between the two countries, one might have expected the careful selection of a man eminently qualified to negotiate with the Colombian leadership. However, Bryan rather cavalierly chose sixty-year-old Thaddeus Thomson, who had graduated from the Texas Military Institute, had been a successful lawyer and rancher, but never had held a governmental position.[38] Actually, the Austin, Texas, native had been considered for an Internal Revenue collectorship, but, in the confusion of assigning appointments, that position had been filled. To resolve the conflict, Thomson, on the recommendation of Edward House, was given the Bogotá post, while the other appointee received the collectorship. Upon learning of Bryan's choice, Wilson wondered not about Thomson's diplomatic skills but whether or not too many persons from the Austin area were receiving governmental positions. Bryan, who already had received Colombia's assurance that his proposed nominee would be acceptable, reaffirmed his support for Thomson despite his candidate's Texas background. Wilson, accepting his secretary's recommendation, submitted the name to the Senate, and, on 10 June, Thomson became the new minister to Colombia.[39]

Although the treaty negotiations were to be conducted in Bogotá, Thomson initially had no specific instructions. He had embarked for Bogotá prior to the receipt of the Colombian note of 19 August, which proposed a settlement by direct negotiation, not by arbitration. Immediately upon receiving the message, Bryan telegraphed Thomson that "proper instructions" would soon follow.[40] However, not until early September did the minister learn that President Wilson was willing to offer $15 million to settle all claims and differences between Colombia and the United States, including any claims Colombia might have against Panama.[41]

Meeting with both the minister for foreign affairs and the Colombian President, Thomson quickly discovered that they considered $15 million insufficient. President Restrepo, "most anxious" to reach an arrangement, suggested that the United States submit a detailed treaty proposal concerning all contentious questions, not just an indemnity. Before Thomson could relay this request to Washington, Bryan telegraphed that, if Colombia believed the offer too low, it should make an appropriate counterproposal. While Bryan had thought in terms of $25 million since August, more could be gained by initially proposing a much lower sum.[42] The secretary wanted the Restrepo government to receive credit for any increase in the size of the indemnity. By enhancing the prowess of Colombian negotiators, Bryan explained to Wilson and Thomson, "their government will be in a better position to deal with their people" and may be able to avoid a repetition of the earlier congressional defeat in 1909.[43] Impressed with this logic, Restrepo, abandoning his request for a detailed proposal, agreed to receive a formal indemnity offer. He then could outline his nation's demands for a higher indemnity, specific canal concessions, and an appropriate boundary settlement.[44]

According to this scenario, Thomson delivered an American offer of $20 million on 1 October, the same day he received Bryan's warning about the Pearson-Murray contract. Three weeks later Colombia countered with its own proposals. An acceptable treaty, Bogotá declared, should contain an expression of regret for the isthmian affair, a new boundary line with Panama at the 79th longitude west of Greenwich, an indemnity of $50 million, and special canal concessions.[45] Although discussions would continue during the next five months over the exact nature of the special concession demands, that topic never posed a major negotiating problem. The other three Colombian proposals, however, formed a basis for more serious discussions.

In his talks with Colombian officials, Thomson had learned that an expression of sincere regret would assist the passage of any proposed treaty. He therefore submitted to the State Department a draft proposal that he believed should accompany the initial U.S. offer of indemnity to Colombia. "The Government and the people of the United States," he wrote, "sincerely regret that anything should have ever occurred to mar, in any way, whatsoever, the close and traditional friendship" of our two countries.[46] As Secretary Bryan read Thomson's draft, he felt uneasy. He wanted to go as far as possible in lamenting past occurrences, but he did not want to anger Republican senators by apologizing for, or indicating disapproval of, the actions of the Roosevelt administration. Given the delicate nature of such a clause, Bryan forwarded Thomson's dispatch to President Wilson, suggesting that he might want to rewrite it to reflect his own ideas more accurately.[47] Three days later Bryan received the president's response; the Thomson draft indeed had been unsuitable. Instead, Wilson rephrased it to read: "The Government and people of the United States sincerely desire that everything that may have marred or seemed to interrupt [their] close and long established friendship . . . should be cleared away and forgotten."[48] Using the presidential formula, the Bogotá legation was instructed to proceed with negotiations.

The Colombian response came on 22 October. Wilson's "apologies" did not seem to go far enough; after all, the United States had not only interfered with Colombia and Panama in 1903 but also had reaped the benefits of an independent isthmian republic. It had been in the wrong, not Colombia. Therefore, the regret clause, according to Colombia, should be more forceful in extending apologies to the wronged state. Bogotá diplomatically refrained from pointing out these particular justifications to the Wilson administration. Rather, it simply suggested a more acceptable phraseology by which the United States "sincerely regrets and invites the Government and people of Colombia to forget anything that may have occurred to mar or to interrupt [their] close and long established friendship."[49] By including this clause in the treaty, the United States not only would apologize for past events but also would directly ask for Colombia's forgiveness. Such action would certainly salve the past injuries Colombia had received at the hands of Washington.

Bogotá's phrasing exceeded that of either the president or even Thomson. In transmitting the Colombian message to Washington, Thomson had noted that "great stress is laid upon the word 'regrets.' . . . Your approval . . . in this form would go far toward a settlement of the whole question which is largely a matter of satisfying Colombian pride and quixotism."[50] The negotiations heretofore had gone smoothly in an atmosphere of friendship and compromise, not of belligerency and antagonism. The secretary certainly did not want that to change, yet he could not accept Colombia's proposal. To resolve the dilemma, Bryan asked State Department Counselor John Bassett Moore to draft a compromise article. Moore retained the term "regret," while eliminating the "forgiveness" section. By mid-November both the president and the secretary had approved Moore's substitute article: "The Government of the United States of America . . . expresses . . . sincere regrets that anything should have occurred to interrupt or to mar [our] relations of cordial friendship."[51] It means, Secretary Bryan wrote, exactly what it says; the United States regrets any interruption of friendly relations but does not apologize for past American actions.[52] In responding to Colombian counterproposals one month later, Bryan informed the Bogotá legation that the "President feels that [this] article goes as far as this government should be asked to go. Aside from the President's unwillingness to use his position to criticize a former President he could not do so without jeopardizing the ratification of the treaty which requires approval of two-thirds of the Senate."[53] Faced with America's determination to grant no more liberal phraseology, Bogotá accepted Moore's modified regret clause on 17 January 1914.[54] One of the three major obstacles for a successful treaty had been overcome.

The second area of disagreement involved the exact Panama-Colombia border, a problem that had faced previous American negotiators.[55] In its original October proposals, Colombia had argued that the border should be along the 79th longitude, a line that would have given it approximately one-third of all Panamanian lands. No doubt the Restrepo administration was testing the State Department to see just how far it would go. Within three weeks, Washington had decided that such a boundary was unacceptable; instead, Wilson and Bryan were willing to reaffirm former Secretary of State Elihu Root's boundary proposal of August 1907. The Colombians indicated approval of the suggested modification, provided the line be altered slightly in their favor near the Pacific coast. Washington refused. Not wanting to jeopardize the entire treaty because of an insignificant section of territory, Colombia relented and accepted the American boundary demarcation.

Only one other article posed major problems for the two governments: the amount of indemnity the United States would pay Colombia. As in their boundary proposal, the Restrepo administration initially urged an inflated $50 million, double the amount Secretary Bryan thought justifiable.[56] Two months after receiving that exorbitant demand, Bryan reaffirmed his 1 October offer of $20 million. Replying on 5 February, Colombia dropped its demand to $30 million and a $250,000 annual installment for 100 years. Even though Bogotá later halved the length of annual installments to only 50 years, the combined total payment was still too high to satisfy Washington.[57] Within one week of Colombia's modified offer, Thomson received the State Department's last word: $25 million "is to be considered final as to amount. Department cannot add an annuity."[58] Realizing that they could obtain no greater sum, Colombian officials agreed on 31 March to the American offer.[59] With that approval the terms of the treaty were complete.

Six days later Minister for Foreign Affairs Francisco José Urrutia and Minister Thomson signed the final treaty and prepared to submit it to their respective legislative bodies. This was the second time Colombian and American officials had signed an agreement resolving the tension between the two nations arising out of the Panamanian episode. The first time both sides had been optimistic of rapid passage but had been sorely disappointed when the Colombian Congress refused to give its approval. Now each side was again optimistic and expected legislative approval.

There was, however, one major difference between the 1909 situation and that of 1914. Colombian leaders had learned a significant lesson from the Root-Cortés-Arosemena fiasco. Early in the negotiations, President Restrepo had decided to work closely with a congressional commission in order to assure eventual legislative acceptance. This consultative body, known as the Suárez Commission, was composed of five prominent Colombians representing all the major political parties.[60] They worked intimately with Foreign Minister Urrutia in formulating Colombia's stance. Not only had they been consulted at every turn, but also their suggestions and thoughts had been noted and incorporated into the final treaty. These five commission members and Urrutia had jointly carried the negotiations to their successful conclusion. While not fully content with the final solution, the members acknowledged that this was the best possible agreement attainable and urged their congressional colleagues to grant approval to the document. Given the unified recommendation of both the Restrepo administration and the leaders of the various political factions, the Thomson-Urrutia Treaty gained official congressional approval on 9 June 1914.[61] Ten years of effort finally seemed to have brought tension between the United States and Colombia near its formal end.

The Wilson and Restrepo administrations had negotiated in one year an agreement that had eluded their predecessors. Although lacking diplomatic experience as he entered the presidency, Woodrow Wilson had evoked an idyllic vision of hemispheric unity, cooperation, and friendship. The Colombians, by refusing to negotiate with the outgoing Republican leaders, had gambled on the sincerity of that new rhetorical vision. While complications later arose over the proposed Murray contract, an atmosphere of friendship and compromise generally had characterized the U.S.-Colombian negotiations that eventually led to the signing of the Thomson-Urrutia Treaty on 6 April 1914.

Notes

[1]J. P. Tumulty to Secretary of State William Jennings Bryan enclosed the 11 March 1913 press release, RG 59, SD 710.11/106. Also see Bryan to ALB, 13 March 1913, RG 84: GC; *Bulletin of the Pan American Union*, "Notable Address by President Wilson," November 1913, 684–87; and Wilson address at Philadelphia, 4 July 1914, in Ray Stannard Baker and William E. Dodd, eds., *The Public Papers of Woodrow Wilson: The New Democracy* (New York: Harper & Brothers, 1926), 1:143.

[2]Harley Notter, *The Origins of the Foreign Policy of Woodrow Wilson* (Baltimore: Johns Hopkins Press, 1937), 653. Arthur Link, Wilson's foremost biographer, agrees. See his comments in J. Joseph Huthmacher and Warren I. Susman, eds., *Wilson's Diplomacy: An International Symposium* (Cambridge: Schenkman Publishing Company, 1973), 8–9. Also see Wilson's comments at Annapolis, 5 June 1914, Baker and Dodd, *Public Papers: The New Democracy* 1:130.

[3]Betancourt to Bryan, 3 May 1913, Julio Betancourt Papers, New York-Historical Society, New York. Also see RG 59, SD 711.21/169.

[4]Bryan to Betancourt, 18 July 1913, RG 59, SD 711.21/169; Bryan to Wilson, 18 July 1913, box 66, William Jennings Bryan Papers, Library of Congress Manuscripts Division (hereafter cited as Bryan Papers).

[5]Betancourt to Bryan, 19 August 1913, RG 59, SD 711.21/183. For a view of Bryan's role in the Colombian negotiations see Paolo E. Coletta, "William

Jennings Bryan and the United States-Colombian Impasse, 1903–1921," *Hispanic American Historical Review* 47 (November 1967):486–501.

[6]Harrison to Bryan, 17 April 1913, RG 59, SD 821.6363/1.

[7]Murray to Martin Ribon, 7 December 1912, box C 26, S. Pearson and Son Archives, Science Museum Library, London (hereafter cited as SPS Archives).

[8]Cowdray (Pearson) to Ribon, 14 July 1913, box C 25, SPS Archives.

[9]Text of so-called Murray contract, 23 April 1913, RG 59, SD 821.6363/6. The contract did not stipulate specific boundaries for the concession. Rather it permitted Pearson and Son to select the potential petroleum areas it desired. For information on the British firm's actions in Colombia, especially negotiations between it and Bogotá, see boxes C 25, 26, 27, correspondence dated 3 October 1912 to 25 January 1914, SPS Archives.

[10]Unless otherwise noted the background information on Pearson comes from J. A. Spender, *Weetman Pearson, First Viscount Cowdray, 1856–1927* (London: Cassell & Company, 1930); and Desmond Young, *Member for Mexico: A Biography of Weetman Pearson, First Viscount Cowdray* (London: Cassell & Company, 1966).

[11]Merrill Rippy, *Oil and the Mexican Revolution* (Leiden: E. J. Brill, 1972), 153.

[12]Bryan to ALB, 1 October 1913, RG 59, SD 821.6363/8.

[13]Article 76, subsection 14 of the 1886 constitution granted Congress authority to approve or reject contracts.

[14]For information concerning the General Asphalt-Pearson rivalry see boxes C 25, 26, 27, correspondence dated 7 June to 29 September 1913, SPS Archives. Also see Cowdray to Murray, 27 June 1913, Lord Murray Papers, National Library of Scotland, Edinburgh.

[15]See chap. 3, p. 75 in this volume.

[16]Hibben to Knox, 10 August 1909, vol. 903, 14858, NMF; Adee to Northcott, 13 October 1909, RG 84: Instructions from the Department of State (IFD), National Archives.

[17]Acting Secretary of State Moore to ALB, 6 October 1913, RG 84: Cables and Telegrams Received and Sent (CR&S), National Archives.

[18]RG 59, SD 821.6363/8.

[19]For material regarding Wilson's Mexican policy see Peter Calvert, *The Mexican Revolution, 1910–1914: The Diplomacy of Anglo-American Conflict* (Cambridge: Cambridge University Press, 1968), chaps. 4–7; Arthur S. Link, *Wilson: The New Freedom* (Princeton: Princeton University Press, 1956); George M. Stephenson, *John Lind of Minnesota* (Port Washington: Kennikat Press, 1971 [1935]); Larry D. Hill, *Emissaries to a Revolution: Woodrow Wilson's Executive Agents in Mexico* (Baton Rouge: Louisiana State University Press, 1973); Josephus Daniels, *The Wilson Era: Years of Peace, 1910–1917* (Chapel Hill: University of North Carolina Press, 1944); and Ray Stannard Baker, *Woodrow Wilson, Life and Letters*, vol. 4 (Garden City: Doubleday, Page & Company, 1935). By early summer the other major European powers also had recognized Huerta.

[20]Lind to Bryan via Assistant Secretary of the Navy Franklin D. Roosevelt, 13 September 1913, RG 59, SD 812.00/10502. The largest non-American firm was Águila. Both Calvert and Baker note that Wilson may have first become suspicious of Cowdray after reading a report by Delbert Haff, attorney

for American interests in Mexico, and discussing it with him personally. See Calvert, *Mexican Revolution*, 182; and Baker, *Life and Letters* 4:245–49. For the Haff memorandum dated 12 May 1913 see RG 59, SD 812.00/7576.

[21]This information had been received from the American oil man, Henry Clay Pierce, who met with Boaz Long, head of the Latin American Division, in New York on 24 and 25 August, RG 59, SD 812.00/8693-1/2, Long to Bryan, 26 August 1913. Pierce and Cowdray had clashed over oil rights in Mexico earlier. Also see Magdaleno Ostos de Loinaz to John Lind to State Department, 12 September 1913, RG 59, SD 812.00/8963. American officials already were aware that Cowdray and the British government had close ties. In July, Cowdray had received a major contract for oil from the British navy, oil that would come from his Mexican holdings.

[22]Lind to Bryan, 8, 15, 23, and 25 October 1913, RG 59, SD 812.00/9127, 9128, 9355, 9401; Lind to Bryan 22, 24, and 28 October 1913, reel 2, frames 72–74, 121–24, 200, John Lind Papers, Minnesota Historical Society. Lind sent similar disquieting reports on Cowdray in November as well. See reel 2, November 1913 correspondence, ibid.

Also see Stephenson, *John Lind*, 240; Hill, *Emissaries*, chap. 5; Calvert, *Mexican Revolution*, chaps. 4–7; Baker, *Life and Letters* 4; and Link, *The New Freedom*, 371–72. For subsequent attitudes of the Wilson administration toward Cowdray and Britain see Charles Seymour, *The Intimate Papers of Colonel House* (Boston: Houghton Mifflin Company, 1926), 199–200; Burton J. Hendrick, *The Life and Letters of Walter H. Page* (New York: Doubleday, Page & Company, 1925 [1921]), 206–8, 218; and Viscount Grey of Fallodon, *Twenty-Five Years, 1892–1916* (New York: Frederick A. Stokes Company, 1925), 100.

[23]Arthur S. Link, *The Papers of Woodrow Wilson* (Princeton: Princeton University Press, 1978), 28:388. For a discussion of Britain's Mexican policies see Calvert, *Mexican Revolution*; and the following Public Record Office collections: F.O. 115/1742, 1749; F.O. 204/417, 421; and F.O. 800/83, 84, 94, 241.

[24]Text of address in *Pan American Bulletin*, November 1913, 684–87.

[25]28 October 1913, series 2, reel 51, Wilson Papers.

[26]RG 59, SD 812.00/9625A.

[27]Page to Bryan, 13 November 1913, RG 59, SD 812.00/9703; Bryan to Page, 13 November 1913, RG 59, 812.00/9703; Calvert, *Mexican Revolution*, 264–67.

[28]House to Page, 14 November 1913, in Hendrick, *Life and Letters*, 207–8; Calvert, *Mexican Revolution*, 269–73.

[29]Link, *Papers of Wilson* 28:528. Also see Grey to Lionel Carden, 10 November 1913, F.O. 115/1742-489, PRO. On 17 November 1913, Cowdray publicly denied interference in Mexican political affairs. See Cowdray press release, box A 3, SPS Archives.

[30]19 November 1913, RG 59, SD 821.6363/19. Before this final decision had been made, the legation had been urged not to relax its vigilance on the matter. See Bryan to ALB, 29 October 1913, RG 84: CR&S.

[31]Percy C. Wyndham to Grey, 29 April 1913, F.O. 135/349-8, Commercial, PRO.

[32]Thomson to Bryan, 3 October 1913, RG 59, SD 821.6363/9; Thomson to Bryan, 14 October 1913, RG 84: CR&S.

[33]Thomson to Bryan, 23 October 1913, RG 59, SD 821.6363/13; Harrison to Bryan, 14 November 1913, RG 84: CR&S; Harrison to Bryan, 22 November 1913, ibid. Also see Manning to Bryan, 5 December 1913, RG 59, SD 821.6363/28.

[34]The Puerto Wilches Railroad also was known as the Great Northern Central Railroad. For examples of British and Colombian arguments in this case see Wyndham to Grey, 14 October 1913, F.O. 135/351-G72, PRO; Murray to Cowdray, 14 October and 1 November 1913, box C 26, SPS Archives; Urrutia to Pedro Maria Carreno, 17 October 1913, F.O. 135/351-G79; Murray to Simon Araujo, 22 October 1913, F.O. 135/354-G71; and Grey memorandum, 4 November 1913, F.O. 371/1631-49810. For a more detailed discussion of this controversy see the relevant correspondence in F.O. 135/344, 345, 349, 350, and F.O. 371/1630, 1631, 1951, 2921, 2343, 2659, 3192.

[35]For an analysis of the Murray episode in Colombia see boxes C 25, 26, 27, correspondence dated 3 October 1912 to 25 January 1914, SPS Archives; and Peter Calvert, "The Murray Contract: An Episode in International Finance and Diplomacy," *Pacific Historical Review* 35 (May 1966): 203–24. For further information see A. C. Veatch, *Quito to Bogotá* (New York: George H. Doran Company, 1917), 272–74; Page to Bryan, 26 November 1913, RG 59, SD 821.6363/23; Page to House, 26 November 1913, Hendrick, *Life and Letters*, 217; Young, *Member for Mexico*, 4, 184; Page to Wilson, 8 January 1914, series 2, reel 53, Wilson Papers; Page to Wilson, 19 March 1914, reel 55, ibid.; Spender, *Weetman Pearson*, 210; and Harrison to Bryan, 25 November and 4 and 10 December 1913, RG 59, SD 821.6363/24, 27, 29.

[36]Baker, *Life and Letters* 4:24; Paolo E. Coletta, *William Jennings Bryan: Progressive Politician and Moral Statesman, 1909–1915* (Lincoln: University of Nebraska Press, 1969), 2:239.

[37]E. David Cronon, ed., *The Cabinet Diaries of Josephus Daniels, 1913–1921* (Lincoln: University of Nebraska Press, 1963), entry of 22 April 1913, 50–51. Also see Katharine Crane, *Mr. Carr of State: Forty-Seven Years in the Department of State* (New York: St. Martin's Press, 1960), 162.

[38]For information on Thomson see AF-Biography-Thomson Family, in the Austin-Travis Collection at the Austin Public Library, Austin, Texas.

[39]For information relating to Thomson's appointment see Edward House Diary, 8 and 14 March and 15 May 1913, Edward M. House Papers, Sterling Memorial Library, Yale University; House to T. W. Gregory, 15 May 1913, Select Correspondence, series 1, group 466, box 51, ibid.; Bryan to Wilson, 23 May 1913, series 4, reel 286, Wilson Papers; Wilson to Bryan, 29 May 1913, series 3, reel 133, ibid.; Bryan to Wilson (undated, written between 29 May and 2 June), series 4, reel 286, ibid.; Senator Morris Sheppard to Wilson (undated, probably around 1 June), series 4, reel 286, ibid.; and Bryan to Wilson, undated, series 2, reel 53, ibid.

[40]20 August 1913, RG 59, SD 711.21/183.

[41]Bryan to Thomson, 5 September 1913, RG 59, SD 711.21/183A. Also see Coletta, "United States-Colombian Impasse," 486–501.

[42]Thomson to Bryan, 12 September 1913, RG 59, SD 711.21/187; Bryan to Thomson, 12 September 1913, RG 59, SD 711.21/187; Bryan to Wilson, 20 August 1913, box 66, Bryan Papers.

[43]Bryan to Wilson, 15 September 1913, box 43, Bryan Papers; Bryan to Thomson, 12 September 1913, RG 59, SD 711.21/187.

[44]Thomson to Bryan, 17 September 1913, RG 59, SD 711.21/189; Bryan to Thomson, 19 September 1913, ibid.; Thomson to Bryan, 24 September 1913, RG 59, SD 711.21/197.

[45]Thomson to Bryan, 22 October 1913, RG 59, SD 711.21/199.

[46]Thomson to Bryan, 23 September 1913, RG 59, SD 711.21/191.

[47]Bryan to Wilson, 26 September 1913, box 66, Bryan Papers.

[48]Wilson to Bryan, 29 September 1913, ibid. Also see Bryan to Thomson, 29 September 1918, RG 59, SD 711.21/191.

[49]Thomson to Bryan, 22 October 1913, RG 59, SD 711.21/199.

[50]Ibid.

[51]Bryan to Wilson, 13 November 1913, series 2, box 52, Wilson Papers; Bryan to Thomson, 19 December 1913, RG 59, SD 711.21/199.

[52]Bryan to Wilson, 13 November 1913, series 2, box 52, Wilson Papers.

[53]Bryan to ALB, 14 January 1914, RG 59, SD 711.21/220.

[54]Harrison to Bryan, 17 January 1914, series 2, reel 53, Wilson Papers.

[55]See chap. 3 in this volume.

[56]Thomson to Bryan, 22 October 1913, RG 59, SD 711.21/199.

[57]Bryan's offer is found in Bryan to Thomson, 19 December 1913, ibid.; Colombia's initial response is contained in Harrison to Bryan, 5 February 1914, RG 59, SD 711.21/226; and Colombia's second proposal is in Thomson to Bryan, 7 March 1914, RG 59, SD 711.21/234.

[58]Bryan to Thomson, 14 March 1914, series 2, reel 55, Wilson Papers.

[59]31 March 1914, RG 59, SD 711.21/240.

[60]Thomson to Bryan, 6 April 1914, RG 59, SD 711.21/242. For comments on the Suárez Commission and its remarks to Congress see República de Colombia, *Tratado entre la República de Colombia y los Estados Unidos de America* (Bogotá: Imprenta Nacional, 1914). Also see Uribe, *Colombia y los Estados Unidos*, 186–203. The following prominent Colombians sat on the special commission:

Marco Fidel Suárez
former minister for foreign affairs; served as president (1918–22); moderate Conservative

José M. González Valencia
former congressman, senator, and minister of state; ultra Conservative

Antonio José Uribe
president of the House of Representatives; former minister for foreign affairs; Conservative

Nicolás Esguerra
lawyer, former congressman, and minister of state; candidate for president in 1914; Liberal

Rafael Uribe Uribe
famed Liberal general who led one of the defeated revolting armies in the War of a Thousand Days

[61]The treaty passed the first of three readings on 2 May and then was referred to a Senate committee of seven, which eight days later unanimously urged its passage. Following two weeks of debate, the treaty passed the second crucial reading by a 3-to-1 margin. After passing its third reading the next day, the document went to the House, where in less than two weeks it had passed all three readings. For a discussion of Colombian and U.S. press reaction to the treaties see Mount, "American Imperialism," 189–92; and Richard, "Panama Canal," 296–337.

Chapter V

The Ratification Process: Phase I

Under the constitutions of Colombia and the United States, all treaties, in order to be binding, must be approved by their respective legislative branches. In signing the Thomson-Urrutia Treaty in April 1914, both governments acknowledged that the agreement must be approved in accordance with those laws.[1] As it had entered the discussions in 1913, the Wilson administration had vividly remembered the Colombian legislature's opposition to the tripartite agreements in 1909, the outburst of anti-Americanism coupled with anti-Reyesism, and how the optimistic Roosevelt and Taft administrations had helplessly watched those agreements go down in defeat. Hoping to stave off any renewal of that legislative hostility, or another outburst directed against the Colombian executive, Secretary of State William Jennings Bryan desired to enhance the negotiating acumen of Colombia's officials, making it appear as though, by diligence and craft, they had extracted the best possible terms from the United States. One of the major factors in that effort included his suggestion for a series of proposals and responses that would give the Colombian negotiators credit for securing a much higher indemnity. Such sensitivity reflected an astute perception of that nation's domestic scene. However, either from apathy, ignorance, or supreme self-confidence, neither Bryan nor President Woodrow Wilson bothered with their own Senate, in whose hands success equally lay.

The most probable explanation for that negligence lies in Wilson's conception of the presidency. In his study of constitutional government, published in 1908, Wilson had reflected upon the relationship between the executive and the legislative branches in treaty matters. At that time he believed that

> one of the greatest of the President's powers . . . [is] his control which is very absolute, of the foreign relations of the nation. The

> initiative in foreign affairs, which the President possesses without any restriction whatever, is virtually the power to control them absolutely. The President cannot conclude a treaty with a foreign power without the consent of the Senate, but he may guide every step of diplomacy, and to guide diplomacy is to determine what treaties must be made, if the faith and prestige of the government are to be maintained. He need disclose no step of negotiation until it is complete, and when in any critical matter it is completed the government is virtually committed. Whatever its disinclination, the Senate may feel itself committed also.[2]

Given this attitude, it is not surprising that Wilson and Bryan retained absolute control over negotiations with Colombia, nor that they both expected the Senate to agree routinely to the terms approved by the administration. In fact, leaders in the executive branch exhibited a remarkable disinterest in the attitude of senators toward the proposed treaty. Between 2 May and 9 June 1914, when that document was under consideration by the Colombian Congress, no poll was taken to ascertain the position of U.S. senators, and one was not even taken after the treaty passed its second crucial reading in the Colombian Senate on 26 May. Secretary Bryan simply assured Minister Thomson in Bogotá on 9 June that "there is no reason to doubt the ratification of the Colombian treaty."[3] The document's fate seemed so secure that no one in the executive branch apparently felt the need to lay the groundwork for senatorial approval. Maintaining that complacency, seven days later Wilson submitted the convention to the Senate, where, after the cursory first reading, it was referred to the Foreign Relations Committee.

Preoccupied with crises in the Dominican Republic and Haiti, with intervention in Mexico, and with their normal load of domestic legislation, the senators exhibited little interest in this agreement with Colombia, an agreement that in some form had been in progress for ten years. It did not appear to require their immediate and individual attention.[4] That attitude was clearly reflected in a letter to former President Theodore Roosevelt from the new Democratic chairman of the Senate Foreign Relations Committee, William Joel Stone of Missouri. Writing on 23 July he reported that, although he had urged his colleagues by special note to attend a committee meeting on the treaty, only four of seventeen bothered to show up.[5]

In addition to outright apathy, the Colombian treaty faced major opposition. Certainly one of the most vocal critics of the Thomson-Urrutia agreement was Roosevelt. Convinced that American actions on the isthmus in 1903 were correct in every detail, he regarded the settlement as a "crime against the United States."[6] On 11 July, in a vituperative letter to Senator Stone, which the Missouri chairman described as a "very ferocious screech," the former president sought permission to appear before the Foreign Relations Committee to discuss the Colombian agreement.[7] Only two options remained, Roosevelt charged, for the Senate and the American people:

> Either the course we took in 1903 was right, in which case it is worse than an outrage now to pay blackmail, or it was wrong, in which case we have now no right to be on the Isthmus. . . . If, as is unquestionably the truth, we have the right to be on the Isthmus, it would be a shameful thing cringingly to put ourselves in the wrong by the payment of blackmail.[8]

In case the senators had missed any of his earlier explanations of the 1903 episode, Roosevelt concluded by pointing out that "every action we took was not only open but was absolutely straight and was rendered absolutely necessary by the misconduct of Colombia and the dignity of the United States and the interests not only of the United States but of the world in having the canal built. Every action we took was in accordance with the highest principles of public and private morality."[9] As president he had gone as far as discretion allowed in dealing with Colombia but had been rudely rebuffed in 1909. The United States, therefore, should not pursue the matter further, certainly not to the extent of bribing Colombia with an expression of regret and an outrageous sum of money.

The most effective opposition to the Thomson-Urrutia Treaty came not from Roosevelt but from his old friend Senator Henry Cabot Lodge. As ranking minority member of the Foreign Relations Committee, he was in an ideal position to obstruct approval of any unsatisfactory accord with Colombia. This intelligent, dedicated, industrious scholar-politician from Massachusetts for the next four years would effectively stymie the efforts of the Wilson administration to secure senatorial approval of the Colombian agreement. Having received his doctorate in history from Harvard in 1876 and having taught there between 1878 and 1879, Lodge was familiar with the historical interaction of the branches of the federal government. That knowledge, coupled with his congressional experience, had convinced him by 1902 that the Senate should take an active role in any treaty-making process. "The action of the Senate upon a treaty," the senator indicated, "is not merely to give sanction to the treaty, but is an integral part of the treaty making, and may be taken at any stage of a negotiation."[10] His interpretation differed drastically from that of Wilson who believed that the executive was solely responsible for negotiating and signing an agreement, after which the Senate was "virtually committed" to ratification.

While Lodge sought to grant the president wide authority in foreign affairs and agreed that he legally did not need to seek senatorial advice during treaty negotiations, he could not justify blindly approving any treaty referred by the executive. He certainly did not feel committed by presidential action during the Colombian negotiations. To Lodge, he and his fellow senators would be negligent of their duties as elected representatives of the people if they approved without scrutiny each and every treaty submitted to them. It was their duty to study those documents to determine whether or not the president had acted wisely and in the best interests of the whole nation.

The outright opposition of such powerful Republican leaders as Roosevelt and Lodge, as well as the apparent disinterest of supposedly friendly senators, delayed consideration of the Colombian treaty. Not only did the administration need every Democratic vote, but to secure passage by the necessary two-thirds majority it also had to win the support of thirteen Republicans,[11] which proved impossible in 1914. By early September, five months after the treaty had been signed, Bryan telegraphed the Bogotá legation that chances of passage in this session of Congress were slight.[12] In a surprising admission of ignorance and inaction, the secretary continued, "I believe a majority of the Senators would favor the treaty if we could get it to a vote, but we have no satisfactory poll upon which to predicate an opinion."[13] How could there be a satisfactory poll? The treaty had been under consideration in the U.S. Senate only since June. Fearful that the Colombian settlement would jeopardize other vital legislation pending before Congress, the Wilson administration had refused to apply political pressure on reluctant legislators. Before raising the potentially divisive Colombian issue, it sought passage of the pending Federal Trade Commission and ship subsidy bills. Writing to Wilson in early December, Bryan, worried over further delay, suggested that the president discuss the treaty in his upcoming State of the Union message.[14] Wilson, however, rejected his secretary's advice. Concerned with Mexican intervention, the outbreak of war in Europe, and passage of the politically explosive ship subsidy bill, the president viewed the energetic pursuit of Senate approval as undesirable at that moment. Perhaps, within a few months, after the tempers of current congressional debates had cooled and after the inflammatory "blackmail" rhetoric had subsided, the administration could secure the necessary two-thirds vote of the Senate.

Opposition to the treaty remained vigorous, however. A threatened filibuster would have prevented action in the spring of 1915, even if the treaty had squeaked out of the Foreign Relations Committee. But, as Chairman Stone noted in the closing days of the 63d Congress, the committee was badly divided between pro- and antitreaty forces. Further committee action in this session, he warned Wilson, would be unwise. In addition to the Republican opposition in committee, at least two Democrats also had questioned the advisability of the treaty.[15] If all seven Republicans opposed ratification, those two Democratic votes would be decisive; in fact, they would assure the defeat of the agreement in committee by a single vote. With only one week remaining in the third session, Wilson had little choice except to resubmit the treaty to the new Congress convening in December.[16] Apologizing for the delay, Secretary Bryan informed the Colombian government that "the new senate, we are convinced, will be more favorable to the ratification of the treaty than the senate which has just adjourned."[17]

Bryan's optimism proved unfounded. While the new Senate Foreign Relations Committee did report out the treaty in February 1916 by a narrow 8-to-7 vote, its passage still seemed doubtful.[18] Viewing Republican opposition in the full Senate, the Democratic leadership wisely decided to postpone further consideration until some more suitable date. Since this was a presidential election year, and Wilson already had aroused enough controversy over his Mexican policies, there was no desire to initiate a major, potentially unsuccessful, floor fight in the Senate over ratification. Charges of paying Colombia blackmail, together with assertions that the treaty admitted America's guilt in securing the Panama Canal and therefore stained American honor, would not be popular campaign issues for the president or other Democrats.

The opposition's persistence, as well as Wilson's desire to avoid a major political battle, postponed serious consideration of the Thomson-Urrutia document until February 1917. Even then the president's narrow defeat of Charles Evans Hughes in the November elections threatened to complicate the ratification process. Robert Lansing, who upon Bryan's resignation in June 1915, had been promoted from counselor to secretary of state, informed Wilson in late January 1917 that Republican "resentment and disappointment" over their recent loss made ratification unlikely. Delay would now be the wisest course to pursue.[19]

Within two weeks, growing antagonism between Germany and the United States forced a reconsideration of Lansing's delay policy. Responding to the outbreak of war in Europe in August 1914, President Wilson had sought to maintain American neutrality, but, once Germany initiated submarine warfare in February 1915, true neutrality proved difficult. Secretary Bryan, objecting to Wilson's stiff notes to Germany over its sinking of the *Lusitania*, on which 128 Americans had died, resigned in mid-1915. Confident that he correctly pursued a policy of firmness toward Germany, the president refused to be moved by Bryan's resignation. In April 1916 he went even further when he warned Germany that continued submarine attacks, in violation of the rules of cruiser warfare, would force the United States to sever diplomatic relations. Reacting quickly, the German government had banned U-boat strikes in the war zone surrounding Britain. An intense internal struggle between German civilian and military leaders during the ensuing months had resulted in the resumption of unrestricted submarine warfare on 1 February 1917. As threatened, President Wilson responded two days later by severing relations with Germany.

The unexpected crisis with the German government focused Washington's attention on Latin America, especially Colombia. If the United States should become actively involved in a war, the strategic importance of the Panama Canal and its approaches would be of inestimable value. By 6 February, Secretary Lansing, abandoning his former stand, urged the immediate consideration of the Colombian treaty. He informed the president that "the question of having all the nations of Northern South America, and particularly Colombia, which is nearest to the Canal, friendly to the United States is most important, in view of probable eventualities." Furthermore, "opposition to the treaty can be overcome by impressing upon the opposition leaders the great importance of having the nations bordering on the Canal friendly, and not hostile."[20] Wilson, who shared Lansing's concern, wrote Senator Stone on 17 February, urging him to press for immediate ratification. While acknowledging the primary purpose for approving the treaty should be to render justice to Colombia, he quickly added that "we need now and it is possible shall need very much more in the immediate future all the friends we can attach to us in Central America where so many of our most critical interests lie."[21] Stone, reacting to the president's uneasiness, called the Foreign Relations Committee into session three days later.

Unmoved by the fluctuating relations with Germany, Senator Lodge remained obdurate. He did not doubt that Germany was active in Colombia, but those actions could not justify approving a bad treaty. Writing to Roosevelt on 22 February, Lodge indicated that he would "cheerfully give Wilson 150 millions to spend on Naval preparations, but . . . [not] 25 millions as blackmail to Colombia."[22] Only the day before the senator, supported by his Republican colleagues in committee, had intimidated the Democrats into postponing consideration of the document until the next session.

Spurred by German activity in the Caribbean, the Wilson administration prepared to launch an all-out assault to secure approval of the Colombian treaty. Although the State Department had been concerned earlier with the increased communications between the German embassy in Washington and individuals in Colombia, only in late February did it fear the serious possibility of intrigue in Colombia.[23] Perception of Germany's activities in that nation also was influenced by the alarming German proposal of a military alliance with Mexico contained in the Zimmermann telegram passed to the United States by Britain in late February. More than ever, Colombia's friendship seemed desirable. With the legislators scheduled to adjourn on 3 March, Wilson decided to push for ratification by calling a special session of Congress two days later.[24] To impress the senators with the importance of passage, the State Department warned that "it is greatly feared that should the treaty not be ratified, the United States will have a very unfriendly Northern South America to contend with . . . and if war between the United States and Germany comes, it will find [Venezuela, Ecuador, and Colombia] openly unneutral, if not hostile, to [the United States] and a menace to the defenses of the canal."[25] Approval of the three-year-old Colombian treaty would alleviate part of this hostility and assist the United States in counteracting German activities in the Caribbean.

Acceding to the president's wishes, Chairman Stone spearheaded the effort to secure approval in committee and in the full Senate. To convince skeptics that the document did not question America's honor or its right to the canal zone, supporters of the treaty added two amendments. Rather than having only the United States express sincere regrets that anything had marred or disrupted cordial relations, Article 1 was modified so that both the United States and Colombia expressed mutual regrets.[26] Articles 2 and 3, granting advantageous rights in the canal zone and a payment of $25 million, remained unchanged. In return for those trading and monetary considerations, Colombia, in an identical Article 4, still promised recognition of Panama's independence. Committee Democrats, however, added a new Article 5 stating "that neither the making of this convention nor any of the stipulations herein contained shall be considered to cast any doubt or shadow upon the title of the United States to the Panama Canal, which title the Government of Colombia recognizes as entire, absolute, and complete in the United States of America."[27] With these modifications the Democratic members recommended immediate Senate approval.

Joining with the Democrats on the Foreign Relations Committee, newly elected Senator Philander Knox broke the Republican phalanx against the treaty. Shortly after the United States and Colombia agreed to the Thomson-Urrutia Treaty in April 1914, he had opposed the settlement. The monetary payment of $25 million had seemed entirely too high, especially when accompanied by "an apology that fouls our title to Panama."[28] However, by March 1917, Knox could accept that payment so long as the treaty did not impugn previous American actions or motives on the isthmus. Believing the modified treaty met this vital condition, and concerned that relations should be normalized between the United States, Colombia, and Panama, the senator joined with the Wilson administration to support ratification.[29]

The administration's argument that ratification would undercut Germany's position in Colombia backfired. Senator Lodge suspected a Democratic ploy. Wilson, he wrote Roosevelt, "plans to have the Republicans reject [the treaty] unless he can carry it through by the patriotic plea, and then denounce us for treason."[30] However, Lodge planned to withstand the president's maneuverings. He discounted Lansing's arguments that Colombia might eventually assist Germany unless the treaty passed the Senate, astutely reasoning that publication of the Zimmermann telegram on 1 March would discourage any Caribbean state from entering the German orbit.[31] While various southern republics may have disliked the United States, they were aware of practical realities: that Germany lay across the Atlantic enmeshed in a war with Russia, England, and France, that the German fleet was bottled up by mighty British squadrons, and that naval supremacy in the Caribbean lay with the United States, not Germany or even England.

Lodge, therefore, would not be herded into approving the objectionable Colombian treaty based on fictitious claims of national security. Were Germany a greater threat, the senator still would have opposed "buying" Colombian friendship with passage of the 1914 treaty.[32] As a result, when Wilson on 12 March ordered Stone to push the treaty, Lodge's reaction was immediate. He approached his Republican colleagues, arguing that, in addition to admitting American wrongdoing in November 1903, the United States, by approving the treaty, now would be buying Colombia's questionable friendship. Aware that the Republicans could not stop the favorable report of the treaty out of the Democratically controlled Foreign Relations Committee, Lodge quickly huddled with thirty-three senators, enough to prevent approval. Within hours of Wilson's command to Senate Democrats, the Massachusetts senator had confirmed the opposition of more than one third of the Senate.[33] Hoping to assure Wilson's defeat, he urged Roosevelt to contact those Republicans who seemed to be wavering.[34] There must be no doubt about the final vote.

Having lost the committee fight as anticipated, Lodge and his Republican colleagues successfully moved to block Senate approval. On 16 March, only two days after the favorable committee report, Senator Stone admitted defeat by postponing the treaty until the regular session of Congress in April.[35] However, unless one side or the other indicated a willingness to compromise, prospects for passage seemed remote. Thirty-seven senators already had indicated privately that the present treaty with Colombia was unacceptable,[36] and their continued opposition would destroy any chance of securing ratification by the necessary two-thirds vote. Since both sides agreed on the desirability of a settlement with Colombia, the crucial conflict hinged, as before, upon the exact terms of such an agreement.

Acknowledging the possibilities of a prolonged deadlock, Democratic and Republican leaders initiated discussions aimed at resolving the current impasse. Senator Stone suggested an alteration of Article 3, by which the United States promised to give Colombia $25 million within six months of ratification. Rather than pay one lump sum, he proposed that the United States pay only $5 million within six months, and then $5 million annually for the next four years. Not only would that modification please opposition senators, but it also would give the United States better leverage in its dealings with Colombia. "If we should pay Colombia the full $25,000,000 at once and in one payment," Stone wrote Lansing, "the Government and the people [of Colombia] might feel at greater liberty to act in a spirit less friendly towards us. If we hold back a larger part of the money they would at least be under some restraint."[37] On 19 March, Lansing and the president approved Stone's proposed alteration.[38]

While Democratic leaders considered this modification, Lodge requested a meeting with Assistant Secretary of State William Phillips.[39] The senator hoped that the administration, facing certain defeat next session, would be willing to remove the objectionable features from the treaty. Phillips reinforced Lodge's position when, at their meeting on 18 March, he noted that the administration "consider[ed] the passage of the treaty of the highest importance, in fact imperative." To ensure passage and remove further anxiety over ratification, Lodge responded, the administration only need to incorporate a few modifications. While personally believing $25 million too high, he realized Colombia probably would reject any lesser amount as insufficient; therefore, he would recommend no reduction in the monetary payment. However, other changes were needed: the section expressing regret should be stricken entirely; the privileges granted Colombia in the canal zone should not apply during any future war between Panama and Colombia; Bogotá should agree to use the $25 million for internal improvements aimed at benefiting the people of Colombia and not their lobbyists in Washington; and finally, the United States, in return for approving the treaty, should secure some tangible benefits such as a ninety-nine-year lease on the Atrato route and two Colombian islands—

San Andrés and San Luis de Providencia. Should Secretary Lansing express interest in these proposals, Lodge indicated to Phillips, he would be willing to arrange a conference in which they could discuss the agreement in greater detail.[40]

Lansing, responding to Lodge's initiative, began working on the draft of a new treaty. Consulting at least three Republican members on the Foreign Relations Committee—Frank B. Brandegee, Philander C. Knox, and Henry Cabot Lodge—he rewrote much of the Thomson-Urrutia agreement.[41] Writing to President Wilson on 23 March, Lansing emphasized the need to negotiate a new treaty, one based on his own just completed draft. "I can guarantee," he promised, that such a treaty "will be accepted by the senate."[42] That was not an empty boast since, in altering the original terms, he had incorporated almost every Republican objection.

Lansing's new proposals substantially modified the agreement signed at Bogotá in 1914.[43] Rejecting both the original regret clause and the more recent Democratic "mutual regret" clause, he eliminated Article 1 altogether; by adding a completely new section to Article 2, he met Republican objections that the United States guaranteed preferential canal privileges to Colombia. "The provisions of this article shall be operative even in case of war between Colombia and any other country," Lansing wrote, "but not in case of war between Colombia and the United States or between Colombia and Panama." Wanting to erase all fears that Colombia might assist Germany in its present war, the secretary, on his own initiative, added: "In case of war between the United States and another country other than Colombia, the privileges and immunities provided for in this article shall not be used by Colombia in any manner whatsoever to the advantage directly or indirectly of the enemy of the United States."[44] Such an unsolicited provision certainly pleased the Republicans.

Considering Lodge's desire that the United States should retain firmer control over the use of the $25 million, Lansing incorporated Senator Stone's suggestion of 17 March. Colombia would now receive this sum over a four-year period, materially tying that republic to the United States for the duration of the payments. Thus modified, Article 3 satisfied Republicans and Democrats alike. Since neither side sought any alteration of Article 4, by which Colombia agreed to recognize Panama, Lansing left that last section unchanged.[45]

While eliminating or altering three of the substantive articles in the 1914 treaty, the secretary's draft added two completely new articles. In the first, Colombia would grant to the United States the "exclusive right to construct, operate, and maintain an interoceanic canal over the Atrato or any other route over Colombian territory whenever the two governments shall agree that the construction of such a canal would be conducive to their mutual interests and welfare."[46] This clause would permanently assure the United States of any interoceanic canal option in Colombia, while not requiring it to agree to appropriate funds for actual construction. The second article sought immediate and effective control over the Colombian islands of San Luis de Providencia and San Andrés, lying 145 miles off the Caribbean coast of Nicaragua.[47] Under its terms Bogotá would lease the islands to the American government for 100 years, "renewable in the sole and absolute option of the United States" so long as it may desire. While the United States would acknowledge Colombian sovereignty, it would "exercise over the said islands such rights as it would exercise if it were sovereign."[48] Evidently oblivious to the history of U.S.-Colombian canal negotiations, Lansing failed to realize that even the weaker phrasing relating to sovereignty contained in the Hay-Herrán Treaty of 1903 had ignited a Colombian uproar.

A reluctant Wilson granted permission on 24 March 1917 to broach the subject of a new treaty with the Colombian minister in Washington.[49] Frank Polk, counselor of the State Department, met with Minister Julio Betancourt that same afternoon. While he did not reject outright a new negotiation, Betancourt urged a vote on the 1914 document first, but the official Colombian response to a new treaty would have to come from Bogotá.[50] Even as Polk and Betancourt talked, the American chargé, Perry Belden, was writing that the U.S. Senate's refusal to approve the original Thomson-Urrutia Treaty could cause "a deep set and long standing bitterness towards the United States" throughout Colombia.[51] Upon learning of Lansing's alterations five days later, he cabled that they "would only invite hostility to and the ultimate defeat of the treaty."[52] The minister for foreign affairs quickly confirmed Belden's appraisal on 31 March. His government would withdraw the treaty, he warned, if the United States insisted on the Atrato option and the virtual cession of its two Caribbean islands.[53]

Secretary Lansing had badly miscalculated. In his efforts to conciliate the Republican opposition in the Senate, he unwisely had ignored Colombia, whose threat to withdraw the treaty if his draft articles were accepted placed him in an awkward and embarrassing position. Since its declaration of war against Germany on 6 April, the United States could not afford to antagonize the Colombian republic further. Scrapping his draft, Lansing reverted to the 1914 treaty as recommended by the Foreign Relations Committee in mid-March. On 16 April, Senator Stone again tried to secure approval by the full upper house of that earlier document. Those efforts, encountering the same Republican opposition, failed.

Preoccupied with industrial mobilization and the necessary coordination with its new allies, the Wilson administration devoted little time to the Colombian matter after declaring war on Germany. Secretary Lansing, who in March had held daily conferences on the Thomson-Urrutia Treaty, noted in his desk diary only five meetings on that subject between May 1917 and early February 1918.[54] By the second week in February, however, the State Department once again began preparations to secure passage of the long-delayed treaty.

Keenly aware of their previous mistakes, Lansing and his colleagues proceeded slowly. During the spring and summer of 1918, they met informally with a few key senators, particularly Lodge, in order to resolve existing problems with the 1914 document. At the same time, Lansing sought information on the attitude of the newly elected Colombian president, Marco Fidel Suárez, toward possible modifications.[55] He finally had realized that a successful treaty required careful coordination with both the Colombian government and the Republican opposition in the Senate.

Two obstacles blocked settlement in late 1918. Not only did the Republicans fiercely oppose the regret clause contained in Article 1, but they also found Article 3 unsatisfactory. To be acceptable, they insisted, the latter article must extend the length of the indemnity payment over a four-year period. Furthermore, Colombia must promise that no portion of the indemnity would go to lawyers or lobbyists working in the United States. Accepting Colombia's refusal to consider the Atrato option or the lease of its two islands, the Republicans already had dropped that provision from their demands.[56] Even the first two obstacles seemed less formidable by mid-December 1918. At that time, Betancourt indicated that his government would consider modification of the regret clause, removing the objectionable sections. While not commenting on the period of payment, which was generally understood to be acceptable, he also added that all monies received would be used for internal improvements.[57]

In addition to textual obstacles, administration leaders faced in 1919 a Republican-controlled Congress. The November 1918 elections had proved disastrous for the Democrats, who lost five Senate and twenty-five House seats, thereby giving the Republicans a one-vote majority in the Senate and enabling them to assume control over the various committees. Lodge, who by 1915 had become a personal as well as a political enemy of Wilson, became chairman of the Foreign Relations Committee, which controlled the fate of the Thomson-Urrutia document.[58]

In the absence of both Secretary Lansing and President Wilson, who had sailed for France on 4 December, Acting Secretary of State

Frank Polk labored over a modified treaty acceptable to both Colombia and the Republican majority in the Senate. Rather than alter the regret clause, he eliminated it, and he modified Article 3 so that the United States would pay Colombia $5 million within six months of ratification, with an additional $5 million annually over the next four years. Incorporating Lodge's proposal, he also added a stipulation by which Colombia would agree not to use the $25 million to pay legal fees incurred during the ratification process.[59] Having completed his task, Polk met with Senator Lodge on 25 January 1919, while Minister to Colombia Hoffman Philip conferred with Senator Knox. Outlining the new proposals, Polk discovered that both Lodge and Knox approved of his recent efforts and would support his modifications.[60]

The heated Senate debate over the proposed League of Nations covenant in the Versailles Treaty threatened, however, to delay approval of the new Colombian agreement.[61] Despite Lodge's support, consideration of Polk's draft, which officially reached the committee on 19 May, was postponed.[62] The senators were too busy debating a League covenant that neither had been formally signed nor submitted for their approval. Those debates further intensified upon Wilson's arrival in the United States from Europe on 9 July. Not until the thirty-first, two days after Senator Lodge had completed his two-week oral reading of the Versailles document, did the Senate agree to take up the modified Thomson-Urrutia Treaty on 4 August.[63]

Colombian leaders, anxious to reestablish the fullest cooperation and friendship between the government and people of Colombia and the government and people of the United States, had agreed to the Polk draft on 27 February.[64] The strengthening of ties with their northern neighbor, together with the receipt of $25 million, would measurably aid the much-needed economic development of their country. Therefore, they savored the bipartisan support in the U.S. Senate evident in late July. For a third time within sixteen years, agreement seemed within reach.[65]

If the treaty should fail passage in the Senate, Colombia realized that it could face an unpleasant future since the nation was still financially weak and therefore needed the confidence, stability, and credit rating that a $25 million indemnity could provide. Between 1912 and 1919 its external debt alone hovered near $23 million (U.S.).[66] Not surprisingly, in a nation in which annual government revenues averaged only $14,453,000 (U.S.) between 1910 and 1920, the treaty indemnity looked quite appealing.[67] American diplomats in Bogotá aptly described Colombia's financial situation as "most critical" and "disastrous." By Christmas 1917, for example, they noted that the three-year-old Concha administration was two months behind in its pay to the army and national police; even the most fortunate governmental officials were receiving only partial salaries. Colombian President Suárez also reported that the sizable deficit he inherited from his predecessor "crushed" his administration from the outset.[68] A government unable to meet its own payroll and already deeply in debt could hardly be expected to undertake the desirable, although expensive, internal improvements to communication and transportation that were needed to stimulate the nation's economic life.

Even if Colombia had had a full treasury, it still would have been unalterably tied to the United States and would have found it eminently desirable to reach a settlement over Panama. As noted in Chapter 2, between 1906 and 1911 the United States received an average of 46 percent of all Colombian exports each year. When the economic welfare of one nation depends that greatly upon another country, the dependent state must make efforts to maintain an atmosphere of amity and goodwill. This became even more essential between 1912 and 1919, for Colombia's economic reliance on the United States increased dramatically.[69] The outbreak of war in Europe caused the reorientation of merchant shipping and reduced Colombia's exports to England and Germany, its two largest European customers. The United States, much closer by sea and free from the threat of belligerent submarines, began to receive a larger and larger percentage of Colombian exports, taking

Table 3. National Revenue and Expenditures (Col. $): Ordinary Treasury Operations, 1910–20

Year	*Actual Receipts*	*Actual Expenditures*	*Surplus or Deficit*
1910	$10,827,568	$11,501,442	−$673,874
1911	11,527,346	11,793,077	−265,731
1912	13,209,759	14,205,367	−995,608
1913	16,923,223	15,531,643	+1,391,580
1914	13,344,769	14,771,576	−1,426,807
1915	12,054,915	12,824,935	−770,020
1916–17[a]	20,346,702	19,799,608	+547,094
1917–18[b]	13,240,470	15,099,504	−1,859,034
1918–19[c]	10,809,462	18,161,476	−7,352,014
1919[d]	13,602,630	17,243,627	−3,640,997
1920	25,539,248	23,238,789	+2,300,459

Source: Charles A. McQueen, "Colombian Public Finance," in BFDC, *Trade Information Bulletin* 417 (Washington, DC: Government Printing Office, 1926), 21.
[a]1 January 1916–28 February 1917
[b]1 March 1917–28 February 1918
[c]1 March 1918–28 February 1919
[d]1 March 1919–31 December 1919

a record high of 82 percent in 1918. Between 1912 and 1919 the average, although considerably lower than the 1918 high, was still an impressive 67.75 percent. During the war the British share of Colombian exports dropped significantly, from 18 percent in 1914 to under 1 percent by 1918. Naturally, all Colombia's exports to Germany ceased once Britain established its blockade of the Central Powers early in the war. The disruption of its trade forced Colombia to rely more and more heavily upon American markets. Its businessmen could survive during the war only as long as the United States continued to import Colombian products.

Colombia's economic dependence upon political maneuverings in Washington was demonstrated shortly after America's declaration of war against Germany in April 1917.[70] Within six months the U.S. Congress granted the president broad powers to regulate the import and export of goods.[71] Acting under that authority the president during wartime could exercise firm control over the quantity and type of products imported into, or exported from, the United States.[72] Shipping over 81 percent of its exports to the United States during the war meant that Colombia could be critically affected by any presidential proclamation limiting imports. During 1918, Bogotá, aware of Wilson's power, expressed deep concern over rumored restrictions or reductions on the importation into the United States of coffee, bananas, and hides, the three primary Colombian exports.[73] If President Wilson should embargo the importation of those items, Colombia's economy would collapse, placing its farmers and landowners in severe financial straits and stripping its coastal cities of their livelihood. The potential impact of this congressional act vividly demonstrated the extent of Colombia's economic dependence upon the United States.[74]

Even Wilson's restriction of American exports could gravely affect Colombia's treasury. At the turn of the century, Great Britain had been the major source for Colombian purchases; however, by 1911 and 1912 the United States was running a close second.[75] The German attack against France in August 1914, and the subsequent British declaration of war, altered that balance. While Britain continued to export items to Colombia, American exporters seized a golden opportunity and quickly cultivated the growing Colombian market, thereby almost doubling their share between 1914 and 1919, from 31 to 61 percent. As later statistics would demonstrate, the United States had permanently supplanted England as the major source of Colombian imports.[76] Thus, reduction of U.S. exports during the war would be disruptive to Colombian merchants as well as to the government.

Although Colombia's businessmen would survive a major cut in imports from abroad, its government would face a much bleaker future.

Table 4. Total Colombian Exports Including Gold, FOB (Col. $) and Percentages Sent to the United States, England, France, and Germany, 1912–19

		Percentage of Total Exports Sent to			
	Exports	*United States*	*England*	*France*	*Germany*
1912	32.221.746	49.14	13.58	1.94	5.75
1913	34.315.251	54.97	16.22	2.33	9.37
1914	32.632.884	55.97	18.00	1.40	5.45
1915	31.597.131	69.50	11.69	.80	–
1916	36.006.821	75.80	1.81	1.13	–
1917	36.739.882	81.65	1.91	1.22	–
1918	37.443.991	82.22	.71	2.04	–
1919	79.010.983	72.75	3.38	3.03	.27

Sources: For total Colombian exports see *Comercio Internacional de Colombia*, Boletín Numero 3 (Bogotá: Dirección General de Estadística, 1924). The percentages are based on Urrutia and Arrubla, *Estadísticas*, 121.

	Percentage of Coffee and Cattle Hides within Total Colombian Exports	
	Coffee	*Cattle Hides*
1912	52.07	8.26
1913	53.53	9.27
1914	49.34	8.29
1915	57.86	11.65
1916	44.86	11.13
1917	34.43	16.78
1918	55.21	7.98
1919	68.71	10.88

Sources: For coffee percentages see *Comercio Internacional de Colombia*, Boletín Numero 4 (Bogotá: Dirección General de Estadística, 1924); for cattle hides see ibid., Boletín Numero 3, 5. For slightly different percentages see Urrutia and Arrubla, *Estadísticas*, 208A.

Viewing the situation in 1917, or even 1918 before the armistice, the Concha and Suárez administrations could rightfully foresee a drastic reduction in imports. During 1914 and 1915 the national treasury had obtained 75 percent of all revenue from import duties and surtaxes.[77] If the bulk of imports declined, so, too, would government revenue. Again, Colombian officials were reminded how heavily their economy depended on the United States. They were aware that actions in Washington regulating exports and imports provided President Wilson a formidable grip on the people and government of their country.

Table 5. Total Colombian Exports of Coffee and Cattle Hides and Exports of Coffee and Cattle Hides to the United States, 1912–19

	(Colombian Data) Total Colombian Coffee Exports (lbs.)	*(U.S. Data) Colombian Coffee Exports to United States (lbs.)*	*Percentage*
1912	123,442,800	62,912,252	50.96
1913	134,993,300	89,684,514	66.44
1914	136,500,230	91,830,513	67.27
1915	149,247,670	111,077,449	74.42
1916	160,174,020	109,363,456	68.28
1917	138,517,770	93,638,012*	67.60*
1918	151,933,840	118,909,462	78.26
1919	222,723,020	150,483,853	67.57

*estimated

	Total Colombian Cattle Hides Exports (lbs.)	*Colombian Cattle Hides Exports to United States (lbs.)*	*Percentage*
1912	11,392,651	6,303,727	55.33
1913	11,540,194	5,461,505	47.33
1914	10,279,441	5,098,244	49.60
1915	14,182,577	8,385,292	59.12
1916	15,439,323	10,622,874	68.80
1917	17,425,971	14,789,299	84.87
1918	9,976,139	7,064,013	70.81
1919	20,595,183	12,878,893	62.53

Sources: For Colombian data see *Comercio Internacional de Colombia*, Boletín Numero 5 (Bogotá: Dirección General de Estadística, 1924). For U.S. data see U.S. Department of Commerce, *Foreign Commerce and Navigation of the United States, 1912–1919* (Washington, DC: Government Printing Office, 1913–20).

Ratification of the slightly modified Thomson-Urrutia Treaty, therefore, would not only remove a major cloud overshadowing amicable relations with the United States but also would provide Colombia with enough money to revitalize its economic life. Although the alterations were not ideal, they were politically feasible for Colombian leaders, unlike Lansing's abortive proposals in 1917.[78] Bogotá, for example, could cite only one aspect of the country's economic life to justify approval of the Polk modifications: its 5.5 million citizens inhabited an area larger than Texas, Oklahoma, Arkansas, and Louisiana combined, yet in 1917 only 743 miles of railroad existed throughout the entire republic, in which 65 to 70 percent of its population lived not

Table 6. Total Colombian Imports and Percentages Imported from England, France, Germany, and the United States, 1911–19

	Total Colombian Imports CIF (Col. $)	*Percentage of Total Imports Obtained from*			
		England	*France*	*Germany*	*United States*
1911	20.825.000	32.24	9.49	17.91	28.85
1912	27.560.000	32.71	8.40	17.53	31.76
1913	32.816.000	20.46	15.45	14.06	26.74
1914	24.126.000	30.25	5.91	12.25	30.92
1915	20.517.000	30.10	2.68	–	48.55
1916	34.109.000	26.97	3.03	–	52.26
1917	28.464.000	28.28	2.02	–	58.58
1918	25.050.000	26.57	1.15	–	53.06
1919	54.570.000	14.74	1.55	–	60.86

Source: Urrutia and Arrubla, *Estadísticas*, 128.

on the coast but in the interior.[79] National interest required remedies to the delay, frustration, and inconvenience created by such a system, but improvements were costly. Prostrated by its three-year civil war, Bogotá lacked the capital to undertake a large-scale railroad and highway construction program. The proposed $25 million indemnity under the modified Thomson-Urrutia Treaty, however, would enable the central government to begin that full-scale effort.[80] This fact, along with Colombia's economic dependence on the United States, could justify acceptance of the 1919 document.

By August all major obstacles blocking the passage of the revised treaty finally had been overcome. Senator Lodge and his colleagues were satisfied; they had eliminated completely the objectionable regret clause and had retained closer control over the large indemnity. Secretary Lansing had blundered badly by drafting a treaty that had pleased the Republicans but had antagonized the Colombian government. Recovering from that awkward position, he had initiated another joint effort, out of which had emerged the new mutually acceptable draft in which Bogotá would obtain favorable privileges in the use of the canal as well as receive the much-needed $25 million. After six years of effort, the unanimous support of the treaty in the Foreign Relations Committee almost assured eventual passage within the month.

Notes

[1]Article 5 of the treaty specifically stipulated that the document must be ratified in conformity with the laws of each nation. Ratification was governed in Colombia by the 1886 constitution, Article 76, subsection 20, and in the United States by Article 2, section 2, subsection 2 in its constitution.

[2]Woodrow Wilson, *Constitutional Government in the United States* (New York: Columbia University Press, 1908), 77–78. Arthur Link believes that these sentiments, although expressed in 1908, accurately portray Wilson's thinking during his presidency. See Link in Huthmacher, *Symposium*, 12–14.

[3]RG 59, SD 711.21/275. Also see Bryan to ALB, 2 May 1914, RG 59, SD 711.21/253A. Administration personnel may have become overconfident following the impressive Democratic sweep in the 1912 elections. For the first time in twenty years that party controlled both houses of Congress as well as the presidency.

[4]Submission of the treaty to the U.S. Senate in mid-June rated no mention in either the *Washington Post* or the *New York Times*.

[5]Stone to Roosevelt, 23 July 1914, Records of the U.S. Senate, RG 46, 64th Cong., National Archives.

[6]Roosevelt to Stone, 11 July 1914, Morison, *Letters of Roosevelt* 7:778–79. Also see RG 46: 64th Cong.

[7]Stone to Lansing, 8 August 1915, Robert Lansing Papers, vol. 12, General Correspondence, National Archives.

[8]Roosevelt to Stone, 11 July 1914, Morison, *Letters of Roosevelt* 7:778–79.

[9]Ibid. For other Roosevelt comments on a Colombian settlement see Roosevelt to William Roscoe Thayer, 2 July 1915, in Morison, *Letters of Roosevelt* 8:944–45; and Roosevelt editorial, "How the United States Acquired the Right to Dig the Panama Canal," *Outlook* 99 (7 October 1911): 314–18.

[10]Henry Cabot Lodge, *A Fighting Frigate and Other Essays and Addresses* (New York: Charles Scribner's Sons, 1902), 254–55. The entire essay on "The Treaty-Making Powers of the Senate," extends from page 219 to 256. Also see Lodge to Taft, 9 February 1905, Lodge Papers (1905). Lodge did not believe that the U.S. Constitution required the president to take senatorial advice during the negotiations. See Lodge to Emlen Hare Miller, 30 January 1919, PLP, I–Z, Lodge Papers (1919).

[11]Bryan to ALB, 24 September 1914, RG 59, SD 711.21/302.

[12]The current session of Congress would end on 24 October.

[13]5 September 1914, RG 59, SD 711.21/299a. Also see Stone to Bryan, 30 July 1914, and Stone to Reyes, 17 September 1914, RG 46, 64th Cong.

[14]Bryan to Wilson, 3 December 1914, series 2, box 121, Wilson Papers.

[15]Stone to Wilson, 24 February 1915, series 2, reel 68, ibid. The 63d Cong., 3d sess. met from 7 December 1914 to 3 March 1915. For additional correspondence discussing the treaty's status and opposition in the Senate see Bryan to Senator Willard Saulsbury, 12 January 1915, RG 46, 64th Cong.; Stone to Senator Claude Swanson, 14 January 1915, ibid.; Lodge to Roosevelt, 20 January 1915, TR, 1911–18, Lodge Papers; Bryan to ALB, 1 February 1915, RG 59, SD 711.21/310a; Wilson to Thad Thomson, 18 February 1915, RG 84: GC; Bryan to Wilson, 23 February 1915, Correspondence of Secretary of State Bryan with President Wilson, 1913–1915, T-841, roll 3, National Archives; Hannis Taylor to Stone, 23 February 1915, RG 46: 64th Cong.; and Senator James O'Gorman to Stone, 23 February 1915, RG 46: 64th Cong.

[16]The 64th Cong., 1st sess. convened 6 December 1915 and would continue until 8 September 1916.

[17]Bryan to ALB, 6 March 1915, RG 84: CR&S.

[18]Lansing to ALB, 2 February 1916, RG 59, SD 711.21/327.

[19]Lansing to Wilson, 26 January 1917, RG 59, SD 711.21/352-1/2. The Lansing letter was in reply to Wilson to Lansing, 23 January 1917 (711.21/352-1/2) in which the president wondered if there was any other way to secure passage of the treaty than addressing Congress directly.

[20]Lansing to Wilson, 6 February 1917, RG 59, SD 711.21/535. The secretary noted that Chief of Naval Operations Admiral William S. Benson agreed that settlement with Colombia would make canal defense far easier.

[21]Wilson to Stone, 17 February 1917, series 2, reel 86, Wilson Papers. For the senator's reply see Stone to Wilson, 20 February 1917, series 4, reel 297, ibid. Also see Stone's press release, 22 February 1917, in *FRUS, 1917*, 296–97.

[22]Lodge to Roosevelt, 22 February 1917, Lodge Papers (1917–19). Also see "Wilson's Attempt to Force Colombian Treaty Is Blocked," *New York Tribune*, 22 February 1917.

[23]Lansing to Stone, 28 February 1917, RG 46: 65th Cong. For earlier comments and reports on German activities in Colombia see 11 July 1915 memorandum by Lansing in Robert Lansing, *War Memoirs of Robert Lansing* (New York: Bobbs-Merrill Company, 1935), 19–20; Thomson to Wilson, 2 February 1916, RG 59, SD 711.21/331-1/2; Thomson to Lansing, 15 February 1916, RG 59, SD 711.21/332; Thomson to Lansing, 3 February 1916, RG 59, SD 711.21/355; Wilson to Lansing, 1 March 1916, RG 59, SD 711.21/333-1/2; Lansing's analysis of Latin America in early 1917, in *War Memoirs*, 308; and "New Fight to Pass Colombian Treaty," *New York Times*, 20 February 1917.

[24]Lansing to ALB, 28 February 1917, RG 84: CR&S.

[25]Stabler memorandum, 3 March 1917, RG 59, SD 711.21/361. This document, slightly revised, was then sent to the Senate.

[26]Secretary Lansing, in a letter to Wilson on 31 July 1915, had suggested a mutual regret clause, although no action was taken at that time. See RG 59, SD 711.21/328A.

[27]U.S. Congress, Senate, "Settlement of Differences with Colombia," Report 1, pt. 1, 65th Cong., special session, 14 March 1917. This report includes a majority opinion on changes in the treaty by committee Democrats, a concurring opinion by Philander C. Knox, and a dissenting opinion by the remaining Republicans.

[28]Knox to Taft, 20 May 1914, series 3, reel 140, Taft Papers. Also see Taft to Knox, 16 and 25 May 1914, vol. 20, Knox Papers.

[29]Lodge had not wanted the newly elected Knox on the Foreign Relations Committee, but his past service as senator and secretary of state made his appointment almost certain. As minority leader, Lodge feared that Knox would divide the Republicans on the Colombian treaty and thus permit its ratification. See Lodge to Roosevelt, 27 February 1917, TR, 1911–18, Lodge Papers. For Knox's ideas regarding the treaty see Knox to Lansing, 27 March 1917, box 29, Knox Papers.

[30]Lodge to Roosevelt, 12 March 1917, Lodge Papers (1917–19).

[31]Lodge to Roosevelt, 2 March 1917, TR, 1911–18, Lodge Papers.

[32]Ibid. Lodge to Roosevelt, 12 March 1917, Lodge Papers (1917–19); Lodge to Robert S. Hall, 17 March 1917, Lodge Papers (1917).

[33]Lodge to Roosevelt, 12 March 1917, Lodge Papers (1917–19).

[34]Ibid. Also see Roosevelt to Lodge, 13 March 1917, TR, 1911–18, Lodge Papers; Lodge to Roosevelt, 14 March 1917, Lodge Papers (1917–19); Lodge to Roosevelt, March 1917, ibid.; Roosevelt to Lodge, 18 March 1917, Lodge Papers (1911–18).

[35]The *New York Times* reported on 15 March 1917, in an article entitled "Claim 40 against Treaty," that Republican leaders had thirty-nine or forty senators pledged to defeat the Colombian document. The special session of Congress ended on 16 March; Congress would reconvene in regular session on 2 April 1917. The State Department and President Wilson discussed their explanation to Colombia for the postponement. See Polk to Wilson, 17 March 1917, and Wilson to Polk, 17 March 1917, in drawer 89, file 117, Wilson-Polk Correspondence, Frank Polk Papers, Sterling Memorial Library, Yale University. For the formal dispatch to Colombia see Lansing to ALB, 17 March 1917, RG 84: CR&S.

[36]Lansing to Wilson, 23 March 1917, RG 59, SD 711.21/354-1/2.

[37]Stone to Lansing, 17 March 1917, RG 59, SD 711.21/353-1/2.

[38]Lansing to Wilson, 18 March 1917, ibid. Wilson returned Lansing's letter the same day, granting conditional approval of Stone's suggestion. Lansing, in a letter to Wilson on 31 July 1915, had suggested a modification similar to Stone's new proposal. See RG 59, SD 711.21/328A.

[39]Phillips's memorandum to Lansing, 19 March 1917, RG 59, SD 711.21/354-1/2, details his conversation with Lodge on 18 March.

[40]Ibid. Roosevelt approved Lodge's proposal. See Roosevelt to Frank B. Kellogg, 21 March 1917, reel 6, frame 692, Frank B. Kellogg Papers, Library of Congress Manuscripts Division (hereafter cited as Kellogg Papers).

[41]For Lansing's draft see RG 59, SD 711.21/354-1/2. For Lansing's official meetings with senators on the treaty see Lansing Diary, 19 to 23 March 1917, box 65, Lansing Papers.

[42]RG 59, SD 711.21/354-1/2.

[43]The following three paragraphs are based on Lansing's draft treaty, in RG 59, SD 711.21/354-1/2.

[44]Ibid.

[45]Ibid. Lodge informed Roosevelt on 23 March 1917 that Lansing "has framed a treaty embodying all my amendments." See Lodge Papers (1917–19).

[46]Lansing draft, RG 59, SD 711.21/354-1/2.

[47]Neither island was large: San Andrés (12°30′N, 81°42′W), was 7 miles long, and Providencia (13°19′N, 81°23′W) was only 4 1/2 miles long. The United States had obtained a lease from Nicaragua in 1916 to its Great and Little Corn islands, which lay 55 miles off Nicaragua's Caribbean coast.

[48]Lansing draft, RG 59, SD 711.21/354-1/2.

[49]Wilson to Lansing, 24 March 1917, RG 59, SD 711.21/641.

[50]Jordan H. Stabler, head of the Division of Latin American Affairs, wrote a memorandum of the Polk-Betancourt meeting. See 24 March 1917, drawer 77, file 219, Polk Papers.

[51]Belden to Lansing, 24 March 1917, RG 59, SD 711.21/377. Also see Belden to Lansing, 24 March 1917, RG 59, SD 711.21/364.

[52]Belden to Lansing, 29 March 1917, RG 59, SD 711.21/378. Also see Belden to Lansing, 30 March 1917, RG 84: CR&S.

[53]Belden to Lansing, 31 March 1917, RG 59, SD 711.21/379.

[54]Lansing Diary, May 1917–February 1918, box 65, Lansing Papers.

[55]See Lansing Diary, 1918, box 65, Lansing Papers; memorandum on talk between Polk and Lodge, 6 March 1918, RG 59, SD 711.21/468; memorandum of Hoffman Philip conversation with Stone, 1 April 1918, RG 59, SD 711.21/549; memorandum of Philip conversation with Senator Swanson, 8 April 1918, box 24, "Colombian Treaty" folder, Lester Woolsey Papers, Library of Congress Manuscripts Division (hereafter cited as Woolsey Papers); Lansing to Hitchcock, 6 May 1918, RG 46: 65th Cong.; and memorandum on conversation between Lansing and Lodge, 27 August 1918, RG 59, SD 711.21/568. For communications regarding Suárez see Lansing to ALB, 16 March 1918, RG 84: CR&S; Belden to Lansing, 21 March 1918, ibid.; Polk to ALB, 5 June 1918, RG 59, SD 821.51/70a; Polk to Lansing, 31 July 1918, RG 59, SD 821.00/416; Lansing to ALB, 5 July 1918, RG 84: CR&S; Belden to Lansing, 29 July 1918, RG 59, SD 711.21/420; and Belden to Lansing, 15 August 1918, RG 59, SD 821.00/425.

[56]Memorandum on conversation between Lansing and Lodge, 27 August 1918, RG 59, SD 711.21/568; Philip memorandum to Polk, 10 October 1918, box 24, Woolsey Papers.

[57]Stabler memorandum on the meeting, 16 December 1918, drawer 77, file 219, Polk Papers. Also see Stabler memorandum on meeting with Colombian Minister Betancourt, 21 January 1919, drawer 77, file 220, Polk Papers. As early as March 1917, Betancourt had indicated that the indemnity would be used only for public works. However, at that time, Bogotá opposed modification of the regret clause. See Stabler memorandum on meeting with Colombian minister, 16 March 1917, drawer 77, file 219, Polk Papers; and Betancourt to Bryan, 23 March 1917, RG 59, SD 711.21/371.

[58]John Garraty argues that Lodge and Wilson had become personal enemies by the spring of 1915. See Garraty, *Henry Cabot Lodge*.

[59]Polk to ALB, 18 February 1919, RG 59, SD 711.21/445A.

[60]Polk Diary, 25 January 1919, drawer 88, file 13, Polk Papers. In approving the treaty, Lodge did not "betray" Roosevelt, who had died three weeks earlier on 6 January. Writing to the editor of the *Providence Journal* on 5 August 1919, Lodge noted that he and Roosevelt had worked together in seeking changes in the Colombian treaty: "I did nothing and took no step without his approbation. With the article of apology out, he was perfectly willing to let the treaty be ratified although he thought, as I think, that it is desirable for the future that we should have their recognition of the independence of Panama and should close this open sore." See PLP, I–Z, Lodge Papers (1919).

[61]Polk to ALB, 11 June 1919, RG 84: CR&S; Polk Diary, 12 June and 16 July 1919, drawer 88, file 16, Polk Papers. For additional information on the treaty's status see Polk to ALB, 3 March 1919, RG 84: CR&S; Polk Diary, 13 March, 29 May, and 6 and 23 June 1919, drawer 88, file 16, Polk Papers; Polk to Lodge, 19 May 1919, RG 46: 66th Cong.; Polk to ALB, 26 May 1919, RG 84: CR&S; and Polk to ALB, 7 June 1919, RG 59, SD 711.21/471. For an

examination of the Senate fight over the treaty see D. F. Fleming, *The United States and the League of Nations* (New York: Russell & Russell, 1968 [1932]).

[62]Colombian deliberations over the proposals, together with the adjournment of the U.S. Congress between 3 March and 19 May, account for the four-month delay.

[63]Lansing to ALB, 31 July 1919, RG 59, SD 711.21/478a. Also see "Lodge to Hasten Vote on Colombian Treaty," *New York Times*, 26 July 1919.

[64]For a fuller examination of the Suárez administration's view of U.S.-Colombian relations see Jorge Sanchez Camacho, *Marco Fidel Suárez: Biografiá* (Bucaramanga: Imprenta del Departamento, 1955); and Marco Fidel Suárez, *Obras: Sueños de Luciano Pulgar*, vol. 2 (Bogotá: Instituto Caro y Cuervo, 1966). Also see Philip to Lansing, 27 February 1919, RG 59, SD 711.21/448; and Uribe, *Colombia*, 222–25.

[65]To follow proposed changes in the treaty between March 1917 and February 1919 see, in addition to documents already cited in this chapter, Philip memorandum to Lansing proposing three alternative treaties, n.d., box 24, Woolsey Papers; comparison of Lansing, Knox, and Philip drafts, March 1917, box 29, Knox Papers; and a conversation with Senator Knox, 7 February 1918, RG 59, SD 711.21/561. These drafts reflect the opinion of a few key individuals on the entire treaty. For comments, section by section, from State Department officials, senators, and other interested parties see the twenty-seven-page document entitled "Colombian Treaty," in box 24, Woolsey Papers.

[66]See Commercial and Financial Statistics of the Principal Countries of the World, table in *Statistical Abstracts*, 1912–1919. The internal debt by 1918 was approximately $4.5 million (U.S.). See Belden to Lansing, 20 August 1918, RG 59, SD 810.51/880.

[67]See Table 3, National Revenue and Expenditures, p. 120. To convert pesos to dollars, use the yearly rates of exchange found in Urrutia and Arrubla, *Estadísticas*, Table 4, 158. Due to the dislocation of war, Colombian customs receipts declined precipitously between 1913 and 1915. See Wyndham to Foreign Office, 30 June 1916, F.O. 135/380-18, PRO.

[68]For a fuller discussion of Colombian finances and the need for the $25 million indemnity see Suárez, *Obras* 2. Also see Belden to Lansing, 21 December 1917, RG 59, SD 821.51/66; Belden to Lansing, 20 June 1918, RG 84: CR&S; and Philip to Lansing, 15 March 1919, RG 59, SD 711.21/455. For earlier comments on Colombian finances see Thomson to Knox, 29 August 1914, RG 59, SD 711.21/299; Thomson to Lansing, 26 January 1916, RG 84: CR&S; and Belden to Lansing, 24 March 1917, RG 59, SD 711.21/377. For British comments see Wyndham to Foreign Office, 11 June 1915 (F.O. 135/369-14), 13 February 1918 (F.O. 135/407-35), and 11 May 1918 (F.O. 135/407-26), PRO.

[69]See Tables 4 and 5, pp. 122–23.

[70]Colombian historian Jorge Sanchez Camacho believes that America's entry into war sparked a decline in U.S.-Colombian trade, helping to create an economic and fiscal crisis in Colombia. See Sanchez Camacho, *Suárez* 2:152.

[71]*Statutes at Large* 40, pt. 1 (1917–19), "An Act to Define, Regulate, and Punish Trading with the Enemy," 6 October 1917, chap. 106, 422–23; ibid.,

"An Act to Punish Acts of Interference with the . . . Foreign Commerce of the United States," 15 June 1917, chap. 30, 225.

[72]Examples of the president's power can be found in ibid., "An Act to Provide Further for the National Security," 5 October 1918, chap. 181, 1009–10; and ibid., pt. 2, presidential proclamations, 28 November 1917, pp. 1748–49, and 9 July 1917, pp. 1683–84.

[73]Colombian Minister C. A. Urueta to Lansing, 30 April 1918, RG 59, SD 611.216/2; Stabler memorandum re phone conversation with Betancourt, mid-1918, RG 59, SD 611.216/5.

[74]For an example of how the United States used such economic leverage see chap. 6 in this volume.

[75]See Table 6, p. 124.

[76]See Urrutia and Arrubla, *Estadísticas*, 117–18.

[77]McQueen, "Colombian Public Finance," 7–8. For the fiscal year 1913 the *South American Yearbook and Dictionary* (London: Louis Cassier Company, 1915) lists that percentage at 74.09 (p. 516). For more information on customs revenues see McQueen, "Colombian Public Finance," 27–32.

[78]See Suárez, *Obras* 2:1497–99.

[79]Bell, "Colombia: A Commercial and Industrial Handbook," 300. For additional information on Colombian railroad development see W. Rodney Long, "Railways of South America," in BFDC, *Trade Promotion Series* 39 (1927): 27–28; "Colombia: Commerce and Industries, 1922 and 1923," in BFDC, *Trade Information Bulletin* 223 (1924): 16–17; McQueen, "Colombian Public Finance," 32–35; and McGreevey, *Economic History of Colombia*. For the 1918 census by departments see Cruz Santos, *Economía*, 165.

[80]Suárez had long supported the use of the $25 million indemnity for railroad construction.

Chapter VI

The Ratification Process: Phase II*

From the perspective of one who in 1914 or 1919 had questioned U.S. hemispheric intent, the Thomson-Urrutia agreement, instead of heralding a dramatic new era between Colombia and the United States, could symbolize a less humanitarian, more selfish American motivation. It could be a ruse, a foot in the door. Wilson's moral rhetoric could simply camouflage the heretofore more aggressive American economic expansion characterized by the term "dollar diplomacy." It could provide the opening U.S. capital needed to exploit fully Colombia's potential investment and trade markets. Certainly the suspicious could cite the president's enthusiastic backing of America's foreign trade during his two terms in office as support for this interpretation. To understand better Wilson's motivations, it is first necessary to review his general economic policy and then to examine his specific actions toward Colombia.

The Wilson administration's growing economic awareness in 1913 and after was clearly reflected in its policy toward three areas vital to the nation's international commerce. Upon entering the White House, the former New Jersey governor quickly discovered that the United States not only lacked a large, efficient merchant marine capable of serving potential new customers, but it also lacked an international banking network that could finance a growing international trade. Furthermore, Wilson observed that federal law, by restricting industrial, banking, and exporting combinations, deprived the country of a diversified nationwide business community that could benefit from enlarging world markets. Acknowledging the desirability of expanding American exports, he and his administration advisers would attempt to alter or

*Excerpts from Richard L. Lael and Linda Killen, "The Pressure of Shortage: Platinum Policy and the Wilson Administration during World War I," *Business History Review* (Winter 1982): 545–58. Copyright by the president and fellows of Harvard College. Reprinted by permission.

eliminate each of these obstacles over the next few years. They would strive to establish a governmentally subsidized merchant marine and would struggle to reform the banking and antitrust laws, thereby freeing U.S. businessmen to pursue additional markets more actively and effectively.

The most obvious hindrance to America's economic expansion in 1913 was the absence of an effective, efficient merchant marine. Wilson had acknowledged that void as he addressed the enthusiastic Democratic convention that had chosen him as its presidential nominee. "Our industries have expanded to such a point that they will burst their jackets," he warned,

> if they cannot find a free outlet to the markets of the world; and they cannot find such an outlet unless they be given ships of their own to carry their goods—ships that will go the routes they want them to go—and prefer the interests of America in their sailing orders and their equipment. Our domestic markets no longer suffice. We need foreign markets.[1]

However, despite this emphasis as a nominee, Woodrow Wilson, as president, did not immediately pressure Congress to reconsider shipping subsidies. Not until the outbreak of war in Europe in August 1914 had crystalized the need for an American merchant fleet, was he ready to act. As the maritime powers redeployed their commercial vessels during this critical summer, normal trade routes were disrupted and American merchants discovered that they must rely on sporadic, unreliable foreign shipping to transport their products abroad. American ships offered little relief. Even operating at full capacity, the U.S. merchant fleet by 1915 still could carry only 11.8 percent of the country's waterborne exports and just 18.4 percent of its waterborne imports. American firms could muster a fleet totaling only 1.86 million gross tons capable of employment in foreign commerce. In comparison, Britain's merchant fleet in 1915–16 amounted to over 20 million gross tons, Germany's in 1914 to 4.8 million gross tons, and that of France in 1915 to 2.3 million gross tons. Even the small Scandinavian state of Norway maintained a merchant fleet larger than that of the United States, totaling 2 million gross tons in 1916.[2] Faced with the unpleasant reality that foreign ships held a stranglehold on American exports and imports, President Wilson reacted quickly.

Within weeks of Britain's declaration of war on Germany, the president had called two top-level conferences to discuss shipping.[3] To increase the merchant fleet, the administration approved the transfer of foreign ships to American registry and agreed to create a Bureau of

War Risk Insurance, which would guarantee insurability of merchant vessels willing to engage in international trade.[4] In addition, Wilson and his secretary of the treasury, William Gibbs McAdoo, urged support of a federally controlled corporation to purchase or construct merchant ships as needed. Ignoring an anticipated congressional attack that would characterize such a corporation as socialistic, the administration introduced a shipping bill into the House of Representatives on 24 August 1914. Two years later on 7 September 1916, following an intense political struggle in Congress, the bill finally received approval.[5] The people's representatives on Capitol Hill, while noting the deficiency in American shipping, had only reluctantly acknowledged the need for federal subsidies to construct a competitive merchant marine. However, once that decision had been made, governmental machinery moved rapidly. Within a few years the U.S. merchant fleet engaged in foreign commerce had mushroomed from the 1.9 million gross tons in 1914 to 11.1 million gross tons in 1921.[6]

The war in Europe offered American merchants an ideal opportunity to supplant their British and German rivals throughout the world, especially in nearby Latin America. As Secretary McAdoo once described the situation, "The South Americans were like customers of a store that had burned down; they were looking around for a place to spend their money."[7] To take permanent advantage of these new markets, the U.S. government would have to do more than increase the number of ships plying international waters; it also would have to adapt its banking system more closely to the needs of its businessmen and their Latin American customers.

The U.S. banking community was ill equipped to finance a growing trade with Latin America. Federal law not only prevented national banks from establishing foreign branches but also prohibited their use of acceptances, the most common method of conducting international business.[8] Facing these governmental restrictions, an American importer's bank had to operate through a major European banking house—usually a British firm—to arrange contracts with a Latin American exporter. For example, a U.S. firm, after contracting for a shipment of coffee from a Colombian dealer, would confer with his American banker to secure for him a letter of credit. Because federal law prohibited the issue of such a letter, that document had to be obtained from a London bank. The letter of credit simply notified the Colombian exporter that the London institution would guarantee payment for the coffee shipment at the end of an agreed-upon time, usually ninety days. If the Colombian merchant was unable to wait for full payment, he could readily sell the letter of credit at a discount to his local bank, which

Table 7. Value of U.S. Waterborne Imports and Exports of Merchandise, 1908–21

	Total Imports (millions of dollars)	*Percent Carried in U.S. Vessels*	*Total Exports (millions of dollars)*	*Percent Carried in U.S. Vessels*
1908	1123	13.54	1670	7.25
1909	1241	12.17	1481	7.29
1910	1467	10.02	1516	7.52
1911	1436	10.24	1774	7.55
1912	1551	11.03	1880	8.09
1913	1698	11.37	2075	9.06
1914	1738	11.45	2048	8.30
1915	1526	18.41	2466	11.80
1916	2157	24.66	4820	13.80
1917	2590	28.30	5403	17.51
1918	2577	27.82	5226	18.87
1919	3414	35.97	7090	36.61
1920	4731	42.02	7252	43.52
1921	2187	34.98	3888	36.06

Source: Based on Series Q 204–209, in *Historical Statistics of the United States: Colonial Times to 1957*, 452.

would hold it until the end of the ninety-day period and present it at that time to the London bank for redemption. During that three-month interval, the American importer should have received the coffee, sold it, paid his New York banker, who in turn would pay the London banker, who then could redeem the letter of credit held by the local Colombian bank.[9] When Wilson assumed the presidency, therefore, the financing of American commerce hinged on the European banking community acting as a middleman.

The absence of an extensive U.S. network of branch banks in South America placed American merchants at an additional disadvantage compared to their European counterparts. By 1915, Britain's financial institutions maintained seventy-nine branch banks in South America and Germany's, forty-four, but just one American branch existed south of Panama, and that established only in 1913.[10] Those scions of the European financial community could not only deal in acceptances but also could provide valuable information to businessmen in England or Germany. They could relay important credit information on potential customers, assist European merchants in the purchase or sale of merchandise, and report on investment opportunities that might appeal to European firms. Without similar branches, U.S. bankers and businessmen were forced to rely on information received from a native bank or from a European institution, neither of which placed U.S. interests above their own. That Americans lost financial and commercial opportunities to European competitors is therefore not surprising.

Committed to the expansion of foreign trade, as well as to the reduction of European preponderance in such areas as Latin America, the Wilson administration sought to eliminate these restrictions on the nation's banks. Within ten months of his inauguration, the president signed the Federal Reserve Act, which, although primarily aimed at restructuring the domestic banking of the United States, also revolutionized foreign banking activities.[11] For the first time, federally chartered banks could deal in acceptances. Those institutions having capital of over $1 million, upon approval by the newly created Federal Reserve Board, also could establish branches in foreign countries "for the furtherance of the foreign commerce of the United States." The financial logjam finally had been broken. American bankers now were legally equipped to handle international trade and finance more easily, which would prove particularly fortunate as the outbreak of a major world war in 1914 gradually shifted the center of international banking from Britain to the United States. Having already shaken off the legal fetters, an enthusiastic banking community was poised to take full advantage of these new circumstances. Between 1914 and 1920, for example, U.S. financial institutions established at least forty-seven branches throughout South America.[12]

If the Wilson administration hoped to extend American trade successfully and to utilize the war in Europe to best economic advantage, it needed to permit business consolidation and cooperation in foreign trade, in addition to the new shipping bill and the revised banking legislation. Concerned that large businesses would monopolize international trade by use of trusts, interlocking directorates, or combinations, the federal government, as early as 1890, had prohibited such cooperation among American exporters.[13] That concern, that skepticism of business motivation, persisted throughout the first two decades of the twentieth century. By 1916, however, the recently created Federal Trade Commission, whose job was to prevent unlawful and unfair methods of commercial competition, reconsidered the historic limitations on businesses engaged in foreign commerce. Its findings and recommendations reflected a new perception of the growing importance of expanding foreign markets.[14]

In addition to supporting the administration's pursuit of more ships and branch banks abroad, the commission recommended a revision of federal statutes to enable business cooperation and combination in the pursuit of overseas markets. Acting upon that recommendation, Congress approved in April 1919 the Webb-Pomerene Act, which legalized those combinations in foreign commerce that did not restrain trade within the United States or artificially inflate prices.[15] Similarly, Congress, between 1916 and 1919, revised the Federal Reserve Act to permit banks to cooperate closely in foreign banking activities.[16] This relaxation of stringent restrictions on corporations and banks removed the last of the major obstacles threatening to hinder a growing U.S. export-import economy.

The Wilson administration had proven that it was committed to freeing American businessmen from past restrictions and was committed to furthering economic competitiveness abroad.[17] Releasing businessmen from certain federal restrictions, however, did not symbolize unchecked federal support of their operations abroad, nor did it mean that the federal government would use its diplomatic and economic power to pressure foreign governments into signing contracts with them. Undersecretary of State Frank Polk expressed just these sentiments in a communiqué to Bogotá in January 1920. The United States, he reminded his legation, had never contemplated using the Thomson-Urrutia Treaty with its $25 million indemnity as leverage to pressure Colombia to grant contracts to U.S. nationals.[18] Neither had it supported, beyond normal diplomatic aid, nor opposed American firms attempting to secure concessions or contracts from the Colombian government. A commitment to commercial expansion, as envisioned by the president, was not synonymous with commercial exploitation. Wilson's support of such expansion did not violate, at least in his view, the noble sentiments he had expressed shortly upon assuming office.[19]

Not surprisingly, the economic objectives of the Wilson administration influenced discussions over the Colombian treaty. Rather than simply citing moral justifications for a settlement, treaty proponents frequently emphasized economic arguments. Among the papers of the 64th Congress, which considered the document from December 1915 to March 1917, for example, is an unsigned memorandum stressing the tangible economic nature of the agreement, while ignoring the more imprecise ethereal Wilsonian goals of justice, common interests, and honor. "So far it has been impossible for big American corporations to get important contracts in Colombia," the memorandum argued. "Ever since the Panama incident in 1903, the door has been shut against everything American, so that all the big contracts have gone to European firms; and the feeling and prejudice [are] so strong, that it [is] difficult even for American capital to find employment in Colombia." Reminiscent of the China market myth, the unknown author envisioned Colombia as a land of golden opportunity, with untold agricultural and mineral wealth just waiting for development by American firms and capital. Seemingly, the only obstacle preventing this utopian vision from becoming reality was the Senate's reluctance to ratify the Thomson-Urrutia Treaty. If the Senate failed, then aggressive British interests, upon conclusion of the present war, would capitalize on America's inaction.[20]

Similarly, Secretary of State Bryan had informed the Senate Foreign Relations Committee in January 1915 that failure to ratify the Colombian treaty would seriously disrupt America's economic expansion southward.[21] Reflecting that same concern in microcosm, Minister Thomson in Bogotá had warned one year later that it would be "most unlikely that any concession will be granted or any legislation enacted by the Colombian government favorable to the United States until the controversy between the two governments shall have been satisfactorily adjusted."[22] Postponement and delay in approving the treaty could only magnify these fears, not lessen them. Three years after Thomson's warning, for example, Captain J. P. Crawford, a military intelligence officer, was still cautioning Washington that failure to ratify the Thomson-Urrutia agreement could reduce American trade and investment in Colombia and at the same time reopen those markets to European investment capital. "The inference is clear," he said, "that as long as Colombia believes it has a grievance against the United States, English capital is more welcome than American. The British are aware of this condition of affairs and are taking full advantage of it."[23] Common to each of these observations, whether made in 1914, 1915, or 1919, were two interrelated factors. Not only would ratification help undermine any new British commercial ventures, but it also would create a more receptive atmosphere in which U.S. firms could pursue economic concessions in neighboring Latin American states, specifically Colombia.

Economic reasons alone, therefore, seemed to justify speedy ratification by the U.S. Senate, at least some important American corporations believed. In a letter to Vice President Thomas Marshall in 1917, twenty-seven New York businesses, including banks, exporting companies, and industrial firms, urged approval of the Thomson-Urrutia document. "The continued delay in the approval of this treaty," they wrote, "has given rise to misunderstanding and misinterpretation of American motives through the Latin Republics, and retards the development of American commerce with Colombia which is one of the richest countries in South America and offers a splendid field for our business enterprise."[24] Washington needed to act. As administration officials realized, delay could jeopardize both Wilson's wider vision and the more materialistic prospect of profitable new markets in Colombia and its sister republics. Delay could only increase the uneasiness of an already skeptical Latin America.

The German decision in February 1918 to knock Russia out of the war by plunging deep into its heartland paved the way, ironically, for the first tangible test of Wilsonian moral rhetoric matched against important economic considerations as applied to Colombia. Within weeks of the initial assault, the victorious German columns, opposed by tired, disorganized, and dispirited Russian troops, penetrated to within 100 miles of Petrograd in the north and relentlessly swept through the rich Ukraine in the south. With the vanguard of the opposing armies pushing past Rostov, the Bolshevik government sued for peace. With the fateful treaty of Brest-Litovsk, signed on 3 March 1918, the Russians withdrew from the Allied ranks. One reverberation of that military collapse and withdrawal focused Washington's attention on Colombia. In defeating Russia, the Germans had unknowingly deprived the United States of its major supplier of platinum, a most strategic material vital to the war effort.[25] Unless Russia reentered the war, the United States would have to turn to its secondary supplier, Colombia, to obtain this resource for its commercial and military needs.

The military intelligence section of the U.S. General Staff had foreseen just such a possibility. Even before the final German assault, it had submitted a report to Counselor Leland Harrison in the State Department, "analyzing the platinum situation," which, it noted, "may be of interest in connection with the treatment of Colombian affairs."[26] Citing the military and domestic value of platinum, the report revealed that current needs already exceeded available supplies. If Russia were defeated and its exports curtailed or halted, "we must turn to Colombia and establish such relations that a continuance of current production and exploration will be assured, and that new capital will feel warranted in further developing Colombian production."[27] The War Department was worried that a critical shortage of platinum would restrict America's war effort. Reflecting that concern, two months later it would sanction an unorthodox secret mission to Russia aimed at securing, by any means necessary, all available platinum in that politically and militarily divided country.[28]

Even before the receipt of the military intelligence report, the State Department had been aware of the importance of platinum production in Colombia. As early as mid-April 1917, it had advised the Bogotá legation to give all practical assistance to an American firm that was then trying to mine platinum commercially in Colombia.[29] Such action coincided with the dispatch of letters to diplomatic and consular officials throughout that southern republic, stressing the increasing importance of a secure platinum supply and urging that they prevent, whenever possible, "any diversion of the supply . . . to other countries."[30] As Colombian output during the fall of 1917 increased significantly, such a policy appeared to be working.[31] However, aside from those verbal warnings, the United States undertook no positive action to secure Colombia's stocks. Only after Russia's collapse in early 1918, did Washington reconsider its position toward Colombian platinum.

Reacting to the January military intelligence report, Second Assistant Secretary of State Alvey Adee informed the Council of National Defense on 11 February that "the Department believes that the stimulation of platinum production in Colombia by American business interests is of great importance from a military as well as from a political standpoint."[32] The State Department, therefore, would further encourage efforts to expand production and exportation of that valuable mineral to the United States. By urging both Colombian and American firms to greater efforts, the department hoped to offset the Russian losses. However, by mid-1918 disquieting news questioning the permanent availability of Colombia's stocks reached Secretary Lansing.

Washington's recent curtailment of shipping tonnage to Colombia, sparked by its own wartime needs, had evidently rankled. Rumors indicated that the Colombian Congress might establish a governmental monopoly of platinum "in order to enable it to obtain from the United States the tonnage desired by [the] Colombian Government for exportation."[33] Reacting to the threatened curtailment of platinum exportation, Washington ordered Hoffman Philip (the new U.S. minister to Bogotá) to confer immediately with the minister for foreign affairs. You can inform him, Polk noted,

> that if the Colombian Government executes the authorization in this act . . . [it] would undoubtedly have a vital bearing upon the action which the War Trade Board and the Shipping Board might feel compelled to assume in respect to matters concerning exportation and importation from and to Colombia. You will impress upon the Minister for Foreign Affairs the gravity of the situation and express earnest hope that his Government will take no action which would prevent the Government of the United States from receiving the supply of platinum which is required.[34]

Given the already delicate relations with Colombia, State Department officials hoped a verbal warning would deter passage of any such legislation.

On the other hand, it was clear that more decisive measures might eventually have to be taken to assure the flow of platinum from Colombian mines. Those same State Department officials, therefore, listened attentively as a group of businessmen, represented by Earl Harding, presented an ambitious plan to develop fully Colombia's platinum resources.[35] The private group hoped to establish an American trading

Table 8. Colombian-U.S. Platinum Trade, 1913–18

	Colombian Exports to the United States			*Total U.S. Imports*			*Percentage of Colombian Supply in Relation to U.S. Imports*
Fiscal Year	*Unmfged. Troy oz.*	*Mfged. Troy oz.*	*Total*	*Unmfged.*	*Mfged.*	*Total*	
1913	10,461		10,461	49,972	70,771	120,743	8.66
1914	12,387		12,387	40,634	54,189	94,823	13.06
1915	13,121	480	13,601	26,334	14,204	40,538	32.37
1916	25,588	—	25,588	76,011	13,645	89,656	28.54
1917	21,071	207	21,278	23,689	6,418	30,107	70,67
1918	25,365	1,665	27,030	48,745	3,117	51,862	52.18
1917 (1 Jul.– 31 Dec.)	11,951	231	12,182	13,294	1,443	14,737	82.66

Source: U.S. Department of Commerce, *Foreign Commerce and Navigation of the United States, 1913–1918.*

corporation in Colombia for this purpose while, at the same time, wresting its control from German and Turkish interests. To obtain both objectives, American investors needed the cooperation of the U.S. government, particularly the wartime agencies that regulated shipping and international commerce. If those agencies would grant the necessary licenses, the American firm could initiate regular shipping routes between New York and Colombia. That shipping, Harding emphasized, "would be made the basis for negotiating a concession for the exclusive right in Colombia to exploit platinum from Government lands." While stimulating platinum production, the private firm could not only investigate additional business and investment opportunities available to American capital but also could attempt to influence governmental officials to enter the war on the Allied side.[36] This rather tantalizing five-point program stirred the State Department's interest, even though, contrary to Wilson's earlier statements, it would foster a monopolistic concession and would be achieved by using shipping to Colombia as a lever to force Bogotá to grant the necessary platinum concessions. The exigencies of war took precedence over peacetime rhetoric.

Normally the State Department could have acted upon Harding's proposal without interdepartmental consultation. However, since the recently created War Industries Board now coordinated acquisition of such war-related products, he was referred to that authority.[37] Emerging out of their conference with Harding, the board's personnel expressed interest in his platinum proposals. Writing to the State Department shortly thereafter, C. H. Comer, head of the War Industries Board's platinum section, suggested that State coordinate an interdepartmental conference to discuss those proposals in more detail.[38] Officials in State's Latin American Bureau reacted quickly, and within days they had contacted the interested governmental agencies and had scheduled a conference for 30 July.[39]

The representatives of the State Department, the War Industries Board, the War Trade Board, and the War Department who attended that conference were well aware of the strategic value of Colombian platinum. Only four months earlier the War Industries Board had established a platinum section devoted to the study of all aspects of supply and demand for the scarce mineral.[40] Its staff, examining statistics for fiscal year 1917, would have known that Colombia already provided approximately 70 percent of America's platinum imports.[41] Furthermore, a report completed in January 1918 by the War Industries Board's personnel had emphasized the potential shortage of platinum supplies, estimating that the United States would need over 22,000 ounces for commercial use and over 39,000 ounces for governmental requirements in 1918 alone.[42] Even allowing for stringent cutbacks, the board had projected in July that the United States would still need a minimum of 36,000 ounces for essential uses during the next year.[43]

As past statistics revealed, Colombia had never produced that much platinum during a twelve-month period.[44] Likewise, the War Trade Board was aware of the unique importance of platinum. Acting upon the War Industries Board study, the War Trade Board had decreed in March that all platinum imported into the country under governmental licenses had to be sold to the federal government at an established price.[45] Only if federal authorities declined to purchase the mineral would importers be permitted to sell to private customers. Therefore, each of the four agencies represented at the meeting to consider Harding's proposal already had been impressed with Colombia's importance as a platinum supplier.

Two alternatives emerged from the interdepartmental discussion.[46] The federal government could seek a formal agreement with Bogotá by which it would increase shipping allocations to that nation in exchange for a guaranteed continuous supply of platinum, or the United States could bypass the central Colombian government and "strongly encourage" a private American concern, such as that proposed by Harding, to acquire and mine platinum through the competitive private sector. Believing that federal officials in Bogotá were too weak to uphold any promise assuring a steady flow of platinum to the United States, no matter how sincere, the assembled representatives leaned toward support of a private American firm acting within

Table 9. U.S. Platinum Requirements, 1918

Commercial Requirements	
Chemical industry	12,000.00 oz.
Dental industry	—
Electrical industry	10,142.06
Total	22,142.06 oz.
Government Requirements	
Airplane construction	1,658.94 oz.
Trucks, tractors	1,587.98
Sulfuric acid	26,000.00
Nitrogen fixation	8,000.00
Army	2,293.50
Navy	47.20
Total	39,587.62 oz.

Source: War Industries Board, *Final Report*, 477.

Colombia. However, at this meeting they were unwilling to commit themselves irrevocably. Instead, they decided to withhold any final decision until State Department officials could meet informally with Colombian Minister C. A. Urueta in Washington and assess the possible response by Bogotá to a hypothetical formal agreement.

The ensuing informal discussion between the two governments did not prove productive. Colombia's leaders were displeased with the War Trade Board's decision in June to establish stringent import restrictions on hides, which, next to coffee, was the nation's major export. Arguing that the critical lack of shipping forced the curtailments, the board had limited South American hide imports to 57,000 tons. Of that total, Colombia could ship only 400 tons to U.S. markets. To add insult to injury, the board also had ruled that, unless hides contracted for prior to 15 June—the date the order went into effect—had physically arrived in the United States, they would be counted as part of each nation's new tonnage allocation.[47] Probably in belated response to America's wartime commercial restrictions, exemplified by this War Trade Board announcement, the Colombian Congress in mid-September granted President Suárez the authority "to tax, to regulate and to restrict the exportation of gold and other metals of national production [including platinum], and to obtain from one country reciprocal and transitory commercial concessions [to] facilitate the interchange of the national products and the merchandise needed for internal consumption."[48]

Had those powers been delegated in early 1918, rather than in September, a confrontation between Bogotá and Washington would have been almost assured. However, no such confrontation developed in the fall of 1918. German peace feelers in October, coupled with the signing of an armistice in early November, removed the pressure and tension surrounding the platinum issue. By December the wartime demand for the heretofore scarce and valuable mineral had declined sufficiently to enable federal officials to remove all restrictions governing its importation and exportation. At approximately the same time, Washington also decided to lift similar restrictions on the importation of hides.[49] Having resolved the platinum crisis, Colombia and the United States could now continue discussions over modifications to the Thomson-Urrutia Treaty in a more amicable atmosphere.

The platinum incident had demonstrated that under Wilson's leadership there could be exceptions in policy to earlier well-intentioned rhetoric opposing monopolistic concessions in Caribbean states gained by the use of U.S. economic and diplomatic leverage. The realities of war had forced Washington officials to abandon peacetime visions temporarily and revert to methods they had criticized in the past. Just how far the American government would have assisted Harding's private corporation is unclear since the armistice removed the need for federal action. Washington officials, however, had given serious consideration to that five-point program, including the "exclusive right" proviso.

The economic muscle of the United States evident in the platinum crisis and the hides curtailment no doubt helped convince Bogotá to accept Acting Secretary Polk's alterations of the Thomson-Urrutia Treaty in February 1919.[50] When it had agreed to those modifications and the Senate Foreign Relations Committee, now controlled by Republicans, had indicated approval, ratification seemed assured. Therefore, on 4 August 1919, as the Senate committee reported favorably on the treaty, both the Wilson and Suárez administrations eagerly awaited rapid approval. In Colombia that enthusiasm quickly turned to surprise, shock, and apprehension when Senator Lodge and fellow committee members unexpectedly withdrew their support on 7 August, and the full Senate, only seventy-two hours after receiving a favorable report, agreed by voice vote to submit the document to further study.[51] As in 1909 and 1913 the prevailing optimism had been shattered by an unexpected complication.

Senator Lodge's recommitment request on 7 August had been in response to a recent Colombian petroleum decree that supervised oil exploration and asserted federal authority over subsoil rights.[52] Addressing his senatorial colleagues, the Massachusetts legislator warned that the decree "would amount, probably, if enforced, to a confiscation of private property in oil," and therefore "the committee feels that the matter should be examined with care before taking up the treaty."[53] Colombian officials had chosen the worst possible psychological and tactical moment to affirm federal control over subsoil rights on national and private lands. By stressing petroleum and subsoil regulations in mid-1919, they had propelled their nation into a much wider debate, a debate that emphasized the increasing demand and diminishing supply of petroleum resources within the United States and that focused special attention on petroleum exploration and development abroad.[54]

For almost two decades American leaders had acknowledged the need for an effective navy to be used not only for protection but also for economic and territorial expansion. The brief war with Spain in 1898 had proven the value of such a fighting force. The Latin American policies of Roosevelt, Taft, and Wilson, particularly those affecting the Caribbean region, likewise hinged on U.S. squadrons to discourage further European expansion; to supervise unstable republics; and, as canal construction progressed, to guard the isthmian passage. As the

U.S. Navy grew in prestige and power, as its responsibilities extended from the Philippines in the southern Pacific to Cuba and Puerto Rico in the Caribbean, greater emphasis fell on technological innovations that could transform the fleets into even stronger, more effective fighting units.[55]

Prior to 1903 the fleets of the world had burned coal, but that product proved difficult both to load and to store. Furthermore, ships using coal were susceptible to the threat of spontaneous coal dust fires. Therefore, world attention shifted to Great Britain, where in 1903 Sir John Fisher, first sea lord of the Royal Navy, launched a vigorous campaign to convert the already preeminent British fleet from coal to oil. Despite tenacious opposition, the first phase of the conversion had been completed by 1908, when all British torpedo boats burned the new fuel. No sooner had these smaller vessels been refitted than the Admiralty began converting its destroyers.[56]

Civilian and naval officials in Washington were skeptical of such a radical departure in naval propulsion. Nevertheless, by 1910 they too had decided to equip all new destroyers and submarines with oil-burning engines.[57] Battleships, the backbone of the fleet, still would use coal as their primary fuel, but they would be equipped to burn oil as an auxiliary propellant. Not until 1913, under the aggressive leadership of Josephus Daniels, did the Navy Department authorize construction of the newest American dreadnought—the U.S.S. *Nevada*—as the first oil-burning capital ship.[58] Within one year of that decision, the department had committed itself to the construction of an oil-powered fleet, from the smallest gunboat and tender to the largest dreadnought. Secretary Daniels and most of his subordinates had determined that oil was cleaner, safer, and more efficient than coal, and that an oil-burning ship could steam farther and faster with less risk to personnel.[59]

Although efficiency, speed, and range had convinced Daniels that oil power was preferable, he initially had had doubts about supply. Only after Secretary of the Interior Charles Wollcott and Director of the U.S. Geological Survey David T. Day assured him that supplies would be available for at least another twenty years—the expected life of a dreadnought—did Daniels finally agree to conversion for capital ships.[60] By 1915 the navy was burning over 521,000 barrels of fuel oil per year, and by the next year that figure had jumped to over 842,000 barrels.[61] As more and more ships were refitted, future consumption could legitimately be expected to soar. In 1915, for example, capital ships consumed little oil; only nine of America's thirty-six battleships even had the ability to burn oil as an auxiliary fuel. Not one of the fifty-three cruisers in its fleet could use oil. Although more destroyers had converted to oil than any other class of ship, twenty-one of those fifty-six vessels burned only coal.[62] Complete conversion of that class alone would emphasize the significance of adequate and secure petroleum reserves. However, in 1916, Congress further elevated petroleum's importance as it authorized a three-year naval construction program which, when completed, would add to the fleet ten new battleships, sixteen cruisers, fifty destroyers, sixty-seven submarines, and thirteen other auxiliary ships, all to be powered by fuel oil.[63] As Secretary Daniels emphasized in his annual report in 1916, now more than ever "the securing of an adequate supply of oil for the future is a matter of prime importance to the Navy."[64] Few could disagree.

Aside from the navy's needs for petroleum, governmental officials could view with concern the dependence of other military and private sectors upon petroleum products. Paralleling the changing methods of naval power, automobiles, trucks, and buses marked a new era in land transportation. The automotive industry sold a mere 4,192 cars in 1900, but by 1919 dealers across the country had sold over 1.6 million horseless carriages. Add that total to the 6 million already on the nation's highways and motor vehicles consumed over 65 million barrels—2,747,030,000 gallons—of fuel per year.[65] With cars becoming more and more popular, that figure could certainly be expected to rise. In fact, figures for 1920 revealed that consumption had soared from 65 million barrels per year in 1919 to a new high of 82 million barrels.[66] Furthermore, as governmental leaders watched the bloody conflict in western France, they were impressed with the additional long-range need for petroleum products. Motorized transport was proving more effective in supplying troops, tanks were demonstrating their great military potential, and airplanes were revealing that they were useful adjuncts of a progressive military force. Without fuel, these new weapons and support units would be ineffectual.[67]

Prior to 1916 few had expressed anxiety about a continuous supply of crude oil available from American fields. Politicians and oilmen could proudly announce that the United States had produced annually since 1907 over 60 percent of the world's crude petroleum.[68] In 1916, however, that smugness received a ringing blow. For the first time in the twentieth century, Americans consumed more than they produced.[69] During 1916, 1917, and 1918, Washington officials discovered that they must look to other nations for additional petroleum supplies, realizing that stocks of reserve crude oil in the United States had declined over 42 million barrels between 1915 and 1918. Even more impressive, they noted that, in terms of the nation's requirements, those stocks represented in 1918 a 3.5-month supply, compared to a 7.2-month supply in 1915 and an 8.4-month supply in 1909.[70]

Table 10. U.S. Crude Oil Production, 1914–19

	(000,000 gallons)					
	1914	1915	1916	1917	1918	1919
Marked Production	11,162	11,806	12,632	14,083	14,949	15,854
Deliveries to Consumers (domestic crude oil)	10,375	10,874	12,689	14,770	15,970	15,606
Exports	215	158	172	172	206	249
Imports	710	762	873	1,265	1,585	2,215

Source: Based on U.S. Federal Trade Commission, *Advance in the Price of Petroleum Products* (Washington, DC: Government Printing Office, 1920), 19, 26, 27.

Table 11. U.S. Crude Oil Stocks, 1909–20

Year	(000,000 barrels) Stocks at End of the Year	Number of Months Supply Represented by the Stocks
1920	134	3.0
1919	128	3.7
1918	122	3.5
1917	146	4.7
1916	162	6.1
1915	164	7.2
1914	142	6.5
1913	123	5.7
1912	123	6.2
1911	137	7.8
1910	131	8.2
1909	117	8.4

Source: Joseph E. Pogue, *The Economics of Petroleum* (New York: John Wiley & Sons, 1921), 62.

While those Washington officials had no reason to fear an immediate shortage of petroleum products for ships, automobiles, tanks, or aircraft during the war, they became more receptive to disquieting reports questioning America's future petroleum reserves. An early Cassandra, David Day, had warned in 1909 of the depletion of American oil resources, estimating that between 10 and 24.5 billion barrels of oil were still recoverable from domestic fields.[71] In 1915, Ralph Arnold, a respected petroleum engineer, revised Day's estimates.[72] The United

States, he admonished, did not have a 24-billion or even a 10-billion barrel supply of oil remaining. Indeed, Arnold calculated that only 5.763 billion barrels remained, which, if exploited fully, would be depleted by 1937.

Within one year of that most pessimistic projection, the Department of the Interior, issuing its own forecast, estimated future American supplies at 7.4 billion barrels.[73] Three years later, in early 1919, David White, chief geologist for the Geological Survey, considering new drilling techniques and data, projected a reserve falling between 6.74 and 8 billion barrels.[74] Assuming petroleum consumption leveled off at the 1918 level of 380 million barrels, and assuming no external assistance, those reserves would be depleted between 1937 and 1940. White warned that, "barring unexpected good fortune in the search for new supplies, or even less unexpected curtailment of consumption, the petroleum production of the United States is likely not only never again wholly to meet our requirements but even to start soon on the long decline of a waning output."[75] The diplomatic implication of this declining supply had not been overlooked by State Department personnel. Undersecretary of State Polk assured Mark Requa, head of the Oil Division of the U.S. Fuel Administration, in July 1918 that State was "watching the situation carefully."[76] In view of pessimistic estimates about domestic production, the department realized that foreign supplies of crude oil had grown dramatically in significance.

Data would have revealed to both the State Department and the Fuel Administration the phenomenal increase in importation of foreign crude oil between 1910 and 1918. American companies in 1910 had imported only 571,000 barrels of all petroleum products.[77] By 1918 importation of crude oil alone had hit 37 million barrels, an increase of over 6 million barrels from the previous year. During the next twelve months, both agencies would watch as crude oil imports soared to a record high of 52,747,000 barrels. Equally important from the perspective of the State Department, one country—Mexico—supplied most of the available foreign crude: 99.74% in 1917, 99.95% in 1918, and 99.84% in 1919.[78]

As petroleum imports rose, American officials expressed greater interest in worldwide petroleum legislation, specifically in Mexico. Unfortunately, relations with that southern neighbor had deteriorated under the Wilson administration. American troops had intervened at Veracruz in 1914 and two years later, in a separate incident, flagrantly had chased the bandit Pancho Villa deep inside Mexico, almost precipitating a war between the two countries. Not until February 1917 had the last U.S. forces withdrawn. No sooner had these crises passed than on 10 April 1917 the American ambassador in Mexico, Henry P.

Fletcher, reported that the Carranza government might be planning to prohibit the future exportation of petroleum.[79] Secretary of State Lansing immediately counseled the president: "If there is an attempt to prevent the shipment of oil from Tampico, I see no way but to occupy the territory with troops or else to allow the British naval forces to do so, even though it would be a technical violation of the Monroe Doctrine."[80] Although concerned over such rumors, Wilson was unwilling to sanction a third American intervention.[81] Within two weeks of his decision, the Carranza government, acting under the new federal constitution, claimed national ownership of subsoil rights, but it was still unsure of the ramifications of that control. Mexico's fluctuating interpretation of that constitutional proviso during the next three years made Washington officials extremely sensitive to any foreign legislation that affected subsoil rights.[82]

Ignoring America's anxiety over Mexican legislation, Colombia announced its own regulations governing petroleum exploration and ownership of subsoil rights. Two days prior to Lodge's startling recommitment request on 7 August, he had received a telephone call from a disturbed Secretary Lansing explaining the potential implications of the new Colombian decree.[83] Sharing that uneasiness, both the senator and his colleagues on the Foreign Relations Committee considered delay in ratification the wisest possible course. Writing to Bogotá on 9 August, Secretary Lansing explained the Senate's decision to recommit the Thomson-Urrutia Treaty. "The action of the Senate," he wrote,

> was taken because uncertainty exists as to the motives and definite purposes of the Colombian Government with respect to the nationalization, or retroactive application of the principle of nationalization, of oil lands.
>
> Neither the Department nor Congress desire in the slightest degree to interfere with the sovereign rights of Colombia in the disposition of her public lands, mines, or other property.
>
> It is simply desired to make it plain that the interests of American citizens, in any property of whatsoever kind, acquired without notice of limitations or reservations, in good faith, must be protected by Colombia.[84]

Four days later the legation received further explanation of the Senate's action. That august body, the communiqué reported,

> feared that Mexico would be heartened by Colombia's attitude and would be more persistent in forcing her plan of nationalization of oil lands on the ground that it was justifiable as proven by Colombia's action. . . . If Colombia enforces nationalization we must expect other Latin American countries to follow suit and this should be averted.[85]

The State Department wanted to avoid the confiscation of legitimately acquired American investments as well as avoid precedent-setting legislation which other southern republics might utilize. For those reasons it had instructed Minister Hoffman Philip to meet with Colombian officials and discuss an additional amendment to the already modified Thomson-Urrutia Treaty that would safeguard U.S. petroleum contracts signed prior to the issuance of the 20 June decree.[86]

The Colombian proclamation unintentionally unified the State Department and the Republican-controlled Foreign Relations Committee. Their past differences over an acceptable treaty were forgotten, and, during the ensuing months, both groups would work as a unit, often jointly framing important communiqués to Bogotá. That is especially remarkable since, at the same time, President Wilson and Senate Democrats were in a vicious struggle with Senator Lodge and his Republican colleagues over approval of the Versailles Treaty. Secretary Lansing, alienated from Wilson by their disagreement over the League of Nations, did not hesitate to work with the president's political enemies to formulate an acceptable Colombian policy.[87] Preoccupied with the League controversy in August and September 1919, Wilson had no choice but to leave matters completely under Lansing's control. Had the president not suffered a stroke in late September, he might have replaced Lansing and personally supervised the negotiations, but as it was he had no direct impact after June 1919. The State Department and the Foreign Relations Committee, not the president, now controlled policymaking toward Colombia.

Colombian Foreign Minister Hernando Holguín y Caro and Minister for Public Works Carmelo Arango, after conferring with a congressional committee on 14 August, informally reported to Philip that Lansing's proposed petroleum amendment altering the treaty was unacceptable.[88] The desired assurances might be given, they indicated, in a separate protocol. However, not until 19 August did the legation receive Colombia's formal response, which had been formulated in discussions between President Suárez, his cabinet, and congressional representatives. Writing for the administration, the Colombian foreign minister reiterated his earlier informal statement to Philip: a petroleum amendment to the treaty would be impossible. In fact, he argued, an amendment was altogether unnecessary since the government had just suspended the decree. Furthermore, he added,

> my Government is disposed to give to the Government of Washington full guarantees relative to the rights of American citizens in Colombia, rights which like those of all foreigners are guaranteed by us in the same way as are the rights of our own nationals. My Government desires that the Government of Washington shall not have the least doubt about this point.[89]

Colombian officials hoped this statement would reassure their nervous counterparts in Washington.

According to the Bogotá government, no radical, antiforeign legislation had been intended in announcing the decree. Observing Mexico's petroleum legislation, it had simply realized the potential national importance of its own subsoil deposits, which could provide badly needed revenue. To foster exploration and define the legal rights of the nation, departments, and property owners, President Suárez therefore had sought to clarify existing law.[90] This was particularly vital in the summer of 1919, as Minister Arango was in the midst of important negotiations with the American-based Tropical Oil Company.[91] The 20 June proclamation, however, had been aimed as much at Colombian citizens as at foreigners. Neither group had systematically advised federal officials on their exploratory or exploitative activities. To guard national interests and assure maximum production, the Suárez administration had believed that it needed to monitor those developments, and the presidential decree had given it the authority to do so. That short proclamation had been intended only as an interim measure; it would temporarily regulate petroleum development until the Colombian Congress, which would convene in late July, could fully discuss and enact more acceptable legislation.[92] In restating a controversial ninety-year-old statute that vested control over mining properties in the state, the decree had focused national attention on the lack of comprehensive petroleum regulation. That, coupled with immediate temporary supervision of petroleum development, had been the government's goal.

Suárez's decision to rescind the petroleum regulations is less clear. In early August the U.S. linkage of those regulations with the Thomson-Urrutia Treaty forced the Colombian president to reconsider the decree in direct relation with the anticipated, and now jeopardized, $25 million indemnity. In addition, Suárez increasingly realized that many Colombians disliked his action. Even the "friendly" newspaper *El Nuevo Tiempo* had carried articles critical of his government's failure in the decree to respect previously acquired private property rights.[93] Other newspapers, such as *El Tiempo*, were even more condemnatory. However, despite public expressions of dissatisfaction with petroleum regulations, many critics favored the measure provided that it adequately protected private property rights and did not discourage individual economic initiative. However, there were those who disliked any efforts at regulation. One argued, for example, that the decree had been an effort by Bogotá to benefit economically at the last minute from the labors of private citizens who had worked for years to foster petroleum exploration and to secure petroleum contracts.[94] Another critic charged that the decree merely reflected a xenophobic attitude of a minority who "[see] in every citizen who speaks English, a possible Roosevelt."[95] Therefore, by mid-August, with Congress in session, with opposition in both the public and legislative sectors to government ownership of subsoil deposits in private property, and with American discontent, Suárez was quite willing to rescind his controversial decree. After all, he expected a new and more comprehensive measure to emerge out of current congressional deliberations, one that was more sensitive to private property rights.

The basic attitude in Washington regarding a written amendment, or protocol, guaranteeing America's contracts acquired prior to 20 June remained unchanged despite suspension of the decree. "It is felt," Secretary Lansing wrote, "that [the] Colombian treaty will likely remain in Committee until [the] purpose of [the] Colombian Government respecting property rights in question is defined in [a] binding agreement."[96] Minister Philip, who believed that the Colombian statement of 19 August had broken the impasse, was puzzled by this latest telegram; Washington evidently had ignored his recent reports altogether. One week earlier he had cabled his superiors that he was

> assured that the government is endeavoring to bring about legislation which will at the same time amply protect its future interests and offer encouragement to foreign capital and, [he added,] to delay action upon the treaty in the belief that this would influence legislation to favor American petroleum interests, in my respectful opinion would be a lamentable mistake and in all probability would have the contrary effect.[97]

He even had exceeded discretion. Disturbed at Washington's mental density and discouraged that his counsel was being ignored, Philip again had complained on 15 August that departmental policy seemed too narrow and was aimed at supporting American petroleum interests to the detriment of cultivating Colombia's goodwill.[98] Rapid ratification of the Thomson-Urrutia document, not delay, he noted, should govern the State Department's position.

Washington officials knew that the resident minister in Bogotá was disenchanted with their policies. As a result, Secretary Lansing attempted to explain senatorial and departmental actions in its recent handling of the Colombian episode. In light of the Mexican troubles, he began,

> it is but natural that this Government should look with grave concern upon an effort by Colombia or any other Latin American country to adopt a nationalization policy, injurious to American citizens, similar to that now being attempted by Mexico, against the retroactive application of which our Government has repeatedly protested. The disposition of the Senate Committee therefore

> was to make its position clear, not offensively so, but with sufficient definiteness to remove the slightest doubt as to such position.[99]

Lansing did not inform Philip that the head of State's Latin American section also wanted to use this incident to obtain passage in Colombia of "an ideal law with respect to subsoil rights." If this were accomplished, Boaz Long advised, "Colombia's lead might be followed by other Latin American Governments."[100] The American minister understood this departmental logic only after receiving a communiqué one week later that contained just such a protocol.[101]

Before Minister Philip could discuss this new proposal in detail with Colombian officials, Attorney General Ramón Diago urged the Supreme Court to declare unconstitutional the 20 June decree as a violation of property owners' rights.[102] Shortly thereafter, Philip felt justified in reporting that Suárez is "really desirous of promoting closer relations with the United States and that he is not intent upon any policy directly inimical to American interests."[103] Despite the president's amicable expressions, however, hostility persisted in other sectors toward American demands for a separate protocol.

> The unfavorable effect upon the country at large of the action of the Senate of the United States in withholding its vote upon the treaty, the subsequent report of a demand by the United States for further amendment of the treaty to provide for the protection of American oil interests, combined with the violent accusation by the press against the United States have produced a very detrimental state of affairs for American business interests for the time being.[104]

Articles in *El Nuevo Tiempo* in August and September 1919 fully supported Philip's conclusion. Time and again columns condemned U.S. linkage of the treaty and the petroleum decree.[105] In one petition to the legislative chambers in early October, over two hundred eighty women in Bogotá urged that the Thomson-Urrutia Treaty be withdrawn from consideration if the only alternative was to add new clauses that would compromise their country's liberty and independence.[106] Reflecting such popular resentment, as well as its own reservations, the Colombian Senate, in open session on 2 October, unanimously professed

> profound regret that it has been said in the Senate of the United States that Colombia must ratify the obligations contracted by her with the world to always respect rights acquired by foreign citizens. . . . The political institution of the Nation as a civilized people guarantees these rights, our public law has always guaranteed them.[107]

For the American government to insist on written verification of those guarantees would be a slap at the nation's honor. Concluding its pronouncement, the Senate declared "the firmness with which the Nation maintains and will maintain, now and forever, for its honor, respect for the rights of all foreigners."[108] Three days later the State Department learned that Colombia completely rejected the idea of either a special amendment or a protocol that would guarantee foreign rights.[109] Although the Americans had been given a verbal reprimand by the Colombian Senate, they also had received a public commitment to "respect the rights of all foreigners." That assurance, Colombian officials believed, would have to suffice.

The State Department, however, had no plans to slacken its efforts toward a written agreement. Responding to the October declaration, it insisted that the United States neither sought exclusive privileges for Americans in Colombia nor to legislate national policy over lands within the public domain. But it did prefer a written pledge prohibiting the imposition of limitations on U.S. contracts and land titles by ex post facto legislation.[110] Unfortunately, as State's astute Alvey Adee observed in early November, the American government's insistence on a written guarantee had unintentionally transformed the subsoil protocol into an ultimatum that the Colombians, in good conscience, could hardly accept.[111]

The U.S.-Colombian impasse over a written guarantee began to crack on 21 November 1919 when the Colombian Supreme Court ruled that the most questionable sections of the suspended June decree were unconstitutional. The Bogotá government did not have the authority, the justices announced, "to limit in any way the right of the private owner to develop the mines situated in his lands."[112] Five days later President Suárez formally annulled the entire proclamation.[113]

State Department officials were pleased with the court's ruling, but they decided to await the outcome of pending petroleum legislation in the Colombian Congress before urging the U.S. Senate to approve the Thomson-Urrutia Treaty.[114] Not until mid-February 1920 did the department receive a complete copy of that legislation. Conferring with the Bureau of Mines, State immediately scrutinized the new petroleum law,[115] finally deciding that the regulation did not discriminate against Americans, nor "invade vested rights of individuals relative to subsoil deposits."[116] The Colombian government, it concluded, had acted in good faith, and the United States should not further delay ratification of the treaty.

Action by the Foreign Relations Subcommittee, chaired by Senator Albert B. Fall, was essential before the treaty could again be moved to the Senate docket. Detained by congressional business away from Washington, the New Mexico senator learned of the State Department's altered position and of the recent Colombian legislation only on 18 May.[117] Withholding immediate judgment, Fall examined the Colombian law during the following week. Consequently, he and his subcommittee withdrew their objections to the modified treaty.[118] On 3 June the full Senate Foreign Relations Committee urged approval of the Thomson-Urrutia agreement, based on its subcommittee's favorable report.[119] Since Congress planned to adjourn two days later, the treaty could come before the Senate no earlier than 6 December, the scheduled opening date for its third congressional session.

During the intervening six months the national electorate overwhelmingly chose Republican Senator Warren G. Harding as its twenty-fourth president. Perhaps the impressive victory, along with the knowledge that a Republican would be inaugurated on 4 March 1921, made Republican members of the Foreign Relations Committee reluctant to push the Thomson-Urrutia Treaty in the waning days of the Wilson administration.[120] Or, perhaps, Senators Lodge and Fall, aware of underlying discontent within the Senate and elsewhere regarding approval of an agreement that might appear to mar national honor, were still unprepared for a final vote.[121] Whatever the reasons for inaction, Senator Fall informed Secretary of State Bainbridge Colby on 22 February that the treaty would not be considered until after Harding's inauguration. However, the senator added, "I have suggested to the President-elect that if he should call the Colombian treaty matter to the attention of the special session of the Senate [to begin March 4] . . . the treaty would doubtless be ratified in a few days."[122]

Senator Lodge also was cautiously confident of ratification. He had gathered sufficient votes for passage in August 1919 before the unexpected petroleum complication, and he should be able to do it again. Citing his close personal friendship with President Theodore Roosevelt and his eight-year struggle to shape the original Thomson-Urrutia Treaty into an acceptable document, he should be successful in convincing his colleagues that the treaty did not criticize Roosevelt's actions in 1903, or question America's honor. When trying to persuade undecided senators to give approval, economic arguments also could prove effective. In that respect, Lodge could refer doubtful colleagues to the succinct arguments presented by Secretary Colby on 2 March at a gathering of the Southern Commercial Congress in Washington.

> This country can never hope to build the fair structure of cordial and trustful relationships with the people of South America unless we overcome the suspicion of us which lurks in many places, as well as the fear of us, which I regret to say is apparent in some quarters.
>
> Our delay in ratifying the Treaty with Colombia has been most unfortunate. . . . From the single standpoint of our commercial progress in South America, the delayed ratification of the treaty

> is not only an unmixed calamity but an immeasurable one. . . . Wherever Spanish is spoken, our delay in this matter has cost us friends, confidence and commercial opportunity. It has worked automatically to the benefit of our competitors, who have not been slow to take advantage of it. It has caused us to be represented to the Latin American mind as indifferent to justice, willing to be ruthless, aspiring to physical domination and therefore, to be shunned, curbed and resisted. If one were to undertake to estimate the effect upon our trade, upon our commercial position in South America and upon our commercial prospects, of this lamentable policy of delay and postponement, it would make the proposed indemnification of Colombia seem like an inconsiderable sum.[123]

Lodge could not have phrased it better himself.

Consideration of the modified Thomson-Urrutia Treaty was delayed until 12 April, the first full workday of the new 67th Congress. As Senator Lodge initiated discussion on that morning, eight years had elapsed since the signing of the original agreement in 1913. Given the treaty's controversial history, the final debates proved anticlimactic, and, after little more than a week, the Senate voted 69 to 19 to grant the long-awaited approval.[124]

A noticeable lack of enthusiasm characterized Colombia's reaction to the Senate's decision. Two days after the treaty had been submitted to the Colombian Senate, a perceptive Minister Philip observed: "Although I judge that the Colombian Government and Congress may purposely avoid hasty action in approving the treaty, from motives of pride and desire not to be eager in the acceptance of it, yet, from what I learn here, the undoubted intention is to approve it."[125] Acceptance of the treaty would formally acknowledge the loss of Panama and thereby publicly emphasize Colombia's past failure. Neither the special economic advantages obtained in the treaty nor the large monetary indemnity could eradicate that fact. While the treaty would be beneficial in the long run, the Colombian legislature did not have to embrace it with enthusiasm, just accept it. As Philip had foreseen, neither legislative chamber rushed toward final approval. Only after submitting the document to careful study did the Senate vote for ratification on 13 October.[126] House action took even longer, as its deliberations were interrupted by the unexpected resignation of President Suárez stemming from domestic political discord. Only after it had helped select an interim president did the House reconsider the treaty, but by late December it too had voted for ratification.[127] Two months later, on 1 March 1922, the final formal act in a long, exasperating treaty-making process drew to a close as representatives of the two governments exchanged ratifications.

Eight years earlier Woodrow Wilson had entered office seeking a new age in hemispheric relations, an age in which the United States would become a guide and a friend to its southern neighbors, not a selfish, manipulative oppressor. While the economic health of the nation required the continued pursuit of foreign markets, future expansion, Wilson had asserted, would be conducted along nonexploitative, mutually beneficial lines. Twice, however, during the ensuing Colombian negotiations, military and economic considerations outweighed the president's "new era" rhetoric. Concerned with a continuing supply of platinum in the summer of 1918, Washington had flexed its economic muscle to affect Colombia's policy. While the United States could properly reallocate shipping and restrict its imports and exports according to wartime necessity, a similar Colombian effort to regulate platinum exportation had met with hostility, disapproval, and threatened retaliation from Washington.

Within months of that incident, a second, potentially more damaging, crisis had developed. In August 1919, the Wilson administration again had expressed displeasure with Colombia's domestic legislation. This time a presidential regulatory decree supervising petroleum production on public and private lands had raised Washington's ire. In response, American officials had decided to withhold approval of the Thomson-Urrutia agreement until such time as Colombia's petroleum legislation proved satisfactory. Such action, along with the earlier platinum episode, revealed that, although the Wilson administration sought to establish a new hemispheric age, it retained the right to interfere in neighboring republics whenever it considered that its vital national interests were at stake.

Notes

[1]Wilson address, 7 August 1912, Ray Stannard Baker and William E. Dodd, eds., *The Public Papers of Woodrow Wilson: College and State*, 2:471–72; Wilson address at Nashville, 24 February 1912, ibid., 408.

[2]U.S. Federal Trade Commission, *Report on Cooperation in American Export Trade, Part I* (Washington, DC: Government Printing Office, 1916), 29–32. See Table 6, p. 124.

[3]William Gibbs McAdoo, *Crowded Years: The Reminiscences of William Gibbs McAdoo* (Boston: Houghton Mifflin Company, 1931), 296, 304.

[4]Baker, *Life and Letters* 5:111, 112, 135.

[5]*Statutes at Large* 39, pt. 1, "An Act to Establish a United States Shipping Board," 7 September 1916, chap. 451, 728–38. For discussion of the ship subsidy struggle see McAdoo, *Crowded Years*, 294–316; John J. Broesamle, *William Gibbs McAdoo: A Passion for Change, 1863–1917* (Port Washington: Kennikat

Press, 1973), chap. 11; and Jeffrey Safford, *Wilsonian Maritime Diplomacy, 1913–1921* (New Brunswick: Rutgers University Press, 1978).

For administration awareness of the need for ships see Wilson address at Baltimore, 25 September 1916, Baker and Dodd, *Public Papers: The New Democracy* 2:319; Wilson to Stone, 28 March 1916, series 2, reel 78, Wilson Papers; McAdoo to Wilson, 9 October 1915, reel 73, ibid.; McAdoo to Charles Gold, 1 August 1915, reel 72, ibid.; Wilson address, 8 January 1915, Baker and Dodd, *Public Papers: The New Democracy* 1:241–42; Wilson to Congress, 8 December 1914, ibid., 220; and Wilson address at Nashville, 24 February 1912, Baker and Dodd, *Public Papers: College and State* 2:408–9. For an examination of world aid to shipping see Grosvenor M. Jones, "Government Aid to Merchant Shipping: Study of Subsidies, Subventions, and Other Forms of State Aid in Principal Countries of the World," in BFDC, *Special Agent Series* 119 (Washington, DC: Government Printing Office, 1925 [1916]).

[6]U.S. Bureau of the Census, *Historical Statistics of the United States: Colonial Times to 1957* (Washington, DC: Government Printing Office, 1960), 444. For a more detailed examination of activities of the U.S. Shipping Board see its four annual reports, 1917–20, published by the Government Printing Office. See Table 7, p. 134.

[7]McAdoo, *Crowded Years*, 351.

[8]An acceptance is the letter of credit/bill of exchange system described in the remainder of this paragraph. Also see Frank M. Tamagna and Parker B. Willis, "United States Banking Organizations Abroad," *Federal Reserve Bulletin* 42 (December 1956): 1284–95; and Robert Solomon and Frank M. Tamagna, "Bankers' Acceptance Financing in the United States," ibid. 41 (May 1955): 482–94. National banks could not establish branches abroad, but state banks and banking corporations could. By 1913, twenty-three branches operated abroad, mostly in Europe. See Clyde William Phelps, *The Foreign Expansion of American Banks: American Branch Banking Abroad* (New York: Ronald Press Company, 1927), 131–62; Tulchin, *The Aftermath of War*; and Paul Abrahams, *The Foreign Expansion of American Finance and Its Relationship to the Foreign Economic Policies of the United States, 1907–1921* (New York: Arno Press, 1976).

[9]Based on Phelps, *American Banks*; Frederick I. Kent, "Financing Our Foreign Trade," *The Annals of the American Academy of Political and Social Science* 36 (1910): 492–501; and "Long Credits and the New Banking Act," *Bulletin of the Pan American Union* 40 (January–June 1915): 492–94.

[10]William H. Lough, "Banking Opportunities in South America," in BFDC, *Special Agent Series* 106 (Washington, DC: Government Printing Office, 1915) 30, 46; Phelps, *American Banks*, 132–61.

[11]*Statutes at Large* 38, pt. 1, "Federal Reserve Act," 23 December 1913, chap. 6, 251–75. As early as February 1912, Wilson had commented upon the failure of the banking system to cope adequately with foreign trade. See Wilson address at Nashville, 24 February 1912, Baker and Dodd, *Public Papers: College and State* 2:408–9.

[12]Phelps, *American Banks*, 132–61. In their enthusiasm, American banks had entered new markets without sufficient preliminary investigation. As a

result, fifteen of their branches had failed by 1922, and three years later nineteen others were sold to the Royal Bank of Canada. For information on American branch operations in Colombia see ibid.; and Bell, "Colombia: A Commercial and Industrial Handbook," 333.

[13]*Statutes at Large* 26, "An Act to Protect Trade," 2 July 1890, chap. 647, 209–10. For additional restrictive legislation see ibid. 38, pt. 1, "An Act to Create a Federal Trade Commission," 26 September 1914, chap. 311, 717–24; and ibid., "An Act to Supplement Existing Laws against Unlawful Restraints," 15 October 1914, chap. 323, 730–40.

[14]FTC, *Report on Cooperation in American Trade*, pts. 1 and 2. Part one contains the commission's findings and recommendations; part two includes excerpts from its hearings as well as the results of its survey of manufacturers. For Wilson's attitude toward business combinations see his acceptance speech, 7 August 1912, Baker and Dodd, *Public Papers: College and State* 2:464; address at Nashville, 24 February 1912, ibid., 410–11; address to Grain Dealers Association, 25 September 1916, Baker and Dodd, *Public Papers: The New Democracy* 2:318–19; and his State of the Union message, 5 December 1916, series 7B, reel 479, Wilson Papers.

The State Department's foreign trade adviser had urged modification of the anticommerce laws regulating foreign commercial ventures in 1914. Robert F. Rose to Bryan, 15 September 1914, RG 59, SD 610.11/18. Rose's recommendations were forwarded to Wilson by Bryan on 23 September 1914. See series 2, reel 63, Wilson Papers. Commerce Secretary William Redfield also supported a new law. Redfield to Wilson, 3 February 1915, reel 68, ibid.

[15]*Statutes at Large* 40, pt. 1, "An Act to Promote Trade," 10 April 1918, chap. 50, 516–18.

[16]See ibid. 39, pt. 1, "An Act to Amend . . . Federal Reserve Act," 7 September 1916, chap. 461, 755; ibid. 41, pt. 1, "An Act Amending . . . Federal Reserve Act," 17 September 1919, chap. 60, 286; and ibid., "An Act to Amend . . . Federal Reserve Act, 24 December 1919, chap. 18, 378.

[17]For an overview of America's increased economic awareness see Parrini, *Heir to Empire*. In addition to altering legislative barriers, the Wilson administration instituted a series of Pan-American financial conferences to facilitate trade, establish uniform trading laws, and create a spirit of mutual interest and friendship between leading governmental and business leaders of the participating countries. Furthermore, the BFDC of the Commerce Department assumed an ever-increasing role in stimulating international commerce and keeping both government and business posted on available foreign economic opportunities.

[18]Polk to ALB, 24 January 1920, RG 59, SD 711.21/524.

[19]For those sentiments see chap. 4 in this volume.

[20]This memorandum, found in RG 46: 64th Cong., was written between 8 and 16 June 1917.

[21]Bryan quoted in *New York Times*, "Root Attacks Treaty," 14 January 1915. Four years later his successor, Robert Lansing, relayed similar fears to the Senate. See Lansing to Lodge, 24 July 1919, RG 46: 64th Cong. Actually the Lansing letter conveyed the words of Minister Philip in Bogotá, but in

transmission the State Department approved its sentiments. For the original see Philip to Lansing, 15 July 1919, RG 84: CR&S.

[22]Thomson to Lansing, 26 January 1916, RG 59, SD 711.21/334. For additional examples that ratification would aid American penetration in Colombia see DuBois to Knox, 30 September 1912, RG 59, SD 711.21/119; Long memorandum to Lansing, 30 November 1915, RG 59, SD 710.11/261; Belden to Lansing, 29 March 1917, RG 59, SD 821.51/57; and Philip to Lansing, 3 June 1919, RG 84: CR&S.

[23]Crawford to director of Military Intelligence, 27 February 1919, Records of the War Department General and Special Staffs, RG 165, 2317-A-8, National Archives. Too closely tied to the United States, Colombia's actions did not jeopardize commercial and financial ties with its northern neighbor as Bryan, Thomson, and Crawford had feared.

[24]New York firms to Marshall, 27 January 1917, RG 46: 65th Cong. The list included Ingersoll-Rand, Ford Motor Company, W. R. Grace and Company, Westinghouse Electric Export Company, and American Locomotive Sales Corp. Senator Stone informed Secretary McAdoo on 20 January 1915 (RG 46: 64th Cong.) that the Foreign Relations Committee had received a petition from New York export houses favoring the Thomson-Urrutia Treaty, but the names of the firms were not attached. However, McAdoo told Stone on 25 January (RG 46: 64th Cong.) that the names were of "highly reputable and reliable business houses in New York." Lodge indicated that the Senate was under "immense pressure from lobbyists" and from the "big financial interests in New York" urging ratification. See Lodge to Roosevelt, 16 March 1917, TR, 1917–19, Lodge Papers. Also see sixty-nine New York merchants to Stone, submitted to the 65th Cong., special session on 14 March 1917, to accompany Executive H., 63d Cong., 2d sess.

[25]Platinum was used in cable amplifiers, dentistry, airplane construction, in the production of sulfuric acid, and in the fixation of nitrogen. Platinum ranked second in a "List of Strategic Raw Materials for Which the United States is Dependent Entirely or in Part upon Foreign Countries." That list, although undated, probably originated in the Economic Liaison Committee on 4 June 1919. See Records of the Office of the Economic Adviser (ROEA), RG 59, box 2, National Archives.

[26]R. H. Van Deman (chief, Military Intelligence Section of the General Staff) to Harrison, 9 January 1918, RG 59, SD 711.21/644.

[27]Ibid.

[28]Secretary of Commerce Redfield relates the Russian adventure in William C. Redfield, *With Congress and Cabinet* (Garden City, NY: Doubleday, Page & Company, 1924), 190–204. For a fuller discussion of U.S. policy toward Russia relating to platinum see Richard L. Lael and Linda Killen, "The Pressure of Shortage: Platinum Policy and the Wilson Administration during World War I," *Business History Review* 56 (Winter 1982): 545–58.

[29]Polk to Belden, 17 April 1917, RG 59, SD 821.6343/1. The State Department had taken this action upon the recommendation of Redfield. See Redfield to Lansing, 10 April 1917, RG 59, SD 821.6343/1.

[30]Wilbur Carr to Consul Claude Guyant at Barranquilla, 2 May 1917, Carr to Consul Alphonse Lespinasse at Cartagena, 2 May 1917, and Polk to Belden, 24 April 1917, all in RG 59, SD 821.6343/2.

[31]U.S. Department of Commerce, *Foreign Commerce and Navigation of the United States, 1917* (Washington, DC: Government Printing Office, 1918), 220–21. See Table 8, p. 140.

[32]See RG 59, SD 812.6343/14A. The council responded, noting its complete willingness to cooperate with State in this matter. See L. L. Summers to Adee, 15 February 1918, RG 59, SD 821.6343/15.

[33]Rumor reached State from a source other than the Bogotá legation. See Lansing to ALB, 3 June 1918, RG 59, SD 611.216/2A.

[34]Polk to ALB, 17 July 1918, RG 84: CR&S. A similar warning had accompanied the earlier 3 June 1918 telegram to Bogotá, but it had been for the minister's information only.

[35]Untitled memorandum, July 1918, RG 59, SD 821.6343/33. Harding had made an earlier preliminary probe. See 4 June 1918 memorandum, RG 59, SD 821.6343/24.

[36]Ibid. Both the Concha and Suárez administrations favored neutrality during World War I. See Sanchez Camacho, *Suárez*, 133–36. Harding was not the first to propose using shipping as a lever. Concerned that Colombia was too anti-American, the U.S. chargé, Perry Belden, suggested in March 1918 that perhaps withdrawal of Allied shipping from Colombia would help alter Colombia's attitude. Lansing rejected the suggestion. See Belden to Lansing, 5 March 1918, and Lansing to Belden, 16 March 1918, RG 84: CR&S. Also see Wyndham to Foreign Office, 5 March 1918, and Foreign Office to Wyndham, 9 March 1918, F.O. 371/3191-42630, 90097, PRO.

[37]F. Mayer, Latin American Division, memorandum on talk with Harding, 20 July 1918, RG 59, SD 821.6343/32. The War Industries Board had been established on 28 July 1917 but had become an independent agency only in May 1918.

[38]Comer to Stabler, 23 July 1918, RG 59, SD 821.6343/31.

[39]The foreign trade adviser had approved the idea of the meeting. See Office of the Foreign Trade Adviser to Stabler, 25 July 1918, RG 59, SD 821.6343/33. Also see Representative Henry T. Rainey to Polk, 26 July 1918, RG 59, SD 821.6343/29.

[40]U.S. War Industries Board, *Munitions Industry: Final Report of the Chairman of the United States War Industries Board, 1919* (Washington, DC: Government Printing Office, 1935), 468.

[41]*Foreign Commerce and Navigation of the United States, 1917*, 220–21.

[42]*Final Report, WIB*, 477. Also see Table 9, p. 142. In November 1917 the U.S. government attempted to purchase 10,000 ounces of platinum from Great Britain. The British, however, also faced a shortage and were instituting their own conservation measures. See British embassy, Washington to Foreign Office, 6 November 1917, F.O. 115/2302-p. 5; J. J. Broderick to P. C. Anderson, 10 December 1917, F.O. 115/2302-p. 32; Broderick to Anderson, 10 January 1918, F.O. 115/2302-p. 38; and Summers to Anderson, 7 December 1917, F.O. 115/2302-p. 34, PRO.

[43]*Final Report, WIB*, 463.

[44]See Table 8, p. 140.

[45]*Final Report, WIB*, 463. The War Trade Board's licensing power was so extensive, one State Department official could not resist an unofficial comment on a departmental memorandum. Adee wrote that "a telegram today calls upon somebody to exhibit evidence of birth. He might exhibit his navel." An equally serious notation at the bottom read: "License required by W.T.B.?"

[46]Mayer memorandum on the conference, 31 July 1918, RG 59, SD 611.216/22. Also see Polk to Rainey, 2 August 1918, RG 59, SD 821.6343/29.

[47]U.S. War Trade Board, *Report of the War Trade Board* (Washington, DC: Government Printing Office, 1920), 390. For its hide proclamation of 15 June see *War Trade Board Journal*, no. 11 (July 1918): 20. Also see Colombian Minister Urueta to Lansing, 8 October 1918, RG 59, SD 611.216/17; and Lansing to Urueta, 20 October, ibid.

[48]Belden to Lansing, 13 September 1918, RG 59, SD 611.216/12.

[49]Restrictions on platinum were lifted on 12 December 1918; those on hides on 7 January 1919. See *WTB Report*, 393.

[50]See chap. 5 in this volume.

[51]*Congressional Record* 58, pt. 4: 3668.

[52]Decree No. 1255B, 20 June 1919, RG 59, SD 821.6363/51. Lodge immediately appointed a three-man subcommittee, headed by Senator Albert B. Fall, to examine the new petroleum legislation and to coordinate committee efforts with the State Department.

[53]*Congressional Record* 58, pt. 4: 3668.

[54]See John A. DeNovo, "The Movement for an Aggressive American Oil Policy Abroad, 1918–1920," *American Historical Review* 61 (1955–56): 854–76; idem, "Petroleum and the United States Navy before World War I," *Mississippi Valley Historical Review* 41 (1954–55): 641–56; J. Leonard Bates, *The Origins of Teapot Dome: Progressives, Parties, and Petroleum, 1909–1921* (Urbana: University of Illinois Press, 1963); Gerald D. Nash, *United States Oil Policy, 1890–1964* (Pittsburgh: University of Pittsburgh Press, 1968); Cronon, *Daniels Diaries*; Daniels, *Wilson Era*; Tulchin, *Aftermath of War*; and U.S. Department of the Navy, *Annual Reports of the Secretary of the Navy, 1913–1918*. As the military importance of petroleum increased, the government, in a series of politically controversial withdrawals, placed large blocks of oil land under federal control. Initially, 4 million acres were withdrawn in 1909; by 1914 that had increased to 4.6 million acres, by 1917 to 6.3 million, and by 1920 to 6.8 million. See U.S. Geological Survey, *Annual Reports of the Director, 1909–1920*. Also see Secretary of the Interior Franklin K. Lane to Wilson enclosing "Draft of Report of Fuel Oil Supply," 2 September 1919, series 2, reel 104, Wilson Papers; and a petroleum report by the Economic Liaison Committee, 11 July 1919, box 2, ROEA.

For a sample of business fears of nationalization see twenty-two oil companies to Senator Furnifold Simmons, 8 December 1919, RG 59, SD 812.6363/598; and Association of American Producers of Petroleum in Mexico to Lansing, 13 December 1919, RG 59, SD 812.6363/608.

[55]The growing importance of the navy is reflected in congressional authorizations for new ships between 1904 and 1915 which included twenty battleships, five cruisers, seventy submarines, twenty-nine torpedo-boat destroyers, thirty-two destroyers, and twenty-six lesser craft. See *Report of the Sec. Navy, 1916*, 92–93. For a comparison of the U.S. naval expenditures between 1900 and 1915 with those of other world powers see Office of Naval Intelligence Report, 12 December 1914, in George Von Lengerke Meyer Papers, box 20, August–December 1914 folder, Massachusetts Historical Society (hereafter cited as Meyer Papers).

[56]Frederick C. Gerretson, *History of the Royal Dutch* (Leiden: E. J. Brill, 1958 [1957]), 4:250; Leonard Mosley, *Power Play: The Tumultuous World of Middle East Oil, 1890–1973* (London: Weidenfeld & Nicolson, 1973), 11, 12.

[57]*Report of the Sec. Navy, 1910*, 23.

[58]Daniels, *Wilson Era*, 368.

[59]Ibid. Also see *Report of the Sec. Navy, 1914*, 13; *1916*, 34; and DeNovo, "Petroleum before World War I," 648.

[60]Daniels, *Wilson Era*, 368.

[61]*Report of the Sec. Navy, 1916*, 63. One barrel equals forty-two gallons.

[62]Based on "List of Ships of the U.S. Navy Showing Fuel Capacity and Steaming Radius under Different Speeds," compiled by U.S. Navy Paymaster General T. J. Cowie, 5 March 1915, box 20, 1915 folder, Meyer Papers.

[63]*Report of the Sec. Navy, 1916*, 1, 11. As soon as the three-year construction program was completed, Daniels noted that the navy would use 6,721,000 barrels of fuel oil per year in peace and 20,163,000 barrels per year during wartime.

[64]Ibid., 31.

[65]*Historical Statistics of the United States*, 462.

[66]Ibid.

[67]The number of aircraft, for example, had grown rapidly during the war years. The number of new airplanes totaled 681 between 1913 and 1916, 16,168 between 1917 and 1918, and 1,108 between 1919 and 1920. Of that production the U.S. government purchased 196 between 1913 and 1916, 16,004 between 1917 and 1918, and 938 between 1919 and 1920. Ibid., 466.

[68]Even between 1901 and 1906 national production accounted for almost 53 percent of the world production. See Joseph E. Pogue, *The Economics of Petroleum* (New York: John Wiley & Sons, 1921), 52. Pogue was an associate geologist for the U.S. Geological Survey, 1913–14; assistant director, Bureau of Oil Conservation in the U.S. Fuel Administration, 1918; and director, Department of Economic Research, Sinclair Consolidated Oil Corporation, 1919–20.

[69]See Table 10, p. 147.

[70]See Table 11, p. 147.

[71]David T. Day, "The Petroleum Resources of the United States," *United States Geological Survey Bulletin* 394 (1909): 35.

[72]Ralph Arnold, "Conservation of the Oil and Gas Resources of the Americas, Part II," *Economic Geology* 11 (June 1916): 318. This article was originally a paper delivered at the second Pan-American Scientific Conference in Washington, 30 December 1915.

[73]U.S. Bureau of Mines, *Yearbook of the Bureau of Mines, 1917* (Washington, DC: Government Printing Office, 1917), 116–17. Also see the petroleum report prepared by the subcommittee of the Economic Liaison Committee, 11 July 1919, box 2, ROEA.

[74]David White, "The Petroleum Resources of the World," *The Annals of the American Academy of Political and Social Science* 89 (May 1920): 111–12.

[75]Ibid., 111.

[76]Polk Diary, 27 July 1918, drawer 88, folder 10, Polk Papers.

[77]FTC, *Advance in the Price of Petroleum Products*, 19.

[78]During the previous two years the percentage had been slightly lower: 96.36 percent in 1915 and 96.77 percent in 1916. Ibid.

[79]Fletcher to Lansing, 10 April 1917, RG 59, SD 600.129/7.

[80]Lansing to Wilson, 11 April 1917, RG 59, SD 600.129/7.

[81]Wilson to Lansing, RG 59, SD 600.129/12-1/2.

[82]For a more detailed examination of Mexican oil policies and America's responses see Donald C. Baldridge, "Mexican Petroleum and United States-Mexican Relations, 1919–1923" (Ph.D. diss., University of Arizona, 1971); Warrick Ridgely Edwards III, "United States-Mexican Relations, 1913–1916: Revolution, Oil, and Intervention" (Ph.D. diss., Louisiana State University, 1971); Smith, *United States and Revolutionary Nationalism*; Lesta Van Der Wert Turchen, "The Oil Expropriation Controversy, 1917–1942 in United States-Mexican Relations" (Ph.D. diss., Purdue, 1972); Mark T. Gilderhus, *Diplomacy and Revolution*; Gilderhus, "Senator Albert B. Fall and 'The Plot against Mexico,' " *New Mexico Historical Review* (1973): 299–311; Dennis O'Brien, "The Oil Crisis and the Foreign Policy of the Wilson Administration, 1917–1921" (Ph.D. diss., University of Missouri, 1974); and Clifford Trow, "Senator Albert B. Fall and Mexican Affairs, 1912–1921" (Ph.D. diss., University of Colorado, 1966).

[83]Lansing desk diary, 5 August 1919, box 65, Lansing Papers. Also see Lansing to Philip, 5 August 1919, RG 59, SD 711.21/478.

[84]Lansing to ALB, 9 August 1919, RG 59, SD 711.21/478b. Drafted in cooperation with Senators Albert Fall and Porter J. McCumber, who represented the Foreign Relations Subcommittee. See Fall to Lodge, 20 June 1921, folder 1921, A–J, May–August, Lodge Papers.

[85]Lansing to ALB, 13 August 1919, RG 59, SD 821.6363/58. Also see Lansing to ALB, 21 August 1919, RG 59, SD 711.21/481; and Lodge before the Senate, in *Congressional Record* 58, pt. 4: 3668.

[86]Lansing to ALB, 9 August 1919, RG 59, SD 711.21/478b. Drafted in conference with Senators Fall and McCumber.

[87]For an account of Lodge and Wilson's estrangement see Garraty, *Henry Cabot Lodge*; Henry Cabot Lodge, *The Senate and the League of Nations* (New York: Charles Scribner's Sons, 1925); and Widenor, *Lodge and the Search for an American Foreign Policy*. For an account of Wilson and Lansing's estrangement see Joseph P. Tumulty, *Woodrow Wilson as I Knew Him* (Garden City, NY: Doubleday, Page & Company, 1921); Robert Lansing, *The Peace Negotiations* (Boston: Houghton Mifflin Company, 1921); Edith Wilson, *My Memoir* (New York: Bobbs-Merrill Company, 1939); and Daniels, *Wilson Era*. In a memorandum dated 1 August 1919, Lansing considered resigning because of Wilson's treatment of him in

Paris, but he decided to remain. Memorandum entitled "Duty vs. Inclination," box 66, Lansing Papers.

[88]Philip to Lansing, 15 August 1919, RG 59, SD 711.21/480.

[89]Philip to Lansing, 22 August 1919, RG 59, SD 711.21/497, enclosing a copy of the letter from the foreign minister to Philip dated 19 August.

[90]Philip to Lansing, 18 August 1919, RG 59, SD 711.21/482; Philip to Lansing, 26 July 1919, RG 84: CR&S; Suárez address to National Congress, 20 July 1919, RG 59, SD 821.032/25; Bernardo Blair Gutíerrez, *Don Marco Fidel Suárez: Su Vida y Su Obra* (Medellín: Editorial Universidad de Antioquia, 1955); Suárez, *Obras* 2.

[91]The Tropical Oil Company, after two years of exploration, brought in its first well in April 1918. By January 1919 it pumped approximately 8,000 barrels per day, and on 25 August it signed a new contract with the Colombian government. For a copy of that contract see RG 59, SD 821.6363/68. There was only one other major American firm in Colombia—the Colombia Petroleum Company—a newcomer, arriving in 1918. By the end of 1919 it too had obtained rights to explore governmental fields. See RG 59, SD, 821.6363/Barco. Philip informed State that the recent decree did not affect the operations of either company. Philip to Lansing, 16 August 1919, RG 59, SD 711.21/492.

[92]For a copy of the 1255B decree see RG 59, SD 821.6363/51.

[93]For criticisms of the decree see the following 1919 *El Nuevo Tiempo* articles: "La Cuestión Petrolera en Colombia," 17 July; "La Cuestión Petrolera en Colombia," 20 July; "La Cuestión Petrolera," 8 September; "Antonio Torrijos: Su Exposición sobre la Propiedad de los Petroleos," 9 September; "La Cuestión Petrolera," 10 September; "Sobre Petroleo," 14 September; and "El Memorandum de Estados Unidos," 31 October.

[94]Prisciliano Cabrales, "Sobre Petroleo," *El Nuevo Tiempo*, 14 September 1919.

[95]"La Cuestión Petrolera," ibid., 8 September 1919.

[96]Lansing to ALB, 28 August 1919, RG 59, SD 711.21/482. Drafted in consultation with Senator Fall in order to obtain the true sentiment of the Foreign Relations Committee.

[97]Philip to Lansing, 12 August 1919, RG 59, SD 711.21/479.

[98]Philip to Lansing, 15 August 1919, RG 59, SD 711.21/480.

[99]Lansing to ALB, 21 August 1919, RG 59, SD 711.21/481. Approved by Senator Fall before dispatch.

[100]Memorandum by Long to Joseph R. Baker, assistant to the solicitor, 21 August 1919, RG 59, SD 711.21/482. Also see Lansing to Philip, 26 November 1919, RG 59, SD 821.6363/82.

[101]For a copy of the proposed protocol see RG 59, SD 711.21/485.

[102]Unwritten argument of attorney general for Colombia before the Supreme Court, 2 September 1919, RG 59, SD 821.6363/73. Displeased with President Suárez's abandonment of the decree, the foreign minister and the minister for public works resigned two weeks later. Philip to Lansing, 19 September 1919, RG 59, SD 711.21/506.

[103]Philip to Lansing, 19 September 1919, RG 59, SD 711.21/506. Suárez's attitude toward the United States had been consistent. For his reasoning see Suárez, *Obras* 2; and Sanchez Camacho, *Suárez*.

[104]Philip to Lansing, 26 September 1919, RG 59, SD 711.21/509. Also see Philip to Lansing, 1 October 1919 (/505), 4 October 1919 (/510), and 2 October 1919 (/504).

[105]See "El Tratado Colombo-Americano," 15 August; "La Opinión Latino-Americana y el Tratado entre Colombia y los Estados Unidos," 23 August; "Estados Unidos y Colombia," 26 August; "Los Extranjeros en Colombia," 29 August; and "Los Petroleos," 6 September.

[106]"Las Damas de Bogotá y la Soberania de Colombia," *El Nuevo Tiempo*, 8 October 1919. The petition was dated September 1919.

[107]Philip to Lansing, 3 October 1919, RG 59, SD 711.21/507. The acting foreign minister had met with the Senate for five hours on 2 October and approved this declaration, as did President Suárez.

[108]Ibid.

[109]Long to Baker, 6 October 1919, RG 59, SD 711.21/494. The Colombian minister in Washington had relayed this information.

[110]Lansing to ALB, 14 October 1919, RG 59, SD 711.21/504. Also see Fall to Long, 8 October 1919, RG 59, SD 821.6363/75. The State Department already had informed Philip on 16 September 1919 (RG 84: CR&S) that it would not oppose subsoil legislation so long as it only regulated governmental property. Also see Lansing to ALB, 21 November 1919, RG 84: CR&S.

[111]Adee memorandum, 3 November 1919, RG 59, SD 711.21/510.

[112]Philip to Lansing, 22 November 1919, RG 59, SD 821.6363/85; Suárez, *Obras* 2:980–91.

[113]Philip to Lansing, 6 December 1919, RG 84: CR&S.

[114]Lansing to ALB, 9 December 1919, RG 59, SD 711.21/519.

[115]For the terms of the new legislation see *Ley 120 de 1919* (Bogotá: Casa Editorial de Arboleda & Valencia, 1920), pp. 34–62.

[116]Division of Latin American Affairs memorandum on the Colombian treaty, 28 May 1920 (updated to 4 June 1920). See RG 59, SD 711.21/799. Also see Hallett Johnson memorandum to Bainbridge Colby, 12 April 1920, box 2, Bainbridge Colby Papers, Library of Congress Manuscripts Division (hereafter cited as Colby Papers); Office of Solicitor memorandum on the December law, undated, RG 59, SD 821.6363/178; and Colby to Wilson, 13 April 1920, box 2, Colby Papers. For the opinion of oil firms see Henry L. Doherty and Company to Bureau of Mines, 8 June 1920, Prudential Oil to Department of Interior, 2 June 1920, Standard Oil to Bureau of Mines, 28 May 1920, and Sinclair Consolidated Oil to Bureau of Mines, 17 May 1920, all in RG 59, SD 821.6363/116.

[117]Ibid.; Polk to ALB, 9 March 1920, RG 84: CR&S.

[118]Memorandum, RG 59, SD 711.21/799; "Report of the Subcommittee," reel 29, frames 211–18, Albert B. Fall Papers, University of New Mexico, Albuquerque (hereafter cited as Fall Papers). The original manuscripts are located at the Henry E. Huntington Library, San Marino, California.

[119]Colby to ALB, 4 June 1920, RG 59, SD 711.21/537b; "Pave Way to Ratify Colombian Treaty," *New York Times*, 4 June 1920.

[120]Harding had won by 16,143,407 to 9,130,328, representing 60.4 percent of the popular vote. The Republicans also gained ten seats in the Senate and

sixty-five in the House. The new Congress now contained 59 Republicans and 46 Democrats in the Senate, with 301 Republicans and 132 Democrats in the House.

[121]For a sample of opposition see Francis B. Loomis to Senator Frank Kellogg, 14 March 1921, reel 7, frame 473, Kellogg Papers; Gifford Pinchot to Borah, 31 March 1921, box 90, "Colombia Treaty," William E. Borah Papers, Library of Congress Manuscripts Division; and Borah to Thomas Latta, 4 March 1921, box 90, ibid.

[122]Fall to Lansing, 22 February 1921, RG 59, SD 711.21/800. For a slightly different version of that letter see reel 29, frame 256, Fall Papers. Fall and Harding discussed the treaty in letters dated 11 and 14 January 1921, reel 29, frames 80–85, Fall Papers. Harding made clear, however, that if solid senatorial opposition developed he would not wage a major campaign for ratification.

[123]Colby address, 2 March 1921, box 9, Colby Papers.

[124]For a discussion of the treaty see *Congressional Record* 61, pt. 1, 12–20 April, pp. 162–482. For the preliminary votes on each article and on proposed amendments see ibid., 482–86. For the final roll call vote see p. 487.

[125]Philip to Hughes, 24 August 1921, RG 59, SD 711.21/640. Also see Philip to Hughes, 21 September 1921, RG 84: CR&S. The minister reported that the Foreign Relations Committee of the Colombian Senate unanimously favored the document. *El Nuevo Tiempo* had earlier reported on 15 August 1919, in "El Tratado Colombo-Americano," that the majority of the Colombian people "with a lukewarm feeling" seemed resigned to the elimination of the sincere regrets from the treaty and the acceptance of the $25 million indemnity.

[126]Philip to Hughes, 13 October 1921, RG 59, SD 711.21/651.

[127]Philip to Hughes, 22 December 1921, RG 59, SD 711.21/667. For the text of the ratified treaty see *Statutes at Large* 42, pt. 2, "Thomson-Urrutia Treaty," 30 May 1922, pp. 2122–27.

Epilogue

Colombia reflected in microcosm the problem facing America's leaders in the opening decades of the twentieth century. Dedicated to national prosperity, growth, and development, U.S. presidents had to balance national economic and strategic interests against the rights and sovereignty of neighboring states. By adopting a paternalistic attitude; using its economic, military, and moral force to manipulate hemispheric conduct; and trying to transfer its experience and values to Latin America, the United States created growing suspicion, doubt, and distrust in nearby capitals. Each time its perceived interests required intervention or interference, Latin Americans grew more skeptical of their northern neighbor.

As relations with Colombia demonstrate, the United States frequently justified those invasions of sovereignty in benevolent, humanitarian terms. This was no deliberate ruse to cover America's own aggressive ambitions. Roosevelt, Taft, and Wilson, as well as most of their advisers, sincerely believed that they were not only acting in the best interests of the United States but also of Latin America. Perhaps, in retrospect, that is the greatest indictment of their foreign policies toward Colombia in particular and the Caribbean basin in general. The doctrine of the state as parent clearly underlay domestic Progressive reforms in the early decades of the twentieth century and the nation's foreign policy as well. Since the parent was considered stronger, wiser, and more experienced but was concerned and caring too, it could be trusted to act toward its wards with an understanding and compassion that would serve their mutual interests. Such logic formed the basis for Roosevelt's and Wilson's justifications of their actions between 1903 and 1922. So long as Colombian decision making affected only nonsensitive issues, both men had been willing to give nodding support to the principle of equal sovereignty.

However, when Colombian policies affected economic and strategic issues considered sensitive by the United States, that support rapidly diminished. Under these new circumstances, America ceased to be an equal and instead became a reproving parent, willing to pressure Bogotá into adopting policies more in accord with the goals and desires of the United States rather than Colombia. Perhaps Senator Henry Teller hoped to undercut just that attitude when in 1904 he warned that "it will not do" to violate international law or interfere in another state's domestic affairs, citing as means of exculpation the interest of civilization. The purity of one's motivation would not make an illegal act legal, nor, he could have added, would imperialism, no matter how justified, cease to be imperialism.

The vision of America's uniqueness, shared by the Roosevelt, Taft, and Wilson administrations, led them to renounce the type of colonialism and expansionism they attributed to European powers, to disavow national selfishness and greed in foreign policymaking, and to emphasize international cooperation between weak and strong states based on mutual respect, understanding, and friendship. The United States, in dealing with Colombia between 1902 and 1922, sometimes deviated from this rhetorical vision, but its leaders justified those very deviations by citing that same vision. Had Colombians shared that benign perspective of the United States, such deviations might have caused little comment. Unfortunately for the United States, Colombians did not automatically accept that perspective. Nor did either of the three Washington administrations involved in Colombian policymaking between 1903 and 1922 seem to realize that U.S. actions, in contrast to its rhetoric, might be hindering, rather than helping, the nation to achieve its goal of a more secure hemisphere friendly toward the United States. All three were blinded to the differences between action and rhetoric by their own self-deception and their continued reliance on the belief that the United States knew best. That self-assured feeling of superiority all too often led them to act precipitously, without considering Colombian or Latin American sensibilities, and helped create an atmosphere that made compromise and cooperation between Washington and Bogotá more difficult.

In dealing with Colombia, Roosevelt, Taft, and Wilson faced the same dilemma: How could they achieve the economic and strategic interests of the United States and still recognize the rights and sovereignty of a neighboring state? Although they finally succeeded in resolving the isthmian dispute with Colombia in 1922, they never successfully solved this broader question, nor have Washington policymakers in the second half of the twentieth century fared much better. Blinded by the same self-assurance and omniscience that motivated Roosevelt, Taft, and Wilson before them, they all too frequently treat their southern neighbors with the same condescension and paternalism.

Bibliography

Archives and Manuscript Collections

Library of Congress Manuscripts Division, Washington, DC, Papers of:

Chandler Anderson
John Barrett
William Benson
Albert Beveridge
William E. Borah
William Jennings Bryan
Philippe Bunau-Varilla
Andrew Carnegie
Wilbur Carr
Thomas Carter
Bainbridge Colby
William S. Culbertson
Joseph Foraker
Warren G. Harding
Leland Harrison
John Hay
Gilbert Hitchcock
Philander Knox
Robert Lansing
Breckinridge Long
Frank McCoy
John T. Morgan
Key Pittman
Theodore Roosevelt
Elihu Root
John C. Spooner
George Sutherland
William Howard Taft
John Walker
John S. Williams
Woodrow Wilson
Lester Woolsey

Churchill College, Cambridge, England
Cecil Spring Rice Papers

Cincinnati Historical Society, Cincinnati, Ohio
Joseph Foraker Papers

Georgetown University, Washington, DC
Tomás Herrán Papers

Illinois State Historical Society, Springfield, Illinois
Shelby Cullom Papers

Kent State University, Kent, Ohio
Atlee Pomerene Papers

Maine Historical Society, Portland, Maine
William Frye Papers

Massachusetts Historical Society, Boston, Massachusetts
Henry Cabot Lodge Papers
George Von Lengerke Meyer Papers

Minnesota Historical Society Research Center, St. Paul, Minnesota
John Lind Papers

National Library of Scotland, Edinburgh, Scotland
Lord Murray of Elibank Papers

New York-Historical Society, New York, New York
Julio Betancourt Papers

Oxford University, Bodleian Library, Oxford, England
Herbert H. Asquith Papers

Science Museum Library, London, England
S. Pearson and Son Archives

University of New Mexico, Albuquerque, New Mexico
Albert B. Fall Papers
Albert B. Fall Papers of the Huntington Library (microfilm)

University of North Carolina, Southern Historical Collection, Chapel Hill, North Carolina
Hayne Davis Papers

University of Virginia, Alderman Library, Charlottesville, Virginia
Claude Swanson Papers

Western Historical Manuscript Collection, Columbia, Missouri
William Joel Stone Papers

Yale University, Manuscripts Division, Sterling Memorial Library, New Haven, Connecticut
Edward M. House Papers
Frank Polk Papers

National Archives, Washington, DC
RG 40: General Records of the Department of Commerce
RG 46: Records of the U.S. Senate
RG 59: General Records of the Department of State
RG 84: Records of the Foreign Service Posts of the Department of State
RG 151: Records of the Bureau of Foreign and Domestic Commerce
RG 165: Records of the War Department General and Special Staffs

Public Record Office, Kew, England
F.O. 55: General Correspondence to 1905, Colombia
F.O. 115: Embassy and Consular Archives, United States
F.O. 135: Embassy and Consular Archives, Colombia

F.O. 204: Embassy and Consular Archives, Mexico
F.O. 288: Embassy and Consular Archives, Panama
F.O. 368: General Correspondence: Commercial, 1906–1920
F.O. 371: General Correspondence: Political, 1906–1941
F.O. 800: General and Miscellaneous Collections:
Ministers and Officials Papers Relating to Arthur Balfour, James Bryce, Edward Grey, the Marquess of Lansdowne, and Cecil Spring Rice

Government Documents

U.S. Bureau of the Census. *Historical Statistics of the United States: Colonial Times to 1957*. Washington, DC: Government Printing Office, 1960.

U.S. Bureau of Mines. *Yearbook of the Bureau of Mines, 1917*. Washington, DC: Government Printing Office, 1917.

U.S. Bureau of Statistics. *Statistical Abstract of the United States, 1907, 1912–1919*. Washington, DC: Government Printing Office, 1908, 1913–1920.

U.S. Congress. *Investigation of Mexican Affairs*. Washington, DC: Government Printing Office, 1920.

———. *Report of the Isthmian Canal Commission, 1899–1901*. Sen. Doc. 222, 58th Cong., 2d sess., 1903–04.

———. "Settlement of Differences with Colombia," Report 1, pt. 1, 65th Cong., special sess., 14 March 1917.

———. *Use by the United States of a Military Force in the Internal Affairs of Colombia*. Sen. Doc. 143, 58th Cong., 2d sess., 1904.

U.S. Department of Commerce. Bell, P. L. "Colombia: A Commercial and Industrial Handbook." In Bureau of Foreign and Domestic Commerce, *Special Agent Series* 206. Washington, DC: Government Printing Office, 1921.

———. Brown, W. Duval. "Caribbean Markets for American Goods: Colombia." In Bureau of Foreign and Domestic Commerce, *Trade Information Bulletin* 342. Washington, DC: Government Printing Office, 1925.

———. Bynum, M. L. "International Trade in Coffee." In Bureau of Foreign and Domestic Commerce, *Trade Promotion Series* 37. Washington, DC: Government Printing Office, 1926.

———. "Colombia: Commerce and Industries, 1922 and 1923." In Bureau of Foreign and Domestic Commerce, *Trade Information Bulletin* 223. Washington, DC: Government Printing Office, 1924.

———. Filsinger, Ernst B. "Commercial Traveler's Guide to Latin America." In Bureau of Foreign and Domestic Commerce, *Miscellaneous Series* 89. Washington, DC: Government Printing Office, 1922.

———. *Foreign Commerce and Navigation of the United States, 1912–1919.* Washington, DC: Government Printing Office, 1913–20.

———. *Investment in Colombia: Conditions and Outlook for United States Investors.* Washington, DC: Government Printing Office, 1953.

———. Jones, Grosvenor M. "Government Aid to Merchant Shipping: Study of Subsidies, Subventions, and Other Forms of State Aid in Principal Countries of the World." In Bureau of Foreign and Domestic Commerce, *Special Agent Series* 119. Washington, DC: Government Printing Office, 1925 [1916].

———. Long, W. Rodney. "Railways of South America." In Bureau of Foreign and Domestic Commerce, *Trade Promotion Series* 39. Washington, DC: Government Printing Office, 1927.

———. Lough, William H. "Banking Opportunities in South America." In Bureau of Foreign and Domestic Commerce, *Special Agent Series* 106. Washington, DC: Government Printing Office, 1915.

———. McQueen, Charles A. "Colombian Public Finance." In Bureau of Foreign and Domestic Commerce, *Trade Information Bulletin* 417. Washington, DC: Government Printing Office, 1926.

———. ———. "Foreign Exchange in Latin America: A Survey of Conditions since 1914." In Bureau of Foreign and Domestic Commerce, *Trade Information Bulletin* 316. Washington, DC: Government Printing Office, 1925.

———. Mood, James R. "Handbook of Foreign Currency and Exchange." In Bureau of Foreign and Domestic Commerce, *Trade Promotion Series* 102. Washington, DC: Government Printing Office, 1930.

———. "Packing for Export." In Bureau of Foreign and Domestic Commerce, *Miscellaneous Series* 4, 5. Washington, DC: Government Printing Office, 1909, 1911.

———. Paton, William A. "The Economic Position of the United Kingdom: 1912–1918." In Bureau of Foreign and Domestic Commerce, *Miscellaneous Series* 96. Washington, DC: Government Printing Office, 1919.

———. *Reports of the Department of Commerce, 1913–22.* Washington, DC: Government Printing Office, 1913–22.

———. Snow, Chauncey Depew. "German Foreign Trade Organization." In Bureau of Foreign and Domestic Commerce, *Miscellaneous Series* 57. Washington, DC: Government Printing Office, 1917.

———. Snow, Chauncey Depew, and Krall, J. J. "German Trade and the War." In Bureau of Foreign and Domestic Commerce, *Miscellaneous Series* 65. Washington, DC: Government Printing Office, 1918.

———. "Statements on the Latin American Trade Situation." In Bureau of Foreign and Domestic Commerce, *Miscellaneous Series* 18. Washington, DC: Government Printing Office, 1914.

U.S. Department of the Navy. *Annual Reports of the Secretary of the Navy, 1910, 1913–1918.* Washington, DC: Government Printing Office, 1910–18.

U.S. Department of State. *The Lansing Papers, 1914–1920.* Washington, DC: Government Printing Office, 1940.

———. *Papers Relating to the Foreign Relations of the United States, 1903–1922.* Washington, DC: Government Printing Office, 1904–38.

U.S. Federal Trade Commission. *Advance in Price of Petroleum Products.* Washington, DC: Government Printing Office, 1920.

———. *Foreign Ownership in the Petroleum Industry.* Washington, DC: Government Printing Office, 1923.

———. *Report on Cooperation in American Export Trade, Part I.* Washington, DC: Government Printing Office, 1916.

U.S. Geological Survey. *Annual Reports of the Director of the United States Geological Survey, 1909–1920.* Washington, DC: Government Printing Office, 1909–20.

U.S. Shipping Board. *Annual Reports, 1917–1920.* Washington, DC: Government Printing Office, 1917–20.

U.S. War Industries Board. *Munitions Industry: Final Report of the Chairman of the United States War Industries Board, 1919.* Washington, DC: Government Printing Office, 1935.

U.S. War Trade Board. *Report of the War Trade Board.* Washington, DC: Government Printing Office, 1920.

Books

Abrahams, Paul. *The Foreign Expansion of American Finance and Its Relationship to the Foreign Economic Policies of the United States, 1907–1921.* New York: Arno Press, 1976.

Anderson, Donald F. *William Howard Taft: A Conservative's Conception of the Presidency.* Ithaca: Cornell University Press, 1973 [1968].

Anguizola, Gustave. *Philippe Bunau-Varilla: The Man Behind the Panama Canal.* Chicago: Nelson-Hall, 1980.

Arias, Harmodio. *The Panama Canal: A Study in International Law and Diplomacy.* New York: Arno Press, 1970 [1911].

Bacon, Robert, and Scott, James Brown, eds. *Addresses on International Subjects by Elihu Root.* Cambridge: Harvard University Press, 1916.

———. *Latin America and the United States: Addresses by Elihu Root.* Cambridge: Harvard University Press, 1917.

———. *Miscellaneous Addresses by Elihu Root.* Cambridge: Harvard University Press, 1917.

Baker, Ray Stannard. *Woodrow Wilson, Life and Letters.* 8 vols. Garden City, NY: Doubleday, Page & Company, 1927–39.

Baker, Ray Stannard, and Dodd, William E., eds. *The Public Papers of Woodrow Wilson.* 6 vols. New York: Harper & Brothers, 1925–27.

Bates, J. Leonard. *The Origins of Teapot Dome: Progressives, Parties, and Petroleum, 1909–1921.* Urbana: University of Illinois Press, 1963.

Becker, William H., and Wells, Samuel F., Jr., eds. *Economics and World Power: An Assessment of American Diplomacy since 1789.* New York: Columbia University Press, 1984.

Bell, Sidney. *Righteous Conquest: Woodrow Wilson and the Evolution of the New Diplomacy.* Port Washington: Kennikat Press, 1922.

Bergquist, Charles W. *Coffee and Conflict in Colombia, 1886–1910.* Durham: Duke University Press, 1978.

Blair Gutíerrez, Bernardo. *Don Marco Fidel Suárez: Su Vida y Su Obra.* Medellín: Editorial Universidad de Antioquia, 1955.

Brandes, Joseph. *Herbert Hoover and Economic Diplomacy: Department of Commerce Policy, 1921–1928.* Pittsburgh: University of Pittsburgh Press, 1962.

Broesamle, John J. *William Gibbs McAdoo: A Passion for Change, 1863–1917.* Port Washington: Kennikat Press, 1973.

Bunau-Varilla, Philippe. *Panama: The Creation, Destruction and Resurrection.* London: Constable & Company, 1913.

Burton, David. *Theodore Roosevelt: Confident Imperialist.* Philadelphia: University of Pennsylvania Press, 1968.

Caballero, Enrique. *Historia Económica de Colombia.* Bogotá: n.p., 1970.

Caicedo Castilla, José Joaquín. *Historia Diplomática.* Bogotá: Ediciones Lerner, 1974.

Calvert, Peter. *The Mexican Revolution, 1910–1914: The Diplomacy of Anglo-American Conflict.* Cambridge: Cambridge University Press, 1968.

Camacho, Vicente Olarte. *Tratado de 6 de abril.* Bogotá: Imprenta Electrica, 1914.

Cámara de Representantes. *Investigación sobre la Rebelión del Istmo de Panamá.* Bogotá: Imprenta Nacional, 1913.

Cameron, Ian. *The Impossible Dream: The Building of the Panama Canal.* New York: William Morrow & Company, 1972.

Campbell, Charles, Jr. *Anglo-American Understanding, 1898–1903.* Baltimore: Johns Hopkins Press, 1957.

Carles, Rubén. *Reminiscencias de los Primeros Anõs de la República de Panamá, 1903–1912.* Panamá: La Estrella de Panamá, 1968.

Caro, Miguel Antonio. *Discursos y Otras Intervenciones en El Senado de la República, 1903–1904.* Bogotá: Instituto Caro y Cuervo, 1979.

Carter, Purvis. *Congressional and Public Reaction to Wilson's Caribbean Policy, 1913–1917.* New York: Vantage Press, 1977.

Castillero Pimentel, Ernesto. *Panamá y los Estados Unidos.* Panamá: Editora Panamá América, 1953.

Castillero Reyes, Ernesto. *Historia de Panamá*. Panamá: Editora Panamá América, 1962.

———. *Panamá y Colombia: Historia de su Reconciliación*. Panamá: Instituto Nacional de Cultura, 1974.

Cavelier, German. *La Política Internacional de Colombia*. Bogotá: Editorial Igueima, 1959.

Challener, Richard D. *Admirals, Generals, and American Foreign Policy, 1898–1914*. Princeton: Princeton University Press, 1973.

Clarke, Charles E. *My Fifty Years in the Navy*. Boston: Little, Brown & Company, 1917.

Coletta, Paolo E. *The Presidency of William Howard Taft*. Lawrence: University of Kansas Press, 1973.

———. *William Jennings Bryan: Political Evangelist, 1860–1908*. Lincoln: University of Nebraska Press, 1964.

———. *William Jennings Bryan: Progressive Politician and Moral Statesman, 1909–1915*. Lincoln: University of Nebraska Press, 1969.

Collin, Richard. *Theodore Roosevelt, Culture, Diplomacy, and Expansion: A New View of American Imperialism*. Baton Rouge: Louisiana State University Press, 1985.

Comercio Internacional de Colombia. Boletín Numero 3, 4, 5. Bogotá: Dirección General de Estadística, 1924.

Cooper, John Milton, Jr. *The Warrior and the Priest: Woodrow Wilson and Theodore Roosevelt*. Cambridge: Harvard University Press, 1983.

Cortés, Enrique. *Los Tratados con los Estados Unidos y Panamá*. London: n.p., 1909.

Crane, Katharine. *Mr. Carr of State: Forty-Seven Years in the Department of State*. New York: St. Martin's Press, 1960.

Cronon, E. David, ed. *The Cabinet Diaries of Josephus Daniels, 1913–1921*. Lincoln: University of Nebraska Press, 1963.

Cruz Santos, Abel. *Economía y Hacienda Pública*. 2 vols. Bogotá: Ediciones Lerner, 1966.

Cuff, Robert D. *The War Industries Board: Business-Government Relations during World War I*. Baltimore: Johns Hopkins University Press, 1973.

Daniels, Josephus. *The Wilson Era: Years of Peace, 1910–1917*. Chapel Hill: University of North Carolina Press, 1944.

Delpar, Helen. *Red against Blue: The Liberal Party in Colombian Politics, 1863–1899*. University, AL: University of Alabama Press, 1981.

Dennett, Tyler. *John Hay: From Poetry to Politics*. New York: Dodd, Mead & Company, 1934.

Diamond, William. *The Economic Thought of Woodrow Wilson*. Baltimore: Johns Hopkins Press, 1943.

Dyer, Thomas. *Theodore Roosevelt and the Idea of Race*. Baton Rouge: Louisiana State University Press, 1980.

Ealy, Lawrence O. *The Republic of Panama in World Affairs, 1903–1950.* Westport, CT: Greenwood Press, 1970 [1951].

———. *Yanqui Politics and the Isthmian Canal.* University Park: Pennsylvania State University Press, 1971.

Eder, Phanor James. *Colombia.* London: T. Fisher Unwin, 1913.

Farnsworth, David N., and McKenney, James W. *U.S.-Panama Relations, 1903–1978: A Study in Linkage Politics.* Boulder: Westview Press, 1983.

Fleming, D. F. *The United States and the League of Nations.* New York: Russell & Russell, 1968 [1932].

Fowler, W. B. *British-American Relations, 1917–1918: The Role of Sir William Wiseman.* Princeton: Princeton University Press, 1969.

Galambos, Louis. *Competition and Cooperation: The Emergence of a National Trade Association.* Baltimore: Johns Hopkins University Press, 1966.

Garraty, John. *Henry Cabot Lodge: A Biography.* New York: Alfred A. Knopf, 1953.

Gerretson, Frederick C. *History of the Royal Dutch.* Leiden: E. J. Brill, 1958 [1957].

Gibb, George, and Knowlton, Evelyn. *The Resurgent Years, 1911–1927: History of Standard Oil Company (New Jersey).* New York: Harper & Brothers, 1956.

Gibson, William M. *The Constitutions of Colombia.* Durham: Duke University Press, 1948.

Gilderhus, Mark. *Diplomacy and Revolution: U.S.-Mexican Relations under Wilson and Carranza.* Tucson: University of Arizona Press, 1977.

Grayson, Cary T. *Woodrow Wilson: An Intimate Memoir.* New York: Holt, Rinehart & Winston, 1960.

Grey, Viscount, of Fallodon. *Twenty-Five Years, 1892–1916.* New York: Frederick A. Stokes Company, 1925.

Grieb, Kenneth J. *The Latin American Policy of Warren G. Harding.* Fort Worth: Texas Christian University Press, 1976.

———. *The United States and Huerta.* Lincoln: University of Nebraska Press, 1969.

Haley, P. Edward. *Revolution and Intervention: The Diplomacy of Taft and Wilson with Mexico, 1910–1917.* Cambridge: MIT Press, 1970.

Harbaugh, William H. *Power and Responsibility: The Life and Times of Theodore Roosevelt.* New York: Farrar, Strauss & Cudahy, 1961.

Henao, Jesús María, and Arrubla, Gerardo. *History of Colombia.* Translated by J. Fred Rippy. Port Washington: Kennikat Press, 1972 [1938].

Hendrick, Burton J. *The Life and Letters of Walter H. Page.* New York: Doubleday, Page & Company, 1925 [1921].

Hilderbrand, Robert C. *Power and the People: Executive Management of Public Opinion in Foreign Affairs, 1897–1921.* Chapel Hill: University of North Carolina Press, 1981.

Hill, Howard C. *Roosevelt and the Caribbean*. New York: Russell & Russell, 1965 [1927].

Hill, Larry D. *Emissaries to a Revolution: Woodrow Wilson's Executive Agents in Mexico*. Baton Rouge: Louisiana State University Press, 1973.

Hoff-Wilson, Joan. *American Business and Foreign Policy, 1920–1933*. Boston: Beacon Press, 1973 [1971].

Hogan, Michael J. *Informal Entente: The Private Structure of Cooperation in Anglo-American Economic Diplomacy, 1918–1928*. Columbia: University of Missouri Press, 1977.

Houston, David F. *Eight Years with Wilson's Cabinet*. Garden City, NY: Doubleday, Page & Company, 1926.

Huntington-Wilson, Francis M. *Memoirs of an Ex-Diplomat*. Boston: Bruce Humphries, 1945.

Huthmacher, J. Joseph, and Susman, Warren I., eds. *Wilson's Diplomacy: An International Symposium*. Cambridge: Schenkman Publishing Company, 1973.

Jane, Fred T., ed. *Jane's Fighting Ships, 1914*. New York: Arco Publishing Company, 1969 [1914].

Jessup, Philip C. *Elihu Root*. New York: Dodd, Mead & Company, 1938.

Johnson, Willis. *Four Centuries of the Panama Canal*. New York: Henry Holt & Company, 1906.

Jones, Chester Lloyd. *The Caribbean since 1900*. New York: Prentice-Hall, 1936.

Kaufman, Burton I. *Efficiency and Expansion: Foreign Trade Organization in the Wilson Administration, 1913–1921*. Westport, CT: Greenwood Press, 1974.

Kline, Harvey F. *Colombia: Portrait of Unity and Diversity*. Boulder: Westview Press, 1983.

LaFeber, Walter. *Inevitable Revolutions: The United States in Central America*. New York: W. W. Norton, 1984.

———. *The Panama Canal: The Crisis in Historical Perspective*. New York: Oxford University Press, 1978.

Langley, Lester. *The Banana Wars: An Inner History of American Empire, 1900–1934*. Lexington: University Press of Kentucky, 1983.

———. *Struggle for the American Mediterranean: United States-European Rivalry in the Gulf-Caribbean, 1776–1904*. Athens: University of Georgia Press, 1976.

Lansing, Robert. *Notes on Sovereignty from the Standpoint of the State and of the World*. Washington, DC: Carnegie Endowment for International Peace, 1921.

———. *The Peace Negotiations*. Boston: Houghton Mifflin Company, 1921.

———. *War Memoirs of Robert Lansing*. New York: Bobbs Merrill Company, 1935.

Lemaitre Román, Eduardo. *Panamá y su Separación de Colombia*. Bogotá: Banco Popular, 1972.

———. *Rafael Reyes: Biografía de un Gran Colombiano*. Bogotá: Espiral, 1967.

———. *Reyes*. Bogotá: Editorial Iqueima, 1953.

Levin, N. Gordon. *Woodrow Wilson and World Politics: America's Response to War and Revolution*. New York: Oxford University Press, 1968.

Ley 120 de 1919. Bogotá: Casa Editorial de Arboleda & Valencia, 1920.

Link, Arthur S. *The Higher Realism of Woodrow Wilson and Other Essays*. Nashville: Vanderbilt University Press, 1971.

———. *The Papers of Woodrow Wilson*. 55 vols. Princeton: Princeton University Press, 1966–86.

———. *Wilson, The New Freedom*. Princeton: Princeton University Press, 1956.

———. *Wilson, The Struggle for Neutrality, 1914–1915*. Princeton: Princeton University Press, 1960.

———. *Woodrow Wilson: Revolution, War and Peace*. Arlington Heights, IL: AHM Publishing Company, 1979.

———. *Woodrow Wilson and a Revolutionary World, 1913–1921*. Chapel Hill: University of North Carolina Press, 1982.

Liss, Sheldon. *The Canal: Aspects of United States-Panamanian Relations*. Notre Dame: University of Notre Dame Press, 1967.

Lodge, Henry Cabot. *A Fighting Frigate and Other Essays and Addresses*. New York: Charles Scribner's Sons, 1902.

———. *Selections from the Correspondence of Theodore Roosevelt and Henry Cabot Lodge, 1884–1918*. New York: Charles Scribner's Sons, 1925.

———. *The Senate and the League of Nations*. New York: Charles Scribner's Sons, 1925.

McAdoo, William Gibbs. *Crowded Years: The Reminiscences of William Gibbs McAdoo*. Boston: Houghton Mifflin Company, 1931.

McCain, William D. *The United States and the Republic of Panama*. New York: Russell & Russell, 1965 [1937].

McConnell, Grant. *Private Power and American Democracy*. New York: Alfred A. Knopf, 1966.

McCullough, David. *The Path between the Seas: The Creation of the Panama Canal, 1870–1914*. New York: Simon & Schuster, 1977.

McGreevey, William Paul. *An Economic History of Colombia, 1845–1930*. Cambridge: Cambridge University Press, 1971.

Marks, Frederick, III. *Velvet on Iron: The Diplomacy of Theodore Roosevelt*. Lincoln: University of Nebraska Press, 1979.

Martínez Delgado, Luis. *Jorge Holguín o el Político*. Bogotá: Departamento de Divulgación y Publicidad de Caja Agraria, 1980.

May, Ernest. *"Lessons" of the Past: The Use and Misuse of History in American Foreign Policy*. New York: Oxford University Press, 1973.

Mecham, J. Lloyd. *The United States and Inter-American Security, 1889–1960*. Austin: University of Texas Press, 1967.

Mellander, G. A. *The United States in Panamanian Politics: The Intriguing Formative Years*. Danville, IL: Interstate Printers and Publishers, 1971.

Meyer, Lorenzo. *Mexico and the United States in the Oil Controversy, 1917–1942*. Translated by Muriel Vasconcellos. Austin: University of Texas Press, 1977 [1972].

Middlemas, Robert K. *The Master Builders*. London: Hutchinson, 1963.

Miner, Dwight Carroll. *The Fight for the Panama Route: The Story of the Spooner Act and the Hay-Herran Treaty*. New York: Octagon Books, 1966 [1940].

Minger, Ralph Eldin. *William Howard Taft and United States Foreign Policy: The Apprenticeship Years, 1900–1908*. Urbana: University of Illinois Press, 1975.

Ministerio de Relaciones Exteriores. *Boletín*. Bogotá: Imprenta Nacional, 1908–15.

———. *Protesta de Colombia contra El Tratado entre Panamá y los Estados Unidos*. Bogotá: Imprenta Nacional, 1904.

Molina, Gerardo. *Las Ideas Liberales en Colombia, 1849–1914*. Bogotá: Universidad Nacional de Colombia, 1974.

Morison, Elting E., ed. *The Letters of Theodore Roosevelt*. Cambridge: Harvard University Press, 1951.

Morris, Edmund. *The Rise of Theodore Roosevelt*. New York: Coward, McCann & Geoghegan, 1979.

Mosley, Leonard. *Power Play: The Tumultuous World of Middle East Oil, 1890–1973*. London: Weidenfeld & Nicolson, 1973.

Murray, Arthur C. *At Close Quarters: A Sidelight on Anglo-American Diplomatic Relations*. London: John Murray, 1946.

Nash, Gerald D. *United States Oil Policy, 1890–1964*. Pittsburgh: University of Pittsburgh Press, 1968.

Notter, Harley. *The Origins of the Foreign Policy of Woodrow Wilson*. Baltimore: Johns Hopkins Press, 1937.

Ospina, Joaquín. *Diccionario Biográfico y Bibliográfico de Colombia*. 3 vols. Bogotá: Editorial de Cromos, 1927–39.

Ospina Vásquez, Luis. *Industria y Protección en Colombia, 1810–1930*. Medellín: E.S.F., 1955.

Palacios, Marco. *Coffee in Colombia, 1850–1970: An Economic, Social, and Political History*. London: Cambridge University Press, 1980.

Parks, E. Taylor. *Colombia and the United States, 1765–1934*. Durham: Duke University Press, 1935.

Parrini, Carl. *Heir to Empire: United States Economic Diplomacy, 1916–1923*. Pittsburgh: University of Pittsburgh Press, 1969.

Perez-Venero, Alex. *Before the Five Frontiers: Panama from 1821–1903*. New York: AMS Press, 1978.

Perkins, Bradford. *The Great Rapprochement: England and the United States, 1895–1914*. New York: Atheneum, 1968.

Petre, F. Loraine. *The Republic of Colombia: An Account of the Country, Its People, Its Institutions, and Its Resources*. London: Edward Stanford, 1906.

Phelps, Clyde William. *The Foreign Expansion of American Banks: American Branch Banking Abroad*. New York: Ronald Press Company, 1927.

Phillips, William. *Venture in Diplomacy*. Boston: Beacon Press, 1952.

Pizano Salazar, Diego. *La Expansión del Comercio Exterior de Colombia, 1875–1925*. Bogotá: Fondo Cultural Cafetero, 1981.

Platt, D. C. M. *Latin America and British Trade, 1806–1914*. New York: Harper & Row, 1972.

Pogue, Joseph E. *The Economics of Petroleum*. New York: John Wiley & Sons, 1921.

Pringle, Henry. *The Life and Times of William Howard Taft*. New York: Farrar & Rinehart, 1939.

———. *Theodore Roosevelt: A Biography*. New York: Harcourt, Brace & Company, 1931.

Randall, Stephen J. *The Diplomacy of Modernization: Colombian-American Relations, 1920–1940*. Toronto: University of Toronto Press, 1977.

Redfield, William C. *Dependent America: A Study of the Economic Bases of Our International Relations*. Boston: Houghton Mifflin Company, 1926.

———. *With Congress and Cabinet*. Garden City, NY: Doubleday, Page & Company, 1924.

República de Colombia. *Tratado entre la República de Colombia y los Estados Unidos de América*. Bogotá: Imprenta Nacional, 1914.

Restrepo, Carlos. *Orientación Republicana*. Bogotá: Biblioteca Banco Popular, 1972.

Reyes, Rafael. *Escritos Varios*. Bogotá: Tipografía Arconvar, 1920.

———. *Misión Diplomática y Militar, 1903–1904*. Bogotá: Imprenta Nacional, 1904.

Rippy, J. Fred. *British Investments: Latin America, 1822–1949*. Minneapolis: University of Minnesota Press, 1959.

———. *The Capitalists and Colombia*. New York: Vanguard Press, 1931.

Rippy, Merrill. *Oil and the Mexican Revolution*. Leiden: E. J. Brill, 1972.

Rivas, Raimundo. *Historia Diplomática de Colombia, 1810–1934*. Bogotá: Imprenta Nacional, 1961.

Robison, S. S., and Robison, Mary. *A History of Naval Tactics from 1530–1930.* Annapolis: U.S. Naval Institute, 1942.

Robledo, Emilio. *La Vida del General Pedro Nel Ospina.* Medellín: n.p., 1959.

Roosevelt, Theodore. *An Autobiography.* New York: Charles Scribner's Sons, 1927 [1913].

———. *Fear God and Take Your Own Part.* New York: George H. Doran Company, 1916.

———. *Presidential Addresses and State Papers.* New York: Review of Reviews Company, 1910.

Ropp, Steve C. *Panamanian Politics: From Guarded Nation to National Guard.* New York: Praeger, 1982.

Rosenberg, Emily. *Spreading the American Dream: American Economic and Cultural Expansion, 1890–1945.* New York: Hill & Wang, 1982.

Safford, Jeffrey. *Wilsonian Maritime Diplomacy, 1913–1921.* New Brunswick: Rutgers University Press, 1978.

Salazar, Diego Renato. *Historia Constitucional de Colombia.* Bogotá: Librería Jurídicas Wilches, 1979.

Sanchez Camacho, Jorge. *Marco Fidel Suárez: Biografía.* Bucaramanga: Imprenta del Departamento, 1955.

Sanín-Cano, Baldomero. *Administración Reyes, 1904–1909.* Lausana: Imprenta Jorge Bridel & Company, 1909.

Scholes, Walter V., and Scholes, Marie V. *The Foreign Policies of the Taft Administration.* Columbia: University of Missouri Press, 1970.

Schriftgiesser, Karl. *The Gentleman from Massachusetts: Henry Cabot Lodge.* Boston: Little, Brown & Company, 1944.

Seymour, Charles. *The Intimate Papers of Colonel House.* Boston: Houghton Mifflin Company, 1926.

Simon, Maron J. *The Panama Affair.* New York: Charles Scribner's Sons, 1971.

Smith, Daniel. *Aftermath of War: Bainbridge Colby and Wilsonian Diplomacy, 1920–1921.* Philadelphia: American Philosophical Society, 1970.

Smith, Darrell. *The Panama Canal: Its History, Activities and Organization.* Baltimore: Johns Hopkins Press, 1927.

Smith, Darrell, and Betters, Paul. *The United States Shipping Board.* Washington, DC: Brookings Institution, 1931.

Smith, Robert Freeman. *The United States and Revolutionary Nationalism, 1916–1932.* Chicago: University of Chicago Press, 1972.

Soler, Ricaurte. *Formas Ideológicas de la Nación Panameña.* San José: Editorial Universitaria Centro Americana, 1972.

Sosa, Juan B., and Arce, Enrique J. *Compendio de Historia de Panamá.* Panamá: Editorial Universitaria, 1977.

South American Yearbook and Directory. London: Louis Cassier Company, 1915.

Spender, J. A. *Weetman Pearson, First Viscount Cowdray, 1856–1927*. London: Cassell & Company, 1930.

Stephenson, George M. *John Lind of Minnesota*. Port Washington: Kennikat Press, 1971 [1935].

Stratton, David, ed. *The Memoirs of Albert B. Fall*. El Paso: Texas Western Press, 1966.

Suárez, Marco Fidel. *Obras: Sueños de Luciano Pulgar*. Bogotá: Instituto Caro y Cuervo, 1966.

———. *Tratado entre Colombia y los Estados Unidos*. Bogotá: Casa Editorial de 'El Liberal,' 1914.

Taft, William Howard. *Four Aspects of Civic Duty*. New York: Charles Scribner's Sons, 1906.

———. *Present Day Problems*. New York: Dodd, Mead & Company, 1908.

———. *The Presidency: Its Duties, Its Powers, Its Opportunities, and Its Limitations*. New York: Charles Scribner's Sons, 1916.

———. *Presidential Addresses and State Papers*. New York: Doubleday, Page & Company, 1910.

———. *The United States and Peace*. New York: Charles Scribner's Sons, 1914.

Teitelbaum, Louis M. *Woodrow Wilson and the Mexican Revolution, 1913–1916*. New York: Exposition Press, 1967.

Thayer, William Roscoe. *The Life and Letters of John Hay*. Boston: Houghton Mifflin Company, 1915.

Torres Garcia, Guillermo. *Historia de la Moneda en Colombia*. Bogotá: Imprenta del Banco de la República, 1945.

Trani, Eugene P., and Wilson, David. *The Presidency of Warren G. Harding*. Lawrence: Regents Press of Kansas, 1977.

Tulchin, Joseph. *The Aftermath of War: World War I and U.S. Policy toward Latin America*. New York: New York University Press, 1971.

Tumulty, Joseph P. *Wilson as I Knew Him*. Garden City, NY: Doubleday, Page & Company, 1921.

Uribe, Antonio José. *Anales Diplomáticos y Consulares de Colombia*. Bogotá: Imprenta Nacional, 1918.

———. *Colombia y los Estados Unidos de América*. Bogotá: Imprenta Nacional, 1931.

———. *Las Modificaciones al Tratado entre Colombia y los EE. Unidos*. Bogotá: Imprenta Nacional, 1921.

———. *La Reforma Administrativa en Colombia*. Bogotá: Libreria Colombiana, 1917.

Uribe Uribe, Rafael. *Colombia, Estados Unidos y Panamá*. Buenos Aires: n.p., 1906.

Urrutia M., Miguel, and Arrubla, Mario, eds. *Compendio de Estadísticas Históricas de Colombia*. Bogotá: Dirección de Divulgación Cultural Publicaciones, 1970.

Veatch, A. C. *Quito to Bogotá*. New York: George H. Doran Company, 1917.

Vidales, Luis. *Historia de la Estadística en Colombia*. Bogotá: Banco de la República, 1978.

Villegas Arango, Jorge. *Petróleo Colombiano, Ganancia Gringa*. Bogotá: Editextos, 1973.

Villegas Arango, Jorge, and Yunis, José. *La Guerra de los Mil Días*. Bogotá: Carlos Valencia Editores, 1978.

Weinberg, Albert. *Manifest Destiny: A Study of Nationalist Expansion in American History*. Chicago: Quadrangle, 1963 [1935].

Weinstein, Edwin A. *Woodrow Wilson: A Medical and Psychological Biography*. Princeton: Princeton University Press, 1981.

Widenor, William C. *Henry Cabot Lodge and the Search for an American Foreign Policy*. Berkeley: University of California Press, 1980.

Wilkins, Mira, ed. *British Overseas Investments, 1907–1948*. New York: Arno Press, 1977.

———. *The Emergence of Multinational Enterprise: American Business Abroad from the Colonial Era to 1914*. Cambridge: Harvard University Press, 1970.

Williams, Mary. *Anglo-American Isthmian Diplomacy, 1815–1915*. Washington, DC: American Historical Association, 1916.

Williams, William Appleman. *The Tragedy of American Diplomacy*. New York: Dell Publishing Company, 1962 [1959].

Wilson, Edith. *My Memoir*. New York: Bobbs-Merrill Company, 1939.

Wilson, Woodrow. *Constitutional Government in the United States*. New York: Columbia University Press, 1908.

Winkler, Max. *Investments of United States Capital in Latin America*. Port Washington: Kennikat Press, 1971 [1928].

Young, Desmond. *Member for Mexico: A Biography of Weetman Pearson, First Viscount Cowdray*. London: Cassell & Company, 1966.

Zuñiga Guardia, Carlos Ivan. *Dos Tratados*. Panamá: Litho Impresora, 1975.

Articles

Adler, Selig. "Bryan and Wilsonian Caribbean Penetration." *Hispanic American Historical Review* 20 (May 1940): 198–226.

Ameringer, Charles D. "Philippe Bunau-Varilla: New Light on the Panama Canal Treaty." *Hispanic American Historical Review* 46 (February 1966): 28–52.

Arbena, Joseph. "Colombian Reactions to the Independence of Panama, 1903–1904." *The Americas* 33 (July 1976): 130–48.

Arnold, Ralph. "Conservation of the Oil and Gas Resources of the Americas, Part II." *Economic Geology* 11 (June 1916): 299–326.

Baker, George, Jr. "The Wilson Administration and Panama, 1913–1921." *Journal of Inter-American Studies and World Affairs* 8 (1966): 279–83.

Burns, E. Bradford. "The Recognition of Panama by the Major Latin American States." *The Americas* 26 (1969–70): 3–14.

Calvert, Peter. "The Murray Contract: An Episode in International Finance and Diplomacy." *Pacific Historical Review* 35 (May 1966): 203–24.

Chamberlain, Leander T. "A Chapter of National Dishonor." *North American Review* 195 (1912): 145–74.

Clements, Kendrick A. "Woodrow Wilson's Mexican Policy, 1913–15." *Diplomatic History* 4 (Spring 1980): 113–36.

Coletta, Paolo E. "William Jennings Bryan and the United States Colombian Impasse, 1903–1921." *Hispanic American Historical Review* 47 (November 1967): 486–501.

Day, David T. "The Petroleum Resources of the United States." *United States Geological Survey Bulletin* 394 (1909): 30–50.

DeNovo, John A. "The Movement for an Aggressive American Oil Policy Abroad, 1918–1920." *American Historical Review* 61 (1955–56): 854–76.

———. "Petroleum and the United States Navy before World War I." *Mississippi Valley Historical Review* 41 (1954–55): 641–56.

Friedlander, Robert A. "A Reassessment of Roosevelt's Role in the Panamanian Revolution of 1903." *Western Political Quarterly* 14 (1961): 535–43.

Gatell, Frank. "The Canal in Retrospect—Some Panamanian and Colombian Views." *The Americas* 15 (1958–59): 23–36.

Gilderhus, Mark T. "Pan-American Initiatives: The Wilson Presidency and Regional Integration, 1914–17." *Diplomatic History* 4 (Fall 1980): 409–23.

———. "Senator Albert B. Fall and 'The Plot against Mexico.' " *New Mexico Historical Review* 48 (1973): 299–311.

———. "Wilson, Carranza, and the Monroe Doctrine: A Question in Regional Organization." *Diplomatic History* 7 (Spring 1983): 103–15.

"Hide Proclamation." *War Trade Board Journal* 11 (July 1918): 20.

Hill, Larry. "The Progressive Politician as a Diplomat: The Case of John Lind in Mexico." *The Americas* 27 (1970–71): 355–72.

Kaufman, Burton. "United States Trade and Latin America: The Wilson Years." *Journal of American History* 58 (September 1971): 342–63.

Kent, Frederick I. "Financing Our Foreign Trade." *The Annals of the American Academy of Political and Social Science* 36 (1910): 492–501.

Kunz, George F. "Platinum, with Especial Reference to Latin America." *Bulletin of the Pan American Union* 45 (July–December 1917): 606–26.

Lael, Richard L. "Dilemma over Panama: Negotiation of the Thomson-Urrutia Treaty." *Mid-America* 61 (January 1979): 35–45.

———. "Struggle for Ratification: Wilson, Lodge and the Thomson-Urrutia Treaty." *Diplomatic History* 2 (Winter 1978): 81–102.

Lael, Richard L., and Killen, Linda. "The Pressure of Shortage: Platinum Policy and the Wilson Administration during World War I." *Business History Review* 56 (Winter 1982): 545–58.

Latané, John H. "The Effects of the Panama Canal on Our Relations with Latin America." *The Annals of the American Academy of Political and Social Science* 54 (1914): 84–91.

Leuchtenberg, William. "Progressivism and Imperialism: The Progressive Movement and American Foreign Policy, 1898–1916." *Mississippi Valley Historical Review* 39 (1952–53): 483–504.

"Long Credits and the New Banking Act." *Bulletin of the Pan American Union* 40 (January–June 1915): 492–94.

Loomis, Francis B. "Attitudes of the United States toward Other American Powers." *The Annals of the American Academy of Political and Social Science* 26 (July–December 1905): 21–24.

———. "The Position of the United States on the American Continent—Some Phases of the Monroe Doctrine." *The Annals of the American Academy of Political and Social Science* 22 (July–December 1903): 1–19.

Major, John. "Who Wrote the Hay-Bunau-Varilla Convention?" *Diplomatic History* 8 (Spring 1984): 115–23.

Manning, Van H. "International Aspects of the Petroleum Industry." *Transactions of the American Institute of Mining and Metallurgical Engineers* 65 (1921): 78–87.

Marks, Frederick W., III. "Morality as a Drive Wheel in the Diplomacy of Theodore Roosevelt." *Diplomatic History* 2 (Winter 1978): 43–62.

Minger, Ralph. "Panama, the Canal Zone, and Titular Sovereignty." *Western Political Quarterly* 14 (1961): 544–54.

Morgan, John T. "The Choice of Isthmian Canal Routes." *North American Review* 174 (May 1902): 672–86.

Ninkovich, Frank. "Ideology, the Open Door, and Foreign Policy." *Diplomatic History* 6 (Spring 1982): 185–208.

"Notable Address by President Wilson." *Bulletin of the Pan American Union* 37 (July–December 1913): 684–87.

Patterson, John. "Latin American Reactions to the Panama Revolution of 1903." *Hispanic American Historical Review* 24 (1944): 342–51.

Roosevelt, Theodore. "How the United States Acquired the Right to Dig the Panama Canal." *Outlook* 99 (7 October 1911): 314–18.

———. "Nationalism and International Relations." *Outlook* 97 (25 March 1911): 716–20.

Root, Elihu. "An Awakened Continent to the South of Us." *National Geographic Magazine* 18 (January 1907): 61–72.

Scholes, Walter V., and Scholes, Marie V. "Wilson, Grey, and Huerta." *Pacific Historical Review* 37 (May 1968): 151–58.

Smith, Daniel. "Bainbridge Colby and the Good Neighbor Policy, 1920–1921." *Mississippi Valley Historical Review* 50 (1963–64): 56–78.

Smith, George Otis. "Foreign Oil Supply for the United States." *Transactions of the American Institute of Mining and Metallurgical Engineers* 65 (1921): 89–93.

———. "Our Mineral Resources: How to Make America Industrially Independent." *United States Geological Survey Bulletin* 599 (1915): 1–48.

———. "Planning for Tomorrow: A Message from the United States Government to the American People." *Independent* 103 (September 1920): 366–67.

———. " 'Where the World Gets Its Oil' But Where Will Our Children Get It When American Wells Cease to Flow?" *National Geographic Magazine* 37 (January–June 1920): 181–202.

Solomon, Robert, and Tamagna, Frank M. "Banker's Acceptance Financing in the United States." *Federal Reserve Bulletin* 41 (May 1955): 482–94.

Stewart, Watt. "The Ratification of the Thomson-Urrutia Treaty." *Southwestern Political and Social Science Quarterly* 10 (1929–30): 416–28.

Tamagna, Frank M., and Willis, Parker B. "United States Banking Organizations Abroad." *Federal Reserve Bulletin* 42 (December 1956): 1284–95.

Vivian, James F. "The 'Taking' of the Panama Canal Zone: Myth and Reality." *Diplomatic History* 4 (Winter 1980): 95–100.

White, David. "The Petroleum Resources of the World." *The Annals of the American Academy of Political and Social Science* 89 (May 1920): 111–34.

White, K. D. "Oil Development in Colombia, South America." *Bulletin of the Southwestern Association of Petroleum Geologists* 1 (1917): 156–59.

Dissertations

Adams, William R. "Strategy, Diplomacy, and Isthmian Canal Security, 1880–1917." Ph.D. dissertation, Florida State University, 1974.

Anderson, William. "The Nature of the Mexican Revolution as Viewed from the United States, 1910–1917." Ph.D. dissertation, University of Texas, 1967.

Arbena, Joseph L. "The Panama Problem in Colombian History." Ph.D. dissertation, University of Virginia, 1970.

Baldridge, Donald C. "Mexican Petroleum and United States-Mexican Relations, 1919–1923." Ph.D. dissertation, University of Arizona, 1971.

Beyer, Robert C. "The Colombian Coffee Industry: Origins and Major Trends, 1740–1940." Ph.D. dissertation, University of Minnesota, 1947.

Block, Robert. "Southern Opinion of Woodrow Wilson's Foreign Policies, 1913–1917." Ph.D. dissertation, Duke University, 1968.

Cummins, Lejeune. "The Origin and Development of Elihu Root's Latin American Diplomacy." Ph.D. dissertation, University of California, Berkeley, 1964.

Delpar, Helen. "The Liberal Party of Colombia, 1863–1903." Ph.D. dissertation, Columbia University, 1967.

Edwards, Warrick Ridgely, III. "United States-Mexican Relations, 1913–1916: Revolution, Oil, and Intervention." Ph.D. dissertation, Louisiana State University, 1971.

Favell, Thomas Royden. "The Antecedents of Panama's Separation from Colombia: A Study in Colombian Politics." Ph.D. dissertation, Fletcher School of Law and Diplomacy, 1950.

Kaplan, Edward. "The Latin American Policy of William Jennings Bryan, 1913–1915." Ph.D. dissertation, New York University, 1970.

Kist, Glenn J. "The Role of Thomas C. Dawson in United States-Latin American Diplomatic Relations, 1897–1912." Ph.D. dissertation, Loyola University, 1971.

Knott, Alexander W. "The Pan American Policy of Woodrow Wilson, 1913–1921." Ph.D. dissertation, University of Colorado, 1969.

Leal Buitrago, Francisco. "Social Classes, International Trade and Foreign Capital in Colombia: An Attempt at Historical Interpretation of the Formation of the State, 1819–1935." Ph.D. dissertation, University of Wisconsin, 1974.

Mount, Graeme S. "American Imperialism in Panama." Ph.D. dissertation, University of Toronto, 1969.

Mulhollan, Paige. "Philander C. Knox and Dollar Diplomacy, 1909–1913." Ph.D. dissertation, University of Texas, 1966.

Murphy, Donald J. "Professors, Publicists, and Pan Americanism, 1905–1917: A Study in the Origins of the Use of 'Experts' in Shaping American Foreign Policy." Ph.D. dissertation, University of Wisconsin, 1970.

Muth, Edwin. "Elihu Root: His Role and Concepts Pertaining to United States Policies of Intervention." Ph.D. dissertation, Georgetown University, 1966.

O'Brien, Dennis. "The Oil Crisis and the Foreign Policy of the Wilson Administration, 1917–1921." Ph.D. dissertation, University of Missouri, 1974.

Richard, Alfred Charles, Jr. "The Panama Canal in American National Consciousness, 1870–1922." Ph.D. dissertation, Boston University, 1969.

Rosenberg, Emily S. "World War I and the Growth of United States Preponderance in Latin America." Ph.D. dissertation, State University of New York at Stony Brook, 1972.

Seidel, Robert. "Progressive Pan Americanism: Development and United States Policy toward South America, 1906–1931." Ph.D. dissertation, Cornell University, 1973.

Trow, Clifford. "Senator Albert B. Fall and Mexican Affairs, 1912–1921." Ph.D. dissertation, University of Colorado, 1966.

Turchen, Lesta Van Der Wert. "The Oil Expropriation Controversy, 1917–1942, in United States-Mexican Relations." Ph.D. dissertation, Purdue University, 1972.

Newspapers

El Nuevo Tiempo
New York Times
New York Tribune
Washington Post

Index